Books by James Ramsey Ullman

STRAIGHT UP

CARIBBEAN HERE AND NOW *(with Al Dinhofer)*

AMERICANS ON EVEREST

WHERE THE BONG TREE GROWS

FIA FIA

DOWN THE COLORADO

THE DAY ON FIRE

TIGER OF THE SNOWS *(with Tenzing Norgay)*

THE AGE OF MOUNTAINEERING

BANNER IN THE SKY (THIRD MAN ON THE MOUNTAIN)

THE SANDS OF KARAKORUM

ISLAND OF THE BLUE MACAWS

WINDOM'S WAY

RIVER OF THE SUN

THE WHITE TOWER

HIGH CONQUEST

THE OTHER SIDE OF THE MOUNTAIN

MAD SHELLEY

KINGDOM OF ADVENTURE: EVEREST *(editor)*

STRAIGHT UP

JAMES RAMSEY ULLMAN

Doubleday & Company, Inc.

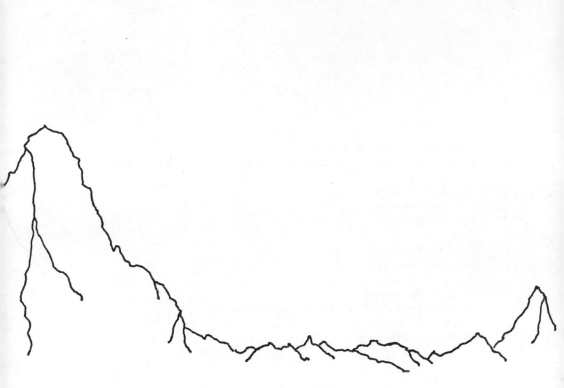

STRAIGHT UP

The Life and Death of John Harlin

Garden City, New York   1968

PHOTO CREDITS

Christian Bonington—※21, 27, 33, 34, 35
Christian Bonington for the *London Weekend Telegraph*—※40, 41, 43, 44, 45,
  46, 47, 49, 50
Dorene Frost—※23
Tom Frost—※24, 25
Hans Hauer—※17
Irish Times—※1
Royal Robbins—※30
Jerry Robertson—※11
Michael Stone—※8, 9, 19, 20
David H. Swanson—※51
Courtesy of Swiss National Tourist Office—※16
Courtesy of Swissair—※39
Bradford Washburn—※15, 22, 26, 31, 32, 42

LIBRARY OF CONGRESS CATALOG CARD NUMBER 68–12193
COPYRIGHT © 1968 BY JAMES RAMSEY ULLMAN

To Marilyn

Acknowledgment

To most of the persons mentioned herein, and to
many who are not, I owe my thanks for their con-
tributions to this, John Harlin's story. Not all will be
pleased by everything. Not all will agree with everything. But I hope all will at least agree that, John
being John, this is inevitable.

J.R.U.

Contents

1	The Wall	15
2	Trans World	23
3	Boy in Golden Shorts	33
4	Horizons	41
5	Two Blond Indians	55
6	Husband	71
7	Fledgling	81
8	Skyways	91
9	Hawk (and Dove)	101
10	The Rover Boys	117
11	Heights (and Valleys)	135
12	Victory	151
13	Farewell to Arms	169
14	Free	183
15	Superjohn	199
16	Perspectives	217
17	The Flame	239
18	The Rope	255
19	"Goodbye John"	275
	GLOSSARY	285

Illustrations will be found following page 144

Straight up is a way of serving a drink.
It is also a way of climbing a mountain,
and of living a life.

1. The Wall

There is no earth anywhere. There is no sky. There is only the grayness of cloud, and through the cloud a gray wall rising from void to void.

This is a mineral world. Of rock, snow, ice, air. It is a frozen world, transfixed in time and space. It is a vertical world. Nothing grows here. No bird alights, no insect crawls, no lichen clings.

It is a world beyond theirs. Beyond man's: high, hidden, forbidden. Yet man is here.

He is hard to see. He is no more than a speck, a midge, glimpsed through a telescope from a mile below. That is when the sky is clear. But now, in the gray cloud, he is not even that. He is gone, lost.

Yet still there.

Sometimes it is a man alone. More often he is with others: two, three, four in all. They have been on the wall for hours. Then for days—and nights. Their progress is slow; so slow that much of the time they are not moving at all but standing, clinging, peering up at the wall above. Their eyes search the verticality of rock and ice, seeking a crack for a finger, a ledge for a toe. At last a hand points. The first man moves again. The rope moves after him, and then the others. Slowly they advance between wall and void.

Theirs is the only life here, but not the only movement. In the void the cloud moves, churning, darkening. The mountain itself moves, spewing down torrents of snow and cannonades of rock. In the torrents the climbers clip themselves into the wall with spike and rope. In the cannonades they press themselves inward and wait, and hope. The rumble above becomes a roar, and the roar envelops them, passes and recedes below. A stillness as vast as the mountain returns, and in the stillness voices call up and down the length of the rope.

"All right?"

"All right."

The words may be English, German, French, Italian. A speaker's name may be Gary, Dougal, Konrad, Hans, Pierre, René, Roberto, Ignazio. But the name of one of them is John. That is the one constant: John. For this is his story.

This is not the first time he has been on this mountain, this wall—or walls—for it is many in one. It is the wall of the Eiger. It is the wall of the Dru, the Fou, the Mönch, the Frêney, the Blaitière, the Grand Capucin, the Grandes Jorasses. He has been on them all. He returns again and again. In the high Alps, among the mountaineers of the world, John Harlin's name has become as well known as those of the peaks he has climbed.

Now on this peak, as on the others, he is not taking the easiest way. He is taking the hardest. Over the years, every summit in the Alps has been reached time without number; the routes of least resistance have become what Baedeker used to call "an easy day for a lady." (If you're a fairly tough lady.) The experts have long since turned to stiffer challenges—the more formidable ridges, the sheer intervening faces— until these too have now been largely mastered. What remains is what Italians call the *direttissima* routes: the most direct routes, straight up, over whatever obstacles. And it is straight up that John and his companions are now climbing through the clouded void.

They are not the first here. Though none before has climbed the wall *direttissima*, others have been on it, following zigzag routes; and a few have succeeded, many have failed, some have died. Well below them already is a rocky bulge over space from which four climbers as expert as they once fell to extinction. A short distance above is a small niche in the precipice on which two others, caught by storm, perished of cold and exhaustion. The disasters and deaths on this mountain are a large part of its history.

John Harlin does not want to die. His companions do not want to die. For this effort they have trained body, mind and spirit to the utmost. They have planned every detail of strategy, tactics, logistics. Now on the mountain they use every refinement of technique and precaution. Still, they well know the nature of the game they are playing; the thin line—as thin as the ribbon of rock providing a toehold—that separates wall from void, *être* from *néant*. With the black humor in which mountaineers are not deficient, they know that a climb, like a drink, can easily be converted from straight-up to on-the-rocks.

"Why, then, do they do it?" asks the man below.

"Yes, why?" John himself has asked, and not long before attempted an answer.

"It is my opinion," he wrote, "that by subjecting oneself to the pure and focused experience of survival, accompanied by careful introspection, one can approach an ultimate in self-control. For example, in climbing, there is the problem of a moment's exertion on a particularly difficult bit of rock or ice, with alternatives of life and death. The movement requires not only strength, the reserves of which . . ."

He had left the sentence unfinished. And here on the wall is not the time to complete it. Though it is the time for care, it is not in introspection. It is the time for those reserves of strength, of skill, of will, and he calls on them. Above, a buttress of rock looms outward. Is there a way over it? He pulls himself up on finger- and toeholds, swings out over space, over *néant*. And yes, there is a way. He finds it, seizes it. He is up and over. At the very last stance there is an icy patch, a slip; if he were alone he might be gone. But he is not alone. His rope leads through a snap ring, fixed to the rock with a metal piton, and from there descends to his partner below, who holds him. This too is part of the game: the partner, the companion. Not only in holding a slip, in doing a job, but simply in being there, in sharing an adventure. Of companions on a climb John has said, "There is a certain oneness, a penetration of one life into another."

A call comes up from below: "Good!"

It could as well be *gut!* or *bon!* or *bono!* and John would like it thus, for it is his firm, indeed passionate belief that mountaineering should be international in its relationships; that its spirit should be as far above the petty differences of state and language as the mountains themselves are above the lowlands.

He climbs on. The others follow. Slowly . . . slowly. For it is late. They began climbing at first light, and now it is dusk, and they are tired. Indeed, John's trained, iron-hard body aches with tiredness. But even the ache, the misery, are not wholly unwelcome, for it is superficial misery. Beneath it, deeper, far more potent, are the strength and will that can master misery, that can force the human body to the utmost limits of performance. And in this John Harlin glories.

He is a tough one, you say? You are right, he is a tough one. But not *only* a tough one, and this is what makes him John Harlin. At the start of the climb, while a companion waited impatiently, he stopped to examine a tiny clump of flowers on a rocky ledge. Now, belaying a ropemate as he comes up from below, he studies the sea of cloud, marveling at its whorls and convolutions. Through the murk a sudden snowflake flies, and he holds it briefly in the palm of his hand.

"Crystals of snow," he muses, "are diamonds, but more delicate." (The crystal vanishes; he turns to the wall and touches it.) "The texture of rock lives." (His ropemate has reached him; he resumes climbing.) "The exercise of muscle is sensuous. The control of fear is spice. Human experience is vitality, and life is passion."

He is not only a tough one but a strange one. Not many Americans of his generation would, as he has, describe an act of supreme physical effort as, above all, "an esthetic experience." He is not afraid of words like esthetic and passion. Without introspection, he believes, experience is meaningless.

They climb on. With each step it grows darker. It is not a single snowflake that now blows in from the void, but a stream, a tide of snow, and the wind is rising. It was on such an evening, years ago, that two of their predecessors reached the niche in the wall, now close above them, and stopped for the night, and froze and died.

At last they too have reached the niche. It is the merest indentation in the soaring rock, above a ledge that slopes steeply into space. Tying themselves in by rope and piton, they work for an hour fashioning a rudimentary bivouac. On such a wall there is room nowhere for even the tiniest tent; the best that can be done is a sack for head and body and another for the feet. Finally they are in them, still lashed to the wall. The rock at their backs nudges them outward, and their muffled feet hang over the abyss.

It is full night now. And full storm. Another hour passes while they struggle with packs and gear, preparing a lukewarm drink and a few bites of dried meat and rusk. Then they sit and wait. In their double sacks they rub their hands and thump their feet together. At intervals they examine the ropes and pitons that hold them to the mountain, and to life.

Crumpled bits of paper protrude from a pocket of John's parka, and he tucks them away. They are letters he received yesterday, before the start of the climb, from his wife Marilyn, his son Johnny, his daughter Andréa. Andréa's says "Come home soon. I love you very much." Johnny's says "Try to make it to the top." Marilyn's says "Still no word. Are you alive? For God's sake *let me know!*"

John Harlin well knows that he has been no paragon as husband and father. He loves his family, but . . . he has been climbing for a month now. One ascent has followed another, and each has required immense planning and concentration. There has simply not been time for writing. . . . Or has there? In any case, from here on he will make time. When he comes down from this climb, the first thing he will do is write. Or phone.

Like the letters, he tucks these thoughts away. He listens to the storm, and the storm is still growing. The wind howls, beating in frenzy on the mountain wall, trying to snatch the tiny bivouac and hurl it off into space. Perhaps it is not when, but *if* he comes down from this climb—alive.

Since pulling his sack over him he has only heard the storm, not seen it. But now he pulls off the sack; he must see it. If this is to be the end, he must watch it coming. Like the user of a psychedelic drug, he seeks the expansion of consciousness and experience to their ultimate limit. It is not a death wish that fills him, but a hunger for life so strong that he will look death in the face and make it part of life.

Even he, however, is made of flesh and blood. Soon the icy wind has numbed his brain. Snow clings and cakes on his eyelids until he cannot see. Again withdrawing into the sack, he resumes rubbing his hands, kicking his feet. And at last he dozes. He does not want to doze.

19

He wants to go on rubbing, kicking. But fatigue fills him, masters him, and in the cold darkness he nods.

In his half-sleep, Marilyn returns. He is with her and the children in their chalet in Leysin, across the Alps; at his work in the Leysin American School, where both he and Marilyn teach. Then older images arise. He is in the cockpit of a jet fighter-bomber of the United States Air Force, cleaving the skies over America, Europe, Africa. He is—of all places—in the atelier of Pierre Balmain in Paris, applying for work as an apprentice dress designer. He is back on a football field at Stanford University in California; back on the craggy rocks near Stanford, exulting in his first climb; back still farther, a boy, a child, in years that took him from California to Ireland, from Missouri to Ethiopia. He is a man of barely thirty, but in his life there are many places, many images. . . .

When he reawakes to the mountain, he knows at once that something is different. The wind is down. Looking out from his sack, he sees that the snow has stopped. Gray clouds still wheel and churn against the mountainside, but the fullness of storm has passed. Death, which has shown its face, has withdrawn it, at least for now.

Night thins into dawn, and John's companions stir. Again there is the laborious business of food and drink; then another tedious hour breaking bivouac. Though the wind is gone, it is bitterly cold, and with chilled, cramped bodies, each simple action seems to take an eternity.

Then at last they are on their way. And almost immediately things are better. The mountain wall still rears above them, on and on without visible end; and now, plastered with new snow, it is even more menacing than before. But nevertheless things are better. With the output of energy, blood courses through artery and vein. They are again performing their function: climbers climbing a mountain. As they move on, the light around them is slowly brightening. Overhead, the cloud is touched with a golden glow.

John looks up. Again, in his imagining, he is back in the cockpit of an Air Force jet, and he recalls how he used to feel as he pushed it on its utmost ceiling. . . . "Sometimes the clouds would reach nearly 40,000 feet. Climbing through them, the bird would be heavy with fuel, and as I approached the tops the rate of climb would sink to less than one thousand feet per minute. I could see the sun straight above, but I could never seem to free myself from that heavy mist . . .

36,000 feet . . . 37,000 . . . 38,000. . . . Minutes would stretch indefinitely. And always that sun was saying, 'I'm here, I'm here. Can't you reach me?'"

Now on a mountain wall he is again climbing, straight up, toward the sun.

2. Trans World

Soon there was no more sun. There was no more John Harlin. Musingly, a while later, his father groped back through the years.

"He was born in Kansas City," he said, "but he was conceived in La Paz, Bolivia." A small smile broke through his sadness as he added, "La Paz is 13,000 feet up. About the same as the Eiger. Sometimes I almost think that's how it got into his blood."

Rear Admiral John E. Harlin, Senior, has never climbed a mountain, but he is no stranger to heights. A flier himself, as well as a flag officer in the U. S. Naval Reserve, he retired in 1966 as a senior jet pilot for Trans World Airlines. The exact date was July 25, his sixtieth birthday, four months and three days after the death of his only son.

He is a Midwesterner, at least in orgin. Born in Puxico, Missouri, he attended Missouri schools and Washington University in St. Louis, graduating in 1928 with a degree in civil engineering. He did not, however, become an engineer. Having had naval flight training in college, he entered the Navy and served a year as bomber pilot on the aircraft carrier *Saratoga*. From this he went on to pilot flying boats for a small airline pioneering the east coast of South America; from this to domestic flying for a fledgling Midwest line; from this, in turn, to a second hitch in the Navy. In 1930, back from South America, he wooed and married Genevieve Sussenbach, from the town of Edwardsville in southwestern Illinois.

"She was a bit of a mouthful," he has conceded. "Not the girl but the name." Presently the Su of Sussenbach became Sue—and Sue she has been ever since.

In 1933, again out of the Navy, John Harlin, Sr., joined TWA— at that time, still Transcontinental and Western Air—which was to remain his basic employer for the rest of his career. But a year later the cancellation of its government airmail contract caused a layoff of personnel, and soon, for the second time, he was forging new air routes in South America. This was for a mining company based in La Paz, and his job was flying men and equipment from the Bolivian altiplano over the Andes to jungle tributaries of the Amazon. On this assignment he brought wife Sue to La Paz, and it was there, toward the end of 1934, that she reported she was pregnant.

In later years, it is safe to guess, their son would have approved of La Paz—or better yet, an Andean mining camp—as a birthplace. But it was not to be. Back home, TWA regained its mail contract; his father was recalled to its operational base in Kansas City, Missouri; and there, on June 30, 1935, John Elvis Harlin II was unspectacularly born in the delivery room of Research Hospital.

There are two points to be noted about his name. First, since it duplicated his father's, it would normally have carried a "Jr." But his parents agreed that he should not run the risk of being *called* Junior; therefore, arbitrarily, the II. As for the Elvis: it was a family name on his father's side, and in a distant deep-South branch thereof, in the same year, there was born another Elvis, also destined to reach certain heights. Whether for this or other reasons, John II never used the name, nor even the initial, except under the duress of official documents.

As with so many Americans, the senior Harlins' ancestry had ramifications. Genevieve (i.e., Sue) Sussenbach's was German on both sides, with known *von* connections and perhaps a faint touch of Hapsburg in the long ago. John I's was English-Scottish-Irish, with—also perhaps—a touch of Cherokee Indian. He himself is inclined to doubt this, and there is nothing in his appearance to suggest it. But John II later enthusiastically endorsed the idea (possibly as compensation for not being born in Bolivia), though he was even more un-Indian-looking than his father.

Child, boy, and man, he would have a small semi-snub nose, a light complexion, blond hair. Indeed, so blond was his hair, so golden-yellow, that many who knew him were under the impression that he had the usual blue eyes to go with it. Though a likely sequitur, however, this was not a fact. For John's eyes were brown. They were keen eyes; throughout his life his vision topped 20/20. But though he himself would grow to be, in certain ways, a hard man, they were not hard eyes. They were soft and deep—"like fresh-plowed warm soil," one of his friends was to say later—able to see many things besides mountain-tops and distant airplanes.

What he saw close around him in early childhood was the middle-class conventional world of the Midwest: the realm that had recently offered Alf Landon to the nation and would presently, and more successfully, present Harry Truman. In those years, the Missouri Valley, like the rest of the nation, was in the toils of the Depression. But it did not strike too harshly at the Harlins, and by the time John was on the scene the worst was over. There was no want or deprivation in his growing up.

Indeed, with an airline pilot for a father, his horizons were wide from the beginning. From the family home in the hills of North Kansas City he could see the planes approaching and leaving the nearby municipal airport, and soon he was visiting it often, as John I flew in and out. Expertise, junior grade, followed quickly. Years later, the clearest memory of one of his mother's friends was of his impatience with her when she could not tell one plane from another. "How many times do I have to tell you, Mrs. Scharz," he would ask despairingly, "that a Stratoliner has *four* engines?"

Planes, however, were still for watching, not for flying, and the general routine of life was of a familiar pattern. By definition, and on the record, his father was engaged in an adventurous, even romantic, profession.[1] But in other aspects of life he was conventional and con-

[1] And no question about it, there was, and is, this side to the senior John Harlin's nature. Aged sixty, he expressed the wish that he could have been a generation younger, so that he would have had the chance to qualify as an astronaut.

servative. A businessman as well as a flier, he was already becoming involved in the administrative end of TWA. On the side, he was a joiner of organizations and active in real estate. In family life, despite his frequent airborne absences, he hewed to traditional lines. And so too did his wife: [a good housekeeper, conscientious mother, and parishioner of the local Unity Church—to which she brought her son when he was old enough to attend.] With two sides to her nature, no less than her husband, she was also an accomplished amateur painter. But of the bohemianism that often accompanies such a talent there was no trace whatever.

Under her influence, young John, early on, began to paint and draw: mostly planes. As a businessman, his major enterprise (unsuccessful) was an attempt to sell a dead snake on a stick.

At the usual five-years-old he went to kindergarten, at six to public school. There were the usual scooter and bike, toy trains and soldiers. There was a big German shepherd called Pal, later another called Billy, and these were important, for all his life he loved animals. The section of North Kansas City in which he lived is today a busy suburb, but around 1940 it was still almost countryside; and this too was important. There were fields for wandering, woods for exploring, a whole realm of nature at his very door.

Inevitably, there were traumas of sorts. At the circus, when he was very young, a balloon burst close behind him, bringing terror and tears, and for some time thereafter he was afraid of sudden loud noises. Then in his first year at school he fell on broken glass, cutting his right wrist so badly that both tendon and nerve were severed. Later, an operation corrected most of the resultant trouble, but he was always to have, from then on, a not quite properly aligned "monkey thumb."

There were also compensations to tip the balance. Foremost among them was a twenty-gauge shotgun, a gift from his father in his seventh year, and with its first wondrous bang beside his ear, his fear of loud noises—and virtually everything else—disappeared forever. His earliest shooting was at clay pigeons in a field near home. But then came a pheasant-hunting trip to South Dakota with family and friends, from which John I proudly reported that he outshot the adults. Also in these years there were other holiday trips: to the Ozarks; to Minnesota lakes for boating and fishing; to the Black Hills, Yellowstone, and the Tetons. One wonders what went through the mind of this boy from

26

the prairies as he gazed for the first time at high mountains; but there is no record save that he looked at them like any other tourist.

The child is father of the man: so say both Wordsworth and the psychiatrists. Granted, it is dangerous to seek rigid cause-and-effect in a thing as volatile as a human life, yet in John Harlin's case it seems safe to say that he was greatly molded by his early experience of the outdoors. And further, on a deeper level, by the fact that he was an only child. His parents would have liked more children. But his mother was unable to have them, and as the usual consequence there was a great focusing upon the *one*—particularly by Sue Harlin, who during her husband's absences strove mightily to be both mother and father. She was not a "spoiler"; she made demands of young John. But her need of him was great. "We were a close family, a very close one," she has said repeatedly. And it may have been this very closeness of loving mother and only child that later impelled her son to adolescent revolt.

John's life was scarcely to be a settled one; his seven childhood years in Kansas City were the most he would ever live in one place. But whatever he brought away from them inwardly, there was to be no outward evidence of attachment. He did not think of Kansas City as "home." He never returned there. Such roots as he was ever to have were put down later, in worlds far away, worlds he made for himself.

The first change, or half-change, of scene came early in 1942. The close of 1941 had brought with it Pearl Harbor and total war, and early the following year Lieutenant John Harlin I of the U. S. Naval Reserve re-entered active service. His initial assignment was, to be sure, not far afield: to the Naval Air Station at nearby Olathe, Kansas. But his small family moved with him the few miles to the southwest, and during the next year John II attended Olathe grade school. Then, in mid-1943, came the first big move, and the Missouri Valley was gone forever.

For the father it was to Hawaii and the Naval Air Transport Service. For mother and son it was to Oakland, California, near the home base of NATS-Pacific where John I was able to visit them briefly at intervals. Here John II went to his third public grade school. He grew— but not fast enough to please him, for he yearned to become an instant

27

man and join his father in the Pacific. During this period his mother gave much time to painting. And he painted too. With the energy if not the technique, of a Michelangelo, he exorcised his martial frustrations by covering the walls of his room with a mural of an epic sea-and-air battle.

Though colleagues in art, Sue Harlin and John II were now having their differences in other fields. A big woman, she was also a strong one. She had firm opinions, a firm will. And though still far from being big, so too did John. As boys go, he was generally quiet and well-mannered. But he had his own way of doing things, and when crossed, a temper that was to grow with the years. What he needed, one imagines, was a brother or sister to play a role in the range of his emotions. As things stood, there was only he and his mother, in that "closeness" that had its dangers as well as its pleasures.

At the other extreme, his father was now mostly absent: the flier-warrior, the doer of deeds, in the boy's mind an almost mythical hero. When he made his home visits, it was not, to John, from a desk in Honolulu, but from such scenes of derring-do as adorned his bedroom wall. And they were marked by exciting interludes of hunting, fishing, and other male pursuits. Johns I and II were not always to agree on everything. But their shared love of the outdoors, of action, of planes and guns and other trappings of the strenuous life, formed a tie between them that was stong and enduring.

When the war ended, so did the Oakland phase. Returning from the Pacific with the rank of commander, and ready for separation from the service, John I was sent across the country to the naval base at Patuxent River, Maryland; and there wife and son joined him in the fall of 1945.

Their travels, however, had barely begun. Back in civilian employment with TWA, John I opted for executive rather than flying duties (though still, as always, maintaining his pilot's rating) and entered the line's new international division. His first assignment, toward year's end, was to Ireland, to start TWA operations in that country. And for several months thereafter the Harlin home was the Royal George Hotel in Limerick, near Shannon Airport.

For a boy of ten, the scenes were changing fast. And so were schools, for now, in quick succession, John went to his fourth, fifth, and sixth

28

in five years. His attendance at the first, a Jesuit institution, ended quickly when his parents one day found him and a classmate lustily beating each other's hands with their belts. "Why are you doing that?" they asked. "To make our hands tough," said John, "so it won't hurt so much when the fathers hit us." And that, for him, was the last of the Jesuits.

For unrecorded reasons, a second Irish school was also found wanting, and then a third was tried that proved satisfactory. Here John was introduced to the mysteries of Gaelic, sterling and rugby, and one of his teachers described him as "a highly intelligent boy . . . but full of wild dreams." On many weekends and holidays, as back in the States, there was fishing and hunting, and it was a source of pride both to him and his father that he was judged good enough with a gun to be allowed to take part in local adult shoots.

In later years, most people who knew John Harlin were to describe him as one of the most formidable physical specimens they had ever seen. But here in Ireland, in his preadolescence, he was almost the antithesis. He was very blond, very thin, a small and choosy eater. Friends of his parents described him as frail, delicate, even ethereal in appearance, an impression probably strengthened by his usually quiet and formal manners. Yet at the same time his energy was immense, his love of sport consuming. Besides hunter and fisherman, he was also an accomplished horseman and swimmer. One day in the countryside, with no adults at hand, he saved a still smaller boy from drowning in a pond, and as a consequence was hailed as a hero. It was a role that, for better or worse, he was to play and enjoy increasingly as time went on.

In TWA, his father was moving up fast. In the spring of 1946, with the Irish installation well established, he was made chief of operations for all of Europe and beyond, and soon afterward the Harlins moved to Paris. Here they presently settled in Versailles—and in Versaillean style—for the home they leased was the Château Montreuil, close by the palace, which had been built by Louis XVI for his sister Elizabeth. During the next three years, John II was to live, if not like a prince, at least like a small boy who was having it good.

Again, of course, there was school: this time the American Community School, in Paris, to which he commuted by train. Here he quickly unlearned his sketchy Gaelic, and in its place learned French.[2] He had the usual schoolboy ups and downs, wins and losses, fights and friendships. Never a classroom star nor a prize grade-getter, he was already showing what was to be his lifelong trait of total absorption in what interested him and total rejection of what didn't.

Among his interests in his new world was Paris itself. With the war barely a year in the past, it was still a city of shortages and half-measures—yet uniquely, unquenchably Paris, a wonderland to a newcomer of any age. The small blond emigrant from the Midwestern prairies and Irish bogs was soon a connoisseur of its streets and boulevards, parks and palaces. He played in the Bois de Boulogne, sailed model boats on the pond in the Tuileries Gardens, and with his mother explored the shops of the Rue de Rivoli and Faubourg St. Honoré.

Best of all, however, were his own home grounds of the Château Montreuil. Here, surrounding the central mansion, were twelve acres of lawn and woodland, paths and gardens, through which he roamed like a lordling on a feudal fief. For a command post there was a cave; for naval maneuvers a pond; for high-level exploits a stand of giant California sequoias, brought to Versailles as seedlings by none other than Ben Franklin, when he was first American Ambassador to the court of France.

It was through these that John first heard the siren call of the heights. And first answered it. Presently he was climbing the sequoias of Château Montreuil, not only in their lower reaches but to their very tops, a hundred and more dizzying feet above the ground. There was no dizzying for him, however. Here was his natural element, as he climbed again and again, alone and exultant, into his private world of the treetops.

In Paris too, one day, there was a climbing episode of note. In the course of a mixed adult-and-children gathering in the apartment of friends of the Harlins, the grownups became aware that their young ones had disappeared. A search disclosed that they had gone out on a small balcony, four stories above the street, and having climbed its railing, were now working their way up the outer wall of the building toward its steep mansard roof. When they were rounded up, it was quickly

2 Later, as an adult living in Europe, his French was still fluent, but ungrammatical. Man and boy, he never made his peace with irregular verbs.

30

determined that John Harlin II had been instigator and leader. "He was old enough to know better," said his mother, "and young enough to spank."

There were adventures farther afield as well. Here, as in Ireland, John I went hunting with friends: now no longer for mere birds or rabbits but for bigger game, wild boar. Yet John II was again held qualified to go along, and more than held his own as gun-handler and marksman.

Then there were trips. Tremendous trips. . . . In his role as overseas operations chief John I moved continually about the expanding TWA network, and on many occasions he took wife and son with him. During his three years based in France, John II got also to Spain, Italy, and Greece. He penetrated beyond the swiftly closing Iron Curtain to Prague and Warsaw. He visited Egypt (riding a camel and partially climbing a pyramid) and newly founded Israel (where he claimed a swim in the Dead Sea cured his athlete's foot). As climax, he went to Ethiopia, where TWA was in charge of operations for the new government airline.

Here, in the land of the Lion of Judah, he also reached the climax of his career as a hunter. But not with a lion; far from it. On a safari for antelope in the bush beyond Addis Ababa, he was again distinguishing himself against adult competition, when suddenly came the chance for the top prize of all. Across the sights of his rifle sped a dik-dik (the smallest of antelopes), a creature so tiny and swift that it is considered among the hardest of all game to bring down. John aimed, fired, hit it. It was his moment of glory—but not for long. Approaching the fallen animal, he found it was not yet dead, and while its brown eyes stared up into his own, he had to stoop and put a bullet in its head. Then, picking it up, he saw that the little thing was strangely swollen in the stomach.

"She was pregnant," someone said.

Twelve-year-old John looked up. "You mean," he said, "she was going to have a baby?"

"Yes."

John turned away. His eyes filled, overflowed. Then he was sobbing. Except for an occasional bout with game birds, he never hunted again.

3. Boy in Golden Shorts

Only twice again, ever, was anyone to see John Harlin cry, and both these times were still far in the future. As of now, the boy in him was fading, the adolescent emerging, and it would not be the sort of adolescent who was given to tears.

During the Paris-and-beyond years he grew rapidly; but not to stringbean dimensions, for he was never quite to reach six feet. As his height increased, so did the rest of him, shoulders broadening, chest deepening, legs fleshing out, until the youngster who had seemed "frail, delicate, even ethereal" was as solid and strong as a shaft of steel. His was an athlete's body. And that was what he now wanted to be—an athlete. American Boy dreams filled his expatriate head, and what he wanted most especially of all was to go home and play football.

He was now reaching high school age, and his parents, too, felt he would be better off back in the States. Making a major decision and sacrifice, John Harlin I gave up his TWA executive position in Europe and returned both to America and to piloting. For the rest of his career he would remain a pilot, flying Trans World for his line from home bases; and for the next ten years his son would live in his native land.

For a while, however, there was no true settling down. In 1949, at the time of the Harlins' return, TWA's main stateside base for overseas operations was in Wilmington, Delaware, and there they made their home for a year. Then, with John I flying largely out of New York, they moved to Clinton, New Jersey. Here, as a side-venture, they bought a working farm, and in a notable change of pace, the erstwhile lordling of Versailles and Ethiopia learned the lore of barns, tractors and fertilizers. Only a few miles away, in total contrast, was the swarm and glitter of metropolis. But in spite of his love of Paris, John was no city boy, and he rarely got there.

In Wilmington he was a high school freshman, in Clinton a sophomore. Studies, as usual, were so-so. But true to his dream, he learned and played football, and for a mid-teenager was an athlete to be reckoned with. As such, he was largely able to counterbalance the "outness" caused by his years abroad; but with only one year at each school he made no close and lasting friends. The most notable tribute to him—which he would have happily renounced—was from an older girl who wrote in his class yearbook, "To the cute little blond fellow who made my heart go bump." There were to be many more such bumps in the future, with John responding in high gear. But in those days Halfback Harlin was more interested in end runs and first downs.

Like so many farms of non-farmers, the Clinton venture was not a financial success. After the one year John I sold out, and another major decision was made—this time to move to California. As an airline pilot, with quick and free commuting available, John Senior was able to live where he chose; and all three Harlins had liked the Bay Area when it was their wartime home. Now in the summer of 1951 they transferred to Redwood City, on the Peninsula south of San Francisco, and John was to be a Californian for the next six years.

With some four thousand students and a plant to match, Redwood City's Sequoia Union High School was a huge institution, but he was not one to be intimidated by size. Robert Rosenaur, a classmate who became one of John's closest friends, said of him later: "He was convinced he could do *anything*—and damn near did."

34

Among the *anythings*, athletically, was of course football, which he played for two years as one of the Sequoia varsity backfield. Also, he was a sprinter and jumper on the track team, competing in the California Junior Olympics, and a first-stringer in wrestling, gymnastics, and swimming. In his second and senior year he became one of a select group of Sequoians deemed worthy to wear the golden-hued running shorts that the school awarded its top-ranking athletes.

At the time, as through the rest of his life, he was thoroughly aware of his physique and blond good looks. Several of his schoolmates remember, not altogether with admiration, his penchant for flexing his biceps and wearing tight T-shirts and shorts (gold or otherwise) that would best display his anatomy. None, however, denies that the display was impressive. So impressive, in fact, that the following year, while a freshman at college, he was offered and accepted a job modeling for photographs for a man's "muscle magazine." This ended in scandal when the magazine crossed the line from muscle to pornography, showing the pictures with John stark naked. Arrests and indictments followed. But John, though square in the spotlight as Exhibit A, had been both innocent and ignorant of what was going on.

Meanwhile, on a less lurid level, his high school life hewed close to the usual pattern. As before, his grades were good to excellent in what interested him (English, language, history); fair to poor in what didn't (math and sciences). The family home, though no château, was comfortable and attractive. He had his beloved sports, friends, two dogs, and presently a car—a used but still usable Jeepster all his own. In it, he had his share of races, chases and all-around motorized adventure, but never to the point where he was relieved of his license. During the summer when he had just passed seventeen he earned money haying on farms in Orgeon. On another vacation he camped and hiked with family friends on the slopes of California's Mount Shasta.

To one who saw him only in action he must have seemed a total extrovert, a hell-for-leather All American Boy. Yet a scant millimeter beneath the surface everything was in turmoil. Such, of course, is the case with most adolescents, locked in youth's classic struggle to come to terms with life and self. But in John Harlin the bubblings and boilings reached an extra degree of intensity. As his physique was stronger than most, so too were his desires, his emotions, his ambitions, his will. In spirit, no less than in body, he was outsize, a little larger than life.

35

With classes and games behind him, he would walk for miles, alone with his dogs, in the hills behind Redwood City. And at home he would now and then withdraw into brown funks. With his father, on hand part-time between TWA missions, his relationship continued as before, firm but rather formal, and visiting classmates made surprised note of his respectful "Sir." With his mother, his rebellion continued apace—typified by his reluctance, and eventual refusal, to go to church —and a tenseness between them was sometimes observable to outsiders. A Sequoia date whom he brought to his home, for instance, later recalled Mrs. Harlin's frequent corrections of his social behavior. "It was John do this, John do that," she said. "He should open the door for me, pull back a chair for me. I used to think any minute he was going to explode. But he only seethed."

Among his contemporaries, he had high visibility. An athlete and junior Adonis, with his golden hair and those golden shorts, he was not easily overlooked, nor later forgotten; yet he was fundamentally a loner, an outsider, and was never a member of one of the "in" groups at Sequoia. To a degree, this was a residue of his semi-European background. But still more it was because of his complex mixture of shyness and aggressiveness. His aggressive side, not unnaturally, showed largely in his relationships with other boys, and particularly other athletes, for he could not bear to be second-best to anyone in activities that truly mattered to him. "That's how we were able to become so close," said his friend Bob Rosenaur. "I was the complete non-athlete and therefore no threat to him. If I got a better mark in class, he didn't give a damn. But if I'd been a better halfback, runner or wrestler, he couldn't have rested until he topped me."

His shyness too was a sometime thing. He loved the limelight of competitive triumph, but hated to stand up and speak in public. He posed with narcissistic pleasure for "muscle" pictures, but was terrified at the suggestion that he join the school dramatic club. Most of all he was shy with girls. "And that's where I came in again," said Bob Rosenaur. "For I wasn't. I was John's pimp right through Sequoia."

The pimping, apparently, was on an eminently respectable level, for there is no record of way-out exploits during John's high school days. On the contrary, the nearest he had to a regular girl was one of the top students and leaders of his class, who in their senior year held the prestigious Sequoian position of "Commissioner of Cultural Activities." Her name was Beth Little, and her reminiscences of John are illuminating.

"I never really thought of him as an athlete," she has said. "With all his size and strength he was still a boy to me, an almost pretty boy trying so hard to grow up. Sometimes he was very much the cosmopolitan world traveler telling about all the things he'd seen and done. Then suddenly he'd be the little boy again, slicking down his blond cowlick." She smiled. "He was always after that cowlick. He was very vain. But also very serious—and very sensitive. About himself, that is; not so sensitive about others. I don't think he really cared much about other people. What he cared about was projects. He had so many projects, so much he wanted to do, to be. . . ." The former Beth Little, now a grown and married woman, thought back over the years to the John Harlin she had known. "He was at battle with those around him and with himself," she said. "I think perhaps he was acting out the conflicts many of us simply accept quietly. His choice to do so may not have been a better one—certainly it was more difficult and more painful—but it was honest. I think the word *determined* described him best of all. It gave him a special quality." She searched for the word. "An aura. . . ."

There were others, too, who felt that aura. His desires were so strong, his energy so vast, that, once within his orbit, many were irresistibly drawn after him. "When he really wanted you to do something," said Bob Rosenaur, "it was almost impossible to say no." Then later, setting down his memories, he added: "John wanted so much, did so much. He was an overgrown boy with a Greek god body, and by the time he was twenty-one he had lived several lives. Being with him in his early years was an unpredictable adventure. Never content to take apart a car's motor, he tried to tear apart the world."

Outwardly it was a small world: the world of Redwood City and Sequoia High. But John Harlin was not built for small worlds. Beneath the façade of unruly cowlick and gung-ho athlete was a mind that ranged out to the ends of the earth. His curiosity was insatiable. He had become a great reader, and a great questioner. The Israeli wife of one of John Senior's TWA associates remembered vividly, years later, the impression he made on her at this time while she was a guest in the Harlin home. "I had thought," she said, "that he was just an average high school youngster, interested mostly in sports, cars, and girls. But then one day we began talking about Israel and its prob-

37

lems as a new nation, and his questions and comments were as penetrating as any I'd ever heard. Later we talked world politics, world-this, world-that. And it was the same. I was amazed at how much he knew, and wanted to know; at his tremendous hunger for knowledge. . . . No, for more than knowledge. For life itself. . . . I remember thinking, 'He is so young, still a boy. Yet his hunger is like a man's who knows he has little time left.'"

Behind the outward image there was also another half-hidden John: John the artist. His boyhood drawings were now relics of the past, his adult painting still in the future. But it was becoming evident that he had extraordinary sensitivity to form, color and texture. As was to happen later in the mountains, companions on a walk would find themselves waiting in astonishment as the Sequoia Strongboy stopped to examine and admire a tiny flower. In the homes he visited he showed awareness and knowledge of interior decor. Most remarkably, he was keenly interested in women's clothing and had definite, detailed opinions on how his dates should dress. One of his mother's friends reported that "when I heard this big hunk of boy in T-shirt and jeans talking about ruching and bouffant skirts, I could hardly believe my ears."

By now, one is ready to ask, "What manner of boy—or man—is this?" . . . And many did. And many would. . . . The only answer, one feels, is that he was multiple; there were many John Harlins in the one that was his sum-total. He was an athlete. He was an intellectual and an artist. He was a man of action and of reverie, an idealist and a schemer, a gladiator who picked violets, an esthete who could crush bones, a man of total sincerity who was also a poseur, a seeker of ultimate truths who was at the same time fated to be, in many ways, a perpetual adolescent.

Potentially, the spectrum was even wider than this. Some who knew him when he was young believe—and John agreed with them—that if he had come from a background of poverty and deprivation he might conceivably have become a criminal. Not a petty criminal. A rip-roaring multi-gunned one. His explosive energy, his intolerance of restraint and his drive toward violence (which were to increase rather than diminish with the years) could in other circumstances, they believe, have pushed him into the role of a total outlaw from society.

Then, at the other extreme, one finds his feminine and narcissistic

38

traits: his photo modeling, his preening, his unabashed pride in his "Greek god" body, as well as his offbeat interest in flowers, furnishings and women's clothes. In spite of his strength and skills, many of the more conventionally molded athletes of Sequoia High School thought him vaguely "girlish." And in a psychiatrically minded world it is not far-fetched to wonder if his later aggressive, almost excessive maleness was not, at least in part, a consequence of early ambivalence.

In the actual living of his life, there is no slightest suggestion that he was ever anything but sexually normal. No more than he was ever a criminal. Yet it is helpful in understanding him to recognize that his nature was so complex, so protean, that it could approach at its edges such disparate poles. In his adult life, many were to think of John Harlin, in his breadths and depths, appetites and diversities, as a Renaissance rather than a twentieth-century man, somehow displaced on the calendar. As a high school graduate, aged just eighteen, he was barely entering into that manhood; but already he was possessed of vast range, vast talents, vast hungers.

Toward what was it all tending for the Boy in Golden Shorts?

Toward the Navy, his ex-Navy father hoped; and during John's senior year at Sequoia plans were made to seek his admission to Annapolis. In preparation, John again crossed the country and spent the summer of 1953 at the Bullis School, a prepping institution for the Naval Academy in nearby Silver Spring, Maryland. But he didn't like it there. He wanted no part of Annapolis, with its drills and uniforms and rigid discipline.

In the fall, returning home to California, he entered Stanford University.

4. Horizons

Here again is a gray wall of rock. But there is no other grayness, no cloud or storm. Below, the earth is green; above, the sky is blue, the sun beaming. This is Yosemite, Valley of the Sun.

At the foot of the wall is a group of young climbers from the Stanford Alpine Club—some experienced upperclassmen, some novice freshmen—and the former are teaching the latter the rudiments of technical rock climbing. One of the leaders points to the sheer rock, indicating the cracks and ledges, humps and hollows that should be used in climbing it; then slowly he works his way up them to a stance above. From there he lowers a rope, calling down that one of the freshmen should follow, and a big blond youngster ties in and begins to climb. As he ascends, the leader shouts instructions, but his words cannot keep pace with his pupil's progress. Moving strongly, surely, swiftly—far more swiftly than his instructor—he has mastered the pitch in a matter of seconds and is perched beside the older climber, breathing easily, grinning slightly. "You mean like that?" he asks.

The instructor eyes the brash freshman, half with respect, half with resentment. But John doesn't mind the resentment. He waits restlessly while the others come slowly up to him; then is off again on the next pitch, again strong, swift and sure. This is his first true climb. Though in the past he has scaled trees and small cliffs, this is his debut on a mountain wall. Yet he climbs like a veteran. Each movement of hand and foot, each swing and thrust of the body, seems wholly natural to him, as if he had been doing this all his life. Indeed, it seems to him that he *has* been doing it: that this is what his life is about, what he was born for.

Up, up he climbs toward the sun on the tall walls of Yosemite. His eyes shine, his blood tingles, his heart sings.

He was introduced to mountaineering by a new friend, Paul Revak. A giant of a young man from Virginia, Revak was an upperclass member of the fraternity to which John was pledged, and a linesman on the varsity football squad. In the normal American scheme of things, football and mountain climbing do not go together. One is in the mainstream of sport, a recognized road to fame and fortune, while the other is for the nonconformists, the way-outs: lovers of the far, the high, the solitary, who couldn't tell a tailback from a touchback or Walter Camp from Y. A. Tittle. Paul Revak, however, played football Saturdays and went climbing Sundays. And John was soon enthusiastically following suit.

The fraternity he had pledged was Theta Chi, but it never became the focus of his college life and interests. At about the same time he entered Stanford his parents moved from Redwood City to Los Altos, in the hills near Palo Alto, and here he lived for the next two years. At the university, as a freshman, he took English, French, history, geology, and art. Overconfident and weak in grammar, he managed to fail French for one term. In art, specifically design, he made an A, and in the other courses he got by. Filling out his schedule was Naval ROTC, partly as a sop to his father for his defection from Annapolis.

Football was both a joy and a frustration. More than ever he loved the physical slambang of the game, and with his big shoulders, slim hips and great speed, had high potential as a star halfback. But his huge intensity of effort made him injury-prone. He suffered damage both to a leg and to a cartilage in his chest, which left him spending as much time on the bench as on the playing field. And a bench—any bench—was the last place in the world John Harlin wanted to be.

Fulfillment came on Sundays. With no violent movement or bodily contact involved, climbing was possible when football wasn't; and he made the most of it. For these one-day campaigns the scene was in various rocky areas in the hills near Stanford. But when the football season ended he was able to take full weekends, driving off to Yosemite or other distant goals. Sometimes he went with only a few companions. One was apt to be Big Paul Revak, the first friend he had had who could match him in sheer physical strength. Another was Jon Lindbergh, son of the flier, a Stanford upperclassman as shy and withdrawn as his father, who loved the mountains with a quiet passion. At other times the climbing was with a larger group from the Stanford Alpine Club (SAC), of which John soon became a member—with Lindbergh conducting the tests that qualified him for acceptance.

The SAC, true to its name, was no mere outing and hiking club. Limited to about thirty members—male and female, graduate and undergraduate—it was dedicated to climbing of high standards, and along with the Harvard Mountaineering Club, it has produced more topflight American mountaineers than any other college group in the country. As for pre-eminence in any field, there was a price to pay: over the years it has had its share of accidents and fatalities. One of these occurred during John's freshman year (on a venture in which he did not participate) when a climber fell to his death on Mount Shasta. Ironically, it received nationwide publicity because one of the members who *was* along was publicity-shunning Jon Lindbergh.

Another irony of this accident was that it happened on an "easy" mountain, a high but gently sloped volcano. For the most part the SAC aimed at the vertical, to be found in miniature on Peninsula cliffs and on the grand scale in Yosemite Park. As any practiced mountaineer knows, however, steepness and danger are by no means synonymous—provided the climber knows what he is about. And it was precisely to the development of the techniques of steepness that the Stanford club was dedicated.

With his tall trees and small cliffs behind him, John was already a natural climber. But now he learned the many refinements of the craft. There was practice in balance and rhythm, in the finding of holds, the choosing of routes; above all in the use of a rope, the

43

climber's lifeline. (In the accident on "easy" Shasta the man who fell was unroped.) Of supreme importance was the belay, the technique of using a rope to catch a fall at its outset. For steep or overhanging descents there was the maneuver of protected self-lowering that the French call *rappel* and the Germans *Abseil*. In the ascent of vertical fissures there was "jamcracking"; on holdless pitches, "friction" and "tension" climbing; for protection, when a human body belay was not enough, metal *pitons* and *carabiners* to fix a rope to the mountain. Finally, for walls so sheer that "free" climbing was no longer possible, there were the methods of "artificial" climbing, employing pitons not only for protection but for direct aid, and hanging from them networks of ropes and ladders.[1]

With its vast precipices, its firm granite and its generally fine weather, Yosemite has proved one of the best places on earth for vertical rock mountaineering. Before World War II, expert cragsmen, using new techniques, had begun forging their way up seemingly impossible walls; and by the time John Harlin was at Stanford artificial climbing had been carried to a point that a few years before would have been wholly incredible. So difficult and complex were some ascents that they took days to accomplish, with the climbers either tying themselves to the walls overnight or descending on fixed ropes to return in the morning. While an attack was in progress, a face would be festooned with hardware like a rising skyscraper.

As with spectacular development in any field, there was controversy. The old guard among American climbers called the new breed "masons," "steeplejacks," "rock engineers"—and worse—averring that these mechanized acrobatics had no faintest relationship to classic mountaineering. To which the new breed replied that they couldn't care less. They were interested not in classic but in *new* mountaineering; not in the already done but the possibly doable. What was classic now was not so much mountaineering as the eternal struggle between old and young, conservative and radical. And as always, when the issue is truly joined, the young and radical prevailed.

Aged eighteen and a college freshman, John Harlin was still some distance from being a top mountaineer, of whatever breed. Yet all who saw him climb, even in his apprenticeship, agreed that here was a

[1] For a more detailed description of mountaineering terms, see the Glossary.

force to be reckoned with. The word *force* has been carefully chosen. He was not, and never would be, a notably graceful climber. In sheer technique—the practice of which was apt to bore him—he was to remain a half-step or so behind the best of his contemporaries. But in drive and power he was unsurpassed and unsurpassable. And in desire and will. "When I climbed," he has said, "life effervesced within me." And that effervescence, charged and channeled, generated a primal force that was awesome to behold.

Football and mountaineering together could not consume his energy. At 5-foot-11 and 190-odd pounds (the weight he would maintain through the rest of his life), his was a coiled-spring body that needed forever to be in action. At home in Los Altos he would sometimes burst from his room and roam the nearby hills. Or bounding into his Jeepster, he would roar down to the Theta Chi house in Palo Alto and enter the upper-floor room of a fraternity brother by way of wall and window. Having read of the "night-climbers" of Oxford and Cambridge, he decided that Stanford, too, was ripe for such exploits, and with assorted fellow adventurers scaled many of the university buildings under cover of darkness. Most ambitious was a project to ascend the high tower of Hoover Library by its inside staircase and then descend the outside wall by rappel, leaving en route the huge painted footprints of an Abominable Snowman. But this master-plan was thwarted by an undersupply of paint and an oversupply of campus police.

When he could not climb mountains, he dreamed mountains. He read mountains. After years of challenge and repulse, Everest had finally been climbed by the British, and in the pages of Sir John Hunt he followed Hillary and the Sherpa Tenzing to their ultimate perch in the sky. Plans were also afoot, he knew, for powerful attacks on the remaining great unclimbed Himalayas. By the time he was a full man, out of college, they would all be gone: a depressing thought. But he was young enough to rally. Somewhere, someday, he would find his own Everest.

In the nether-world of ground level he had adventures too—though more conventionally. Beth Little of Sequoia was now out of his life, but he had the normal quota of dates with Stanford co-eds, and with one he had his first experience of "all the way." With whores or semi-whores, however, he had no truck at all; nor was he to have at any time during the course of his life. His attractiveness to women made it unnecessary, as his ego made it impossible, for him ever to pay money for the act of love.

At athletics he kept his hand in, but with diminishing intensity. At the end of the football season he joined most of his teammates in playing rugby (which he had learned in Ireland); but at Stanford it was a conditioning, not a competitive sport, and offered no high excitements or rewards. Though of first-team caliber in wrestling, swimming, and track, he did not officially participate in them, contenting himself with showing up at an occasional practice—at which, to his satisfaction, he often bested the regulars. Scholastically, he attended the required minimum of lectures and classes. Except for his failure in French, he kept his head above water. And now and then when he was interested, as in art and English, he did far better than that.

One instance was a theme on Conrad's *Heart of Darkness*, for which he got a straight A. He had been much impressed by the story, particularly by the character of the doomed and desperate Kurtz, and in analyzing him used, interestingly, the analogy of a rope. It was not a climbing rope, however. "In the Navy," he wrote, drawing on his ROTC lore, "the extremity of a rope is called the 'bitter' end. If a rope becomes severely weathered, this portion unravels. At the place where one's perceptions and knowledge end, obviously, the unknown begins. But at this point, if one is suddenly pushed into a sea of darkness where escape seems remote, the mind becomes, in a sense, frayed and unraveled. . . ."

It was no eighteen-year-old meathead who wrote this. But sometimes his *own* mind felt frayed and unraveled. There was so much in the world that he wanted to do, and so much that he didn't that he was expected to do. His parents, true to parental tradition, wanted him to get good college marks, and he didn't care about marks, so long as he didn't flunk out. They wanted him to dress, speak, and behave conventionally, but their conventions were of another generation's than his. Hardest of all for him, they shared with most other Americans an almost total non-response to the magic of mountaineering.

He steered by his own stars. He of course went on climbing. He dressed, spoke, and behaved as he pleased. Politically, his parents were conservative, but he had become, if not a radical, a well-left-of-center liberal, with small tolerance for the opposition.[2] And his rejection of his early religious training had become complete. On a college questionnaire inquiring as to his church affiliation, he wrote flatly: ATHEIST.

Perhaps. During the rest of his life, assuredly, he had no interest in formal religion. . . . But there seems little of the atheist in the boy and man who raised his eyes to his beloved mountains and later wrote of them with such a glow of the spirit. He seems rather a pantheist: one far removed from any creed, yet who found divinity in peak and valley, sun and storm, rock and flower, in each and every component of the natural world. Throughout his life he was to believe that action without contemplation was meaningless. And his search for meanings, whether he himself knew it or not, was often not far afield from a search for God.

As a college freshman, to be sure, no one mistook him for a theologian or a philosopher. Whatever his inner quests and questionings, they were well hidden beneath the cloak of his physical energies. Throughout the winter and spring he climbed whenever he could: on the cliffs near Stanford, in the coastal ranges to north and south, best of all in Yosemite in the High Sierra. More than Los Altos or Palo Alto, Yosemite was home. Its soaring battlements—El Capitan, Half Dome, Cathedral Rocks, the Sentinel, the Spires, the Brothers—became more familiar to him than the Stanford campus, as he scaled them again and again by all manner of routes. In American mountaineering, routes are graded from Class I to Class VI, in ascending order of difficulty, and it is perhaps superfluous to say that John, from the outset, steered for the upper brackets. Between V and VI, however, his choice, interestingly, was V. For this represented the ultimate in "free" climbing —which he favored—while VI-graded routes required artificial aids.

Up and down he went, down and up. And in the process he had both triumphs and troubles. Sometimes he would keep struggling with an "impossible" pitch long after his companions had given up and were standing around half-awed and half-laughing. Once, reaching a ledge a thousand feet above the valley floor, he unroped, stepped back

[2] This would seem to have been mainly on his own initiative. The Stanford campus, at the time, was not notably political-minded; and the spectacular doings across the Bay in Berkeley were still a decade in the future.

carelessly, and fell—for ten feet into a cliffside tree. On another occasion, feeling his oats, he showed off before a group of Alpine Club tyros, climbing hand-over-hand up a rope without a protective belay; and the elders of the club, taking a dim view of this, suspended him. He, however, didn't greatly care. He was no organization man.

. . . Nor was another young climber who appeared in Yosemite during that spring of 1954. Gareth Hemming, of the same age as John, was an engineering student at San Diego State College; but this was his only likeness to an engineer, for he was by nature a wanderer, a vagabond, a member of a newly emergent species called beatnik. He was, however, a beatnik with a difference, a vagabond not of pads, pubs, and coffeehouses, but of the wide sky, the high peaks. And he was almost as expert and ambitious a climber as John Harlin.

Now on Yosemite's Lower Cathedral Rock, with a girl partner, he looked up to see John, also with a partner, on the wall above him. "I didn't know who he was then," he said long after. "But I knew this much—that he was a climber. He was leading a crux pitch, a smooth bastard of a slab with nothing but fresh air below, and he was doing it fast and neat and sure, exactly right. That was my first and lasting image of him."

A little later there was a cry in the stillness. There had been an accident on nearby Upper Cathedral, and an injured climber needed bringing down. Park rangers were not trained for such work; it required expert Yosemite cragsmen; so descending separately, John and Gary Hemming joined forces in the valley and volunteered for the job. With a stretcher from park headquarters, they reascended to the scene of the accident on Upper Cathedral and in an operation that took most of the next day succeeded in lowering the injured climber to safety.

This, their first rescue, was not to be their last. Seven years later, in the Alps, they were again teamed in such a venture; and still later, after John's death, Gary was to be the architect of one of the most notable rescues in mountaineering history.[3] But sufficient to the moment was the job just accomplished. Each had found a fellow climber he admired. Each had made a new friend. And for John it was to be the most enduring and stormy friendship of his life.

That too was for the future, however. As of now, Gary meandered

[3] See footnote on page 230.

48

back toward San Diego and John returned to Stanford. It was late in the spring, with the end of the school year approaching. There was cramming, then exams, and he survived. Then the summer lay ahead. He had made various ambitious plans for the summer, and characteristically chose the most ambitious of all—to go to Europe.

It was easier for him than for most. As the minor son of a TWA captain he could fly the whole round trip on the line free of charge; and once abroad, there were many old friends of his parents who could help out with food and shelter. With the decision made, he was soon up and off. Nor was packing a problem, for his luggage consisted of a small camper's pack and a mountaineering ice ax. Eight and a half years before, a boy of ten with his parents, he had left for Europe wondering what sort of birds he would find to shoot in the Irish bogs. Now, almost a man and alone, he was after bigger game.

Indeed, the biggest, the fiercest, the wildest.

Not birds but a mountain. . . .

The Eiger.

Every mountaineer in the world knows the Eiger. It is not the tallest peak in the Alps, nor the most beautiful. But along with Mont Blanc and the Matterhorn, it is the most famous, and in a class by itself, the most infamous. Like every Alpine peak, it has long since been climbed: first by its easiest route, then by successively harder ones, on its various ridges. Throughout its early history, virtually all mountain climbing was on ridges. It was not until after the First World War that pioneering experts in the Alps began venturing onto the vast sheer faces that lay between them. Progress came slowly—with lives lost—but surely; and after progress, success. By the mid-1930s every major face in the range, like every ridge, had been climbed to the top. Except one: the Eiger's: the north wall of the peak called, appropriately, the Ogre, which far from being climbed, had not even been challenged.

Conservative mountaineers were content to leave it at that. True, its summit height was only 13,040 feet, compared to Mont Blanc's 15,780 and more than 14,000 for many other peaks. But the wall beneath the summit was by far the highest in the Alps, six thousand all-but-vertical feet from base to crest. Still worse, it was the northernmost of the great bastions of the range, therefore a magnet for storms;

and its monstrous sweep was forever racked by avalanches of snow and rock. . . . No, said the Old Guard, the wall of the Eiger is no place for men. . . . But as always, there was a New Breed who thought otherwise.

A new breed, in this case, in more ways than one. They were young Germans and Austrians, and if not all-out Nazis themselves, were unquestionably influenced by the mystiques of the Third Reich. "Führer und Vaterland, victory or death!" were their watchwords, as they set out to conquer the "unconquerable"; and in the beginning, what they reaped was mostly death. The first serious attempt was made in the summer of 1935, a few months after John Harlin was born. The participants were two topflight climbers from Munich, and they forged a route about halfway up the face before being overwhelmed by a storm and succumbing to cold and exhaustion. The next year came an even worse disaster, when four men, two Germans and two Austrians, were killed, one of them dying by inches at the end of a rope while dangling a few feet above his would-be rescuers. Then in 1938 came victory. Again the climbers were a four-man German-Austrian team, and their success, after five days and four nights on the wall was a tremendous feat of skill, courage, and endurance. But there were still Nazi overtones to the exploit—all the more strident in the tension of approaching war—and it remained an open question whether it was primarily a triumph or a perversion of mountaineering.

Time, in its usual fashion, gave the answer. During the years that followed, with men fighting and dying elsewhere, the Eiger was left to its austere solitude; and by the time climbers returned to it, in the late 1940s, mountaineering, like the rest of the world, had changed. Techniques and equipment had been vastly improved through wartime mountain training. New frontiers had been opened. The great peaks of the earth, from Everest down, were now far more accessible than they had been before; and even the wall of the Ogre, now de-Nazified, was considered a legitimate challenge to expert climbers.

A new New Breed responded. By 1954, when John Harlin, with overnight bag and ice ax, set out on his pilgrimage, the Eiger's north wall had been scaled by thirteen parties, totaling thirty-eight men—no longer only Germans and Austrians, but Swiss and French as well. It was by no means tamed, however. Still a murderous mountain, it had now taken a dozen lives, and its ascent demanded the ultimate in

50

human resources. To have climbed this wall, this *Eigerwand*, was automatically to rank among the world's top mountaineers. And of this John Harlin was well aware. Just as he was aware that it had never been attempted, let alone scaled, by either an Englishman or an American.

Like myriad tourists before him, he made his way across Europe to the Swiss resort town of Interlaken. Then he rode up on the mountain railway to the smaller, higher resort of Kleine Scheidegg, and there before him rose the awesome trinity of Jungfrau, Mönch and Eiger. The other two, the Virgin and the Monk, were taller peaks than the Ogre, and in their mantles of snow shone dazzlingly white under the summer sun. Yet it was the smallest of the three that held the eye in its spectacular contrast. For it was almost black. Too steep to hold large banks of snow, it cast them down in spuming avalanches, and what remained was six thousand feet of naked rock and iron-hard ice. For sheer power and savagery, there are few sights on earth to match the north wall of the Eiger.

John stared up at it by the hour. Through the telescope at Kleine Scheidegg's hotel he traced the routes of its conquerors and victims, for from his reading he already knew them all. The precipices above him were almost three times the height of anything in Yosemite. But this was the least of their hazards. Yosemite had fine weather, and its rock was firm granite. Here, on a year-round average, was the worst weather in Europe, along with rotting limestone that, like the snow, broke loose and fell in lethal torrents. It was a death trap of a mountain. For almost every three men who had climbed its wall, one man had died. And this too John knew. Yet it was not with fear or apprehension that his eyes went upward, but with an aching of desire.

The boy with the blond cowlick was wildly ambitious. He was often imprudent. But he was not a fool. Realizing that he could not even approach the mountain without a competent companion, he set about seeking one and, in true Harlin style, came up with the unlikeliest partner imaginable—Tenzing of Everest. Fresh from his last year's ascent to earth's highest point, the Himalayan Sherpa was now a world figure and visiting Switzerland as an invited guest. John was an unknown American college boy. But the shyness that afflicted him at the thought of dramatics or public speaking vanished like magic when he was after something he really wanted. In short order he secured an introduction to Tenzing. The veteran from the East and the youngster

51

from the West immediately took to each other, and presently they were climbing together.

There is no fairy story: they did not climb the Eiger. The Sherpa, though a master of the long uphill grind, had had no experience in highly technical climbing such as the north wall demanded, and now aged forty, had no intention of serving an apprenticeship. Along with Swiss companions, he and John climbed the Jungfrau by a conventional route. On a partial ascent of the Eiger's west ridge (which is *its* conventional route) they studied at close hand the complexities of the bordering face. Finally, they did some exploratory scrambling on the lower part of the face itself, but turned back at the point where real difficulties began; and this ended the brief partnership of John Harlin and Tenzing Norgay. The Sherpa continued on his travels. John was unable to find another climber even remotely capable of trying the Eiger with him. And so the curtain fell on his first confrontation with the mountain that was to become the focus of his life.

In another way, and a strange one, the curtain falls—almost—on that whole summer of 1954. John was traveling alone. For the most part he camped out and hitchhiked anonymously, writing to neither family nor friends. As a result, there is no remaining record of what he did on the rest of his trip, in the Alps or elsewhere—except for one story he was to tell later, and this is suspect. It is suspect because John, through all his days, was not unwilling to stretch the truth to his purposes, and prime among these purposes was what might be called the propagation of the Harlin legend. There were always to be legends, ambiguities and conjectures about him. John had done this or that— or hadn't. John had been here or there—or hadn't. And he himself was the principal contributor. Why this should be so for a man in whose life the hard, verifiable facts were so spectacular, it is hard to say. But one of those very facts is that it was. John often gilded the lily. He was a master of what one of his friends called "instant fusion" of truth and fancy, of what had happened with what he wished had happened. Most sensationally, he fused them—or perhaps did not, no one knows—in a story he told of that summer in Europe.

In the beginning (as far as can be ascertained) he told it to only one person: the girl he was soon to meet and later to marry. Then, years afterward, he repeated it to Bob Rosenaur, when his old high school friend was visiting him in Germany. "I haven't told this to many people," he said to him one evening when they were alone together. "But once here in Europe, I killed a man."

It had been in Rome, he went on. He had been walking alone at night in a deserted street when a footpad held him up at knife's point and demanded his money. John made as if to comply; then saw his opening and jumped the man. Getting him around the neck from behind, he applied pressure. He heard an ominous crack. When he released the man he slumped to the ground, lying motionless, and John took off. "He was dead," said John. "I knew he was dead."

That was all. Rosenaur did not know whether to believe him, and neither does one hearing the story at second hand. There were other close friends to whom he never told it. He never told his parents. But in the last two years of his life, after telling Rosenaur, he again repeated it to at least two friends in Switzerland. After so long a time— true or false—one wonders why.

It *could* have happened. He was strong and tough enough. He had an inbred streak of violence that was to show itself throughout his adult life.

Or it could *not* have happened. John could have been legend-building. Assuming some such incident occurred (which seems likely), the holdup man could merely have been injured, with John adding his death to make a better, more Harlinesque story.

Quite possibly he did not know himself. And now no one ever will.

5. Two Blond Indians

It was to be a large weekend for a Stanford junior called Marilyn Miler. In the fall of 1954 the annual football clash with California was in Berkeley, which meant a long Saturday junket across the Bay for visiting Stanfordians. But for Marilyn it meant an even longer one than for most. She was going not just to one game but two: the junior varsity in the morning and the varsity in the afternoon.

Basically, she was not all that much of a fan. On the J.V. level at least, what she went to see was not a football game but a football player. An outdoor girl, though far from a feminine athlete, she was a novice aspirant for membership in the Stanford Alpine Club, and in the course of several outings had become aware of a blond sophomore named John Harlin. She had not met him; the teamings and pairings had not worked out that way. But she had watched him climb, and the more she watched, the stronger was her awareness. From others who knew him she had heard that he was also a J.V. football player. And a few Saturdays later she was watching him in another role, as Halfback Harlin gave his all for the Stanford Indians.

Again, they did not meet. After the game John vanished into a locker room, and at the Big Game in the afternoon he was lost among the thousands. In the evening Marilyn went to a dance. But there was still no John. It remained for Sunday to be *the day*.

Again there was a SAC outing; she went; and at the campus gathering point she found herself suddenly face-to-face with him. Suspended by the club the previous spring, he had now been reinstated, qualifying as a leader-instructor; and today, it developed, he was taking out a small group, separate from the main one, for special practice in rope-handling.

"Well, with which are *you* going?" he asked her.

"The way he said *you*," she was to recall, "implied that he didn't know I had a name, let alone what it was." But simultaneously, being a woman, she realized that her awareness of him had not been a one-way street, and forthwith made some quick calculations. If I say I'll go with him, she told herself, he'll think I'm chasing him. If I say with the others, he'll have to come to me. Yes, that's better: make him come to me. . . . But maybe he won't. . . .

"I'll go with you," she said.

The practice cliff on which they climbed was tall and steep, but she wasn't frightened. There were five of them in the party—three men climbers on one rope, she and John on another—and with John guiding and belaying, she felt a confidence that surprised her. He did not baby her. He saw to it that she climbed, and was not hauled up the cliff. Yet he was *there*, both in body and spirit. Joining him at the top of a pitch, she brushed some earth and leaves from his back and was quickly conscious of his steel-hard frame. But there was no steel in his eyes as, later, they sat on a high ledge and talked. The other men talked only climbing shop: of holds and stances and the use of the rope. John spoke also of the world around them: of trees and foliage, sun and sky. And now again she felt surprise, and pleasure, for she had not altogether expected this from a mountaineering halfback.

Nor was that the end of the far-from-lost weekend. Come evening, a newly familiar voice floated up to her dormitory window, and there outside was John, with another of the SAC climbers, a boy called Dean Johnson. "Can you find a date for Dean?" John called. She could and did. John was *her* date. And before evening's end she had learned still more about him. It began with her confessing her devious female

56

reasoning when he had asked her that morning whom she wanted to climb with; and by the time she was through he was grinning.

"That's not so female," he said.

"No?"

"I was doing the same thing myself."

"You mean—"

"I wanted you to come with me. I was opening my mouth to ask you to, but then I thought no, she'll think I'm chasing her. So I made you make the decision"—John's grin grew wider—"and took my chances."

Now she was called to the phone day and night. A Jeepster came and went. A paper airplane flew in her window and on its wing was written, *Want to go swimming? or skiing? or climbing? or dancing? or . . . ?* LET'S SOMEDAY. *To Mara from J.*

That was what he called her: Mara. And Mara's life was to be far different from that of the former Marilyn Miler.

Not that dates or an eager boy were anything new to her. She was a pretty girl, blonde, blue-eyed, trim-figured, and as a college junior of twenty, a year older than John, she had had her share of experience. Like John's high school girl, Beth Little, however, she was "serious," a hard worker. The holder of one of Stanford's top scholarships, she was majoring in biology, and after hours, to earn her board and lodging, served as a "hasher" in the college dining hall, as well as a sometime cashier and baby sitter. Her home was in the country near Olympia, Washington, and her family background unusual; for her father, though college-educated, had deliberately chosen a withdrawn non-competitive life as a small-scale farmer and rural carpenter. The atmosphere in which she had grown up was simple, high-minded, almost Thoreauvian, and had left her with a deep love of the outdoors and the world of nature. But she was no Amazon, in body or spirit, and was successfully to resist John's efforts to make her one.

Over the long run, that is. In the beginning there was no resisting anything, for she had tangled with a powerhouse. And presently the new Mara Miler found herself involved in an exploit she could not have dreamed of a few weeks earlier. The time was Thanksgiving vacation, the place Castle Crags State Park in northern California, and the occasion a four-day outing of the Stanford Alpine Club, of which she was now a novice member. The Crags were no walls of the Eiger, or even Yosemite, but no molehills either, and a subsequent report in the *SAC Journal* gives a fair idea of what could be, and was, done there. "John Harlin," it noted, "discovered a route directly up [one of the peaks]. The route follows a distinct but shallow gully which appears unclimbable from below and presents the climber with the prospect of a 130-foot Class V lead on a nearly vertical face." What the *Journal* neglected to add was that at John Harlin's heels was Mara Miler.

She had not, of course, expected anything remotely like it. The original idea—or at least *her* idea—was that she would be a camp follower, get some studying done, and perhaps try a few brief scrambles of the sort she had already performed. But John had other notions. First she found herself lured from camp to the foot of a precipice—"just to watch." Then, literally "roped in," she was on her way up, with John in the lead and two other strong SAC climbers as teammates. Though terrified, she was resolved not to show it; and gradually, as on earlier climbs, the worst of her fear wore off in the realization that she was not going to fall. John would not let her fall. On some stretches she was able to climb herself; on others she had to be helped. But always he was there above her, climbing strongly and surely, belaying the rope that held her, shouting down encouragement as they moved higher and higher. Until at last they reached the top of the peak. On her first real climb, incredibly, she had ascended a virgin route, and John's pride in her as she joined him on the summit was enough to compensate for the ordeal.

John's pride. . . .

It was on the Castle Crags that she first felt the full force of that pride: in her, in himself: the pride of the boy "who was convinced he could do anything." And the scene of its happening was more appropriate than she knew. Later, other Stanford climbers dubbed the peak they had scaled Harlin's Horror. But it had an older name, and a strange one, given it in the indeterminate past by someone who, whatever else he may have been, was also a reader of the classics. The name was Hubris. This was Hubris Crag. And in the Greece of Aeschylus and Sophocles *hubris* meant defiance and arrogance before the gods, the pride of man that goes before the fall.

Marilyn Miler did not know this then.

But she knew John's pride as they stood on Hubris' summit.

There were other things in life besides climbing. The LET's SOMEDAY on the paper plane came quickly, as they saw each other almost daily, doing everything together that time and season allowed. When snow came to the Sierras they went skiing—both for the first time—but here there was no two-on-a-rope, as in climbing. While she learned her fundamentals on the novice slopes, he took at once to the steepest runs: zooming down, falling, zooming again: no cautious apprentice but a locomotive without brakes.

Sometimes he half-forgot he was a student with classes and assignments. He still took art courses with enthusiasm, and liked geology to the degree that he vaguely thought of making it his future profession. But he neglected his other courses so badly that he was presently on probation. As before, when in scholastic trouble, he didn't much care. His eye roved occasionally toward the U. S. Army, and specifically the Green Berets, as a likely escape from academe to the world of action and derring-do.

"Serious" Marilyn, however, had no intention of letting either him or herself go down the drain. Her own work meant much more to her than mere getting by, and she was resolved to go on into graduate studies and become a professional biologist. Essentially an organized and methodical person, she strove mightily to bring order into John's helter-skelter ways. Indeed, theirs was, in its fashion, the classic confrontation of the scientific and artistic temperaments; but with a not-so-classic twist, for here Science wore skirts and Art an athlete's sweatshirt.

In point of fact, his interest in art was becoming ever more serious. He painted and sketched both for his courses and his own satisfaction. With occasional divagations toward geology, Green Berets, and of course mountaineering, he was considering design of some sort as a future career.

In his poorer subjects, Marilyn worked with him. She forced *him* to work, to the point where he got off probation, but his impatience with detail and routine made for difficult going. Fortified by wide but uncoordinated reading, he would charge off from the specific to the general, the over-all, the Grand Design (ah, how he loved Grand Designs); and it was all but impossible not to follow him, for when he pursued an idea it was with the drive and force that he attacked a mountain wall. Among people generally, he was not loquacious. With those who bored him, he could be monumentally silent. But with his Mara he loved to talk. And talk they did, with the magic of young talk—about themselves, the future, the world, the universe.

She was a talker too. And she had opinions. When they did not jibe with his there was sometimes trouble, and he would take off in a huff with a goodbye forever. At one or two in the morning the phone would ring for her, waking the dormitory. The next evening there would be flowers. Came the day when a department store delivered an *après-ski* ensemble that he had picked out for her himself.

With other boys who had dated her there had been nothing like this, and the country girl from Washington State was left breathless and dazzled. Nor was the cosmopolite from Paris and points east reluctant to play his role to the hilt. Early on, he spoke of grim doings in night-time Rome. He recounted his Eiger adventure, with a bit of altitude added. His maternal ancestry became definitively Hapsburgian, his parents' Israeli friend a "Middle Eastern princess," and his father one of those unfortunates who pay ninety percent income tax. Further, on one notable occasion, noncosmopolite Mara was briefed on *haute etiquette*, when, as she wrote her family, "At a restaurant, John and I were eating salad. I apologized for eating the lettuce, but insisted I liked it, though one usually leaves it for decoration. John said his family always eat their lettuce—even when dining with ambassadors."

So that was settled.

On a sub-Hapsburg level, and with another side of his nature, he was delighted to learn that she, like he, had a touch of Indian in her lineage. On her mother's side it was straight Finnish, on her father's predominantly British-American, but with a long-ago Iroquois in the background: just as John had—or claimed—a distant Cherokee. They had found another happy point of kinship as two blond Indians.

Like others before and after, Marilyn was bewitched and baffled by the many-Johns-in-one. Far from content with buying her one outfit, he was interested in all her clothes and had definite preferences: among them, slim waists and flaring, though not bouffant, skirts. ("Those that flex with the hips" as he described them.) He liked women's hair long, and as Marilyn compliantly let hers grow, discussed with her how best to wear it. In a room he would note the blends of color and texture, at

60

a table the arrangement of silver and centerpiece. And his love of flowers and animals was stronger than ever. To her pleasure, Marilyn became aware that there were a few soft spots even in his physical weaponry. In casual, as opposed to purposeful, walking, he tired more quickly than she (though this, she conceded, was more from boredom than fatigue). And when swimming, his iron frame shook and shivered in water that she considered merely pleasantly cool.

This was one side of the coin. On the other, more often visible, he was male power incarnate, the irresistible force seeking the immovable object. If with those who bored him he was silent, with those who challenged he was argumentative, even belligerent, and with the confidence of his great strength, he was not above picking a fight for its own sake. Always there was latent violence in him, close beneath the surface. And if it did not often burst out in full dimension—as it had (so he said) in Rome—it showed itself over and over in a fierce competitiveness, a compulsion to excel. John not only drove himself. By both precept and example, he drove others. On as simple a venture as a hike on a forest trail, he would set a pace geared to his own power, and it was for the rest to keep up—or fall behind.

Marilyn Miler tried hard to keep up. "I've been nicknamed 'Harlin's puppy dog,'" she wrote her parents. "But he makes a very good master."

She loved him.
And he loved her.
But there were projects. Always projects.

With the coming of spring it was again time for Yosemite weekends, and they were often together on Stanford Alpine Club outings. Even John, however, was willing to concede that its vaster verticalities were too much for her. She would usually make smaller practice climbs or hike on the scenic trails, while he pushed harder and harder routes up the soaring granite—often in company with Paul Revak, with whom he shared the rank of SAC "superman." Sometimes she would look up to see their tiny figures on a wall high above. Sometimes she would hear John's version of a yodel—a wild and joyous "Y-A-A-A-R-V-O"—descending to her through the still blue air.

In the evenings, at camp, there were bonfires and singing. The favorite song of the club, and of John as well, was a long and lusty ballad called *Jam Crack Joe*, and in the star-strewn nights voices rose in the chorus:

> *That Joe he is a climber from his head down to his heel;*
> *His attack there is no rock can long resist.*
> *He is so tough and callused and his muscles so like steel*
> *That he hammers in his pitons with his fist.*

There were those who recognized affinities between Jam Crack Joe and Jam Crack John. Some to John's glory—but some not. Several of the more conservative SAC climbers disliked his rough-and-tough competitive attitude, and at least one had an unhappy experience with him that he was never to forget. "John was patient and understanding with novices," he recalled years later, "but an all-out rival to anyone he felt was even close to being an equal. I myself wasn't remotely an equal in speed or power, and I knew it. But I was older than John, with longer and wider experience, and on this climb we did together he was out to show me who was top man. Leading the rope, he moved at a tremendous pace. I could nowhere near keep up with him; after each pitch he would have a long wait, belaying, while I followed; and when at last I joined him he would look at me—not say a word, just look at me—with cold contempt in his eyes, like a Nazi storm trooper."

This is a long way from those brown eyes, "soft and deep, like fresh-plowed warm soil." And a long way, too, from the liberal political John who hated all things authoritarian and fascistic. But it is at least a partial measure of his youthful arrogance, of the *hubris* that drove him against both gods and mere men.

Much as he loved them, he was yearning to extend his scope beyond Yosemite walls. And during spring vacation he had the chance: driving with a group of SAC friends—but sans Marilyn—to Wyoming's Tetons. These were the mountains, the first mountains, he had seen as a boy from Kansas City, and he had plans for ambitious ascents. But it proved too early in the year. The range was choked with blizzard and snowdrift, and the team had all it could do digging in and out of its camps. John worked off his energy by breaking trail and toting the heaviest pack. During the night of the biggest snowstorm he slept outdoors in a sleeping bag rather than in a tent—"to toughen himself up."

62

When he returned to Stanford, it was to find that there had been another tragedy in the Alpine Club: Ann Pottenger, a good friend of his and Marilyn's, had succumbed to exhaustion on a climb in Yosemite. Known as a girl who "would rather die than give up," she had done exactly that, attempting an exploit too great for her strength. And there were many who felt that her death was a foolish and pathetic waste of a young life. . . . Not John, however. . . . "He has eternal admiration for Ann, because she *forced* herself," Marilyn wrote to her family. Then later, about her own feelings: "If I must die, I would rather die *living* than live—*dying* of old age and senility."

It would have been hard for her if the future wife of John Harlin had felt otherwise. From beginning to end he believed that "death is part of it all," and that if a woman chose to follow the mountain way it must be on the same terms as a man.

His, one has often heard, was a generation whose goal was security and whose motives were "other-directed." But John had not even read the preamble to its constitution. As he approached his twentieth birthday, security, of any shape, form, or variety, was the last thing on earth he wanted. Nor, short of fame (which he greatly wanted), did he give a damn what people thought of him. Proof of the latter came, spectacularly, toward the end of his sophomore year when he announced that he was going to be a dress designer.

His motivation, one feels in retrospect, was unclear even to himself. To curious outsiders he gave as reason that it was to make money—in clear contradiction of his non-security stand. To the surprised chairman of Stanford's Department of Fine Arts he averred that he "wanted to make women look beautiful." Unquestionably, part of it was that he *was*, strangely but genuinely, interested in women's clothing; that he had a flair for form, color, and texture, and at least a modest talent in drawing. And part, one suspects, was his pleasure in thumbing his nose at what was expected. The reaction was all that a press agent could have hoped for. A columnist in the San Francisco *Bulletin* wrote a story about the football halfback who planned to be a couturier, and in short order John received a letter from the I. Magnin department store inviting him to an interview. As usual, however, he was shooting high. What he wanted first, he decided, was a summer apprenticeship with one of the top Paris dressmakers, and presently his father, through his

TWA connections, was sounding out such firms as Dior, Balmain, and Schiaparelli. To the man who had hoped his son would go to Annapolis, dress designing—though assuredly different—was no stranger a pursuit than mountaineering; and he was getting used to taking things in stride.

In spite of his costly misadventure the previous year, he was still involved in mining ventures, and in June, with young John free of college, father and son went uranium prospecting in Nevada. Meanwhile Marilyn, in pursuance of her biological studies, enrolled for the summer at Stanford's Hopkins Marine Station at Pacific Grove. And toward the first of July John left for Europe. As in 1954, he traveled without charge on TWA; and although he was now presumably bound for the salons of Paris, his meager luggage again included an ice ax.

Unlike the previous summer, this one is well documented. For now there was Mara, and he wrote her faithfully. Indeed, more than faithfully—passionately and possessively—and when once, in one of her own letters, she was indiscreet enough to mention a date with a fellow biologist, he rose stormily to the occasion. "I am jealous of anything that comes close enough to touch you," he wrote back. "Even those lousy fish."

Traveling free on an airline presents its problems as well as its pleasures. Thus his first stop in Europe was Lisbon, because that was the destination of the first plane on which he could hitch a ride. From there he went to Madrid, from Madrid to Rome (with no report of further trouble), and from Rome, finally, to Paris, where he put up at a pension on the Left Bank. By now there had been much communication, through TWA, with various leading couturiers. But none seemed to be exactly falling over itself to acquire the services of a Californian halfback-mountaineer, and he was given the French equivalent of "Don't call us, we'll call you." However, Paris was, as always, full of young people of all nations, and while he waited he made friends and kept busy. In a neighborhood bistro, he challenged and held to a draw "a big blond guy who holds the arm-wrestling championship of Sweden." Perhaps to strike back at Marilyn's biologist friend, he noted for her benefit that he was "continually being confronted with vast numbers of young women up to no good."

But even with such diversions at hand, he was no waiter-around. He eyed his ice ax; he rubbed it; then taking a firm hold, he was off toward the Alps. In Geneva, through the TWA office, he met an American law student by the name of Richard Collins, who was also a mountaineer, and by the same day's end the two were headed for the heights. John's original plan had been to go again to the Eiger, for it had become increasingly his hope and dream to be the first American to climb its fearsome north face. But in that summer of 1955 he was not even to have a look at it. Collins, it developed, had a date with a "very special" girl in Zermatt, with whom he shared a long-standing plan to climb the Matterhorn; and for him, therefore, there was no question of going elsewhere. Though disappointed, John decided to go with him, knowing from previous experience how hard it was to find a climbing partner. And so off they went. Promptly on arrival in Zermatt, Collins discovered that his "very special" one had given him the go-by in favor of a handsome Swiss guide, meaning he and John might as well have gone to the Eiger after all. But by now, there they were, time was short, and the Matterhorn, looming above, was no easy mountain to turn one's back on.

Uncharacteristically for John, they began by following the book. By long tradition, most Matterhorn aspirants preface their climb with a trial run on the nearby, lesser Riffelhorn; and this he and his companion did—with the usual Harlin variations. Though older than John and a mountain lover, "Rip" Collins was far from an experienced cragsman. Yet they set out to climb the Riffelhorn on its hardest side, by a route that had been mastered only a few times previously. Leading throughout, John worked his way up a couloir in the 3000-foot wall, but near the top came to an overhang, and here there was trouble. The only way past the bulge seemed to be a diagonal traverse, and he tried it. But the holds petered out. He could neither get up nor maneuver a retreat. Finally, with fingers stiff and numb, he lost his hold and fell, dropping some eighty feet and dangling free on the rope before he was held by Rip and a protective piton.

Tough and resilient, he was not hurt. Swinging back in to the wall, he climbed up again. But the inexperienced Rip, though he had performed a masterful belay, was badly shaken by the mishap, and they waited a bit for him to regain breath and confidence. Meanwhile other climbers, who had seen the fall from a nearby easier route, were calling down from the summit, offering to lower ropes to help them up; and Rip was all for it. But John would have none of this. Opening

65

what his companion called "his bag of tricks," he brought out pitons, hammer, and carabiners, and with their help again attacked the overhang, and this time cleared it. Reaching the Riffelhorn's summit, they took the easy way down to Zermatt, where word of their climb had preceded them and they were greeted as heroes.

It was not a role they were to play for long, however, for their Matterhorn venture, which now began, was to end quite differently. In fact it must take rank as the one all-out fiasco of John's climbing career.

On the day after the Riffelhorn they hiked up the usual trail to the base of the peak and spent the night there at the well-known Hörnli Hut. In the fine summer weather the hut was crowded with prospective climbers, among them—to Rip's discomfiture—his ex-"special girl" Chris, now not with one guide but three, who were to make a photographic record of her next day's ascent. Their route would be the northeast ridge, straight up from the Hörnli: the way by which the mountain had first been scaled in 1865 by Edward Whymper, but which had since become an easy "tourist trail." And so too would that of the other climbers, mostly with guides. . . . Except for John and Rip. . . . No guides for them, of course. And for John at least, no tourist trail, God forbid. What *he* was after was the Matterhorn's north face, which, if slightly less murderous than the wall of the Eiger, was still one of the classic "impossibles" of the Alps and had been scaled by only a few master climbers. It was largely because of its lure that he had allowed himself to be diverted to Zermatt. And though he would have preferred a stronger partner than Rip Collins, he was not going to let this deter him. After all, he had got them up the Riffelhorn couloir, and he was confident he could do the same on the mighty *Nordwand*.

Such was his plan. What happened was rather different.

In Alpine climbing it is routine to begin major ascents at two or three in the morning, so that a party will be down from its peak before the midday thaw brings rockfall and avalanches. And so it happened next day at the Hörnli. In the darkness, the many climbers, including Chris and her guides, set off up the northeast ridge. As did John and Rip, in another direction. By traversing northwestward from the hut across the mountain's flanks, John had figured, they would emerge on the lower reaches of the north face. But as they moved on it became

66

apparent that something was wrong in his calculations. Instead of carrying them along horizontally, their route led steadily downward. With cliffs and gulfs to either side, there seemed no way to change direction, and in the black of night visibility was almost nil. All they knew was that they were headed down and down, and that if they kept on much longer they would leave the mountain behind them.

They held a council of war, and John admitted defeat. If they waited until daylight it would be too late for a big climb. A day's postponement was impossible because Rip had to be back in Geneva the next evening. The north face was manifestly out, and the best that could be done, if they were to climb the Matterhorn at all, was to retrace their steps and follow the others up the northeast ridge.

So they returned to the Hörnli. They started up the tourist trail. Judging by John's pace on the Riffelhorn, Rip expected them to catch up with the rest in short order. But it didn't happen. John, leading on the rope, moved very slowly, very carefully. At intervals, on the easier going, he gave up the lead and followed. Puzzled, Rip wondered if he had been really shaken by his Riffelhorn fall and it was only now showing. Or if the very easiness of the climb was boring him. In any case, progress was ploddingly slow, and it was full daylight before they reached the tiny Solvay Hut halfway up the peak. Here they rested briefly, then went on. Still slowly, very slowly, while the sun climbed the sky. Then figures appeared above them, descending, and soon they were passing the vanguard of the "tourists" on their way down from the top.

Toward mid-morning something happened to the sun. It paled and vanished. In its place was cloud and grayness, and a shrill wind began to whistle across the rocks of the ridge. For another half hour, then an hour, they climbed on, reaching the shoulder of the Matterhorn, about a thousand feet beneath its summit. But by now the weather had grown worse; it was almost a storm that was blowing. There was another council, another admission of defeat. Not that they could not reach the summit if they tried. But to what purpose? For what pleasure? All that would greet them would be more windblown cloud, and the way down, in the afternoon thaw, would be tricky and dangerous.

They turned. They began the descent. Rip went first on the rope, John second, in belay position, and down they came. Still slowly, still carefully—but not carefully enough. For on a patch of snow below the Solvay Hut Rip lost his footing. The snow slid away; beneath it was ice; and on the ice he tobogganed toward the precipice below. The pitch had not seemed hazardous, and John, above, was not in a secure belaying stance. All he could do as the rope spun out was to search desperately for a hold, and in the last instant he found one. It was behind him and above his head, and when the pull came, one hand was clutching there while the other strained at the rope that led down to Rip. Rip was a big man, but John was a strong one. He held. The rope held. Rip's progress stopped.

But it was not over yet. John was in a spot where he could find no firm position from which to haul Rip up; and Rip, without crampons, began to slip again each time he moved. For several minutes they were pinioned motionless to the mountainside, while the strain on John's arms grew ever greater. . . . Then, all in one, came climax and rescue. . . . Again figures appeared above them, climbing downward, and as they drew near they materialized as Rip's "special girl" Chris and her three-guide escort. It took the guides a matter of seconds to secure John's position and pull Rip to safety, and when a few breaths had been drawn the sextet continued the descent in roped formation. "They drove us down that mountain like a team of horses," said Rip later, not too gratefully. And as a bonus, back in Zermatt that evening, Chris gave a description of the view from the top.

—Thus the Matterhorn story as told by Collins long afterward. But not by John ever, at any time. No lover of fiascos, especially when he himself was at stage center, he again activated one of his "instant fusions" of fact and fancy, with the result that his venture on the mountain assumed the same ambiguous aspects as the previous year's episode of the holdup in Rome.

It began with a postcard to Marilyn, sent from Zermatt, in which he wrote, "I climbed the N. face of the Matterhorn." In a subsequent letter from Paris he amended this, vaguely, to "Whymper's route N. face of Matterhorn." And from then on, for the rest of his life, he told the story as it pleased him to tell it. Rip Collins, becoming a lawyer and later a judge, withdrew from the climbing world, moved to Alaska, and was not readily available to interested questioners. His ex-girl Chris and her guides barely knew John's name at the time and presumably soon forgot the whole incident. The field was free for the mythmaker, and he ran the length of it, going so far, years later, as to list *Matterhorn* (*N. face*) among his climbs in his application for membership in the American Alpine Club. . . . "But by that time," one of his old friends has said, "he probably believed it himself."

At all events, when he came down from the Matterhorn it was never to return. In the same card to Marilyn in which he said he had climbed the north face, the "other John" wrote, "I have never seen flowers so beautiful as here in the mountains. I wanted so for us to gather them together." Then he returned from the heights to the realm of *haute couture*.

Here, no less than on the mountain, Harlin mythology was to be hatched. At the time of his death in 1966, newspapers and magazines throughout the world—drawing on statements made by John at various times—reported that in his youth he had worked as a designer for either Dior, Balmain, or both. But this was simply not true. Dior, along with other dressmakers who had been approached through TWA, turned him down sight unseen. At Balmain's he did have interviews, first with a *sous-directeur*, then with Pierre Balmain himself, and the latter was so taken with him—"he was so completely off-type for a designer"—that he invited him to his country home for the weekend. But after sounding him out and seeing some of his sketches, he told him he did not think he was cut out to be a couturier.

As compensation, John at least had a weekend to remember, meeting fellow guests who ranged from a Nobel Prize winner to Liberace. And he, being John, gave his host something to remember as well. "When he arrived," Balmain recalled after many years had passed, "I showed him to his room and told him to make himself comfortable and come down to the garden, where I was playing cards with two friends. A few minutes later he appeared on the lawn wearing only the briefest of red shorts. He was walking so naturally in the sun that the three of us greatly admired both his physique and his nonchalance at displaying it."

That was the end of Parisian couture—and of his semi-factual, semi-mythological summer in Europe. A week later, with his father and Marilyn, he was again prospecting for uranium in Nevada, telling them of the ascent of the Matterhorn's north face and of draping models in Balmain's atelier.

Back home, things continued to happen fast: some good, some not so good, all factual.

Beginning his junior year at Stanford, he decided, in spite of his disappointment in Paris, to major in fine arts and specialize in dress and costume design—the only male student in the university to do so.

To his chagrin, he was not invited to early practice as a candidate for the varsity football team. The Stanford head coach asked him to report again to the junior varsity, holding out strong hope for future promotion. But John had had enough jayvee and, for the time at least, he gave up football.

When a physical examination disclosed a slight excess of sugar in his urine, he was dropped from Naval ROTC. But with true service logic, the Air Force ROTC forthwith accepted him, and he was pleased with the change.

—As he was pleased with another and greater change in his life when, in October, he and Marilyn were married.

6. Husband

They had talked marriage since back in the spring. From Europe he had brought her not one but two rings: a miniature Swiss watch and an Egyptian scarab. From the time of his return they had considered themselves engaged, and were now unwilling to wait longer.

There was minimal parental opposition. Though they had met John only once, the Milers readily gave their blessing, but they were recluses to the point where they neither staged the wedding nor came down for it to California. As for John I and Sue Harlin, they would probably have preferred a daughter-in-law from a more prosperous and conventional family, and, most certainly, a deferment until their son was of age and out of college. But they too accepted the inevitable with good grace, and the wedding took place in their Los Altos home.

Marilyn was, if anything, even more non-religious than John. Neither wanted a church ceremony, and their choice of minister was a Unitarian. In her father's absence, Marilyn was given away by her younger brother David, a sorely beset young man suffering from both chronic illness and

71

almost total blindness. Best man to the groom was old friend Bob Rosenaur, for whom John was to perform a similar service a year later. Possessing no suit of which coat and trousers matched, John wore a conservative sports jacket with slacks; and Marilyn eschewed full bride's regalia for a white cocktail dress.[1]

With classes and assignments making implacable demands, there was no immediate honeymoon. Through the university placement service they found a home with a well-to-do family in nearby Atherton, with lodging free in exchange for services, consisting of housework for Marilyn and care of the grounds for John—"when he remembered it," she said, "which wasn't often." Basic food money came, to John's embarrassment, from the Milers, and other funds from the senior Harlins and odd jobs. The Jeepster was still at hand. So were friends, many college activities, and—a bit more distantly—mountains.

As in every marriage, there were flies in the ointment. One, for John, was their difference in age; for Marilyn was now twenty-one, he only twenty, and in such matters as liquor buying and car insurance, she was his "legal guardian." Also, she studied harder than he approved of. A college year ahead of him to begin with, she had further made up time so that she would get her degree in December and was now working all-out down the final stretch. Among his less favorite companions were her fellow biologists, with whom, not unnaturally, she enjoyed talking shop; and one evening, at a gathering in the home of one of her professors, he found himself truly at sea. At such affairs it was assumed that the men were biologists, the women wives, and so assuming, another guest started speaking to John of matters protozoan and chromosomic. Said John, in precipitate retreat, "I'm a wife."

For Marilyn, too, there were trials she had not anticipated. As a date, John had always been bursting with life, projects, enthusiasms; but now she saw him in his periodic funks, pacing a room or staring by the hour at television (which he said he hated). When his inner tensions grew unendurable, he would talk grimly of "the thin line between sanity and madness," or, in other moods, lash out at her or pick fights with his friends. Most upsetting of all, perhaps, was his insistence, to her surprise and shock, on sleeping with a gun under his pillow. Happily, it was never used, except as an occasional companion on nighttime

[1] Said Marilyn later (in a documentary rather than romantic mood): "I bought the wedding ring, the flowers, and paid the minister. I had been working, John not."

72

prowlings. Yet it was a disturbing reminder of the dark and violent side of the man she had married.

On balance, though, they were happy together, and in general their life followed normal patterns. As before their marriage, they went out when they could afford to. They both liked the theater and good movies. They liked to dance (though John only conservatively; he never would, or could, hop and bop). And they liked good food, good parties, long evenings of talk. Non-smokers, they also drank little, and that mostly wine or beer. For John this was partly a matter of training; even with football behind him, he had a passion for physical fitness. But with the non-drinking the reason went deeper, and it was simply that he had no need to drink. Though he had his full share of inhibitions and frustrations, they were not of the sort that liquor dimmed or assuaged.

Academically, in his junior year, he was doing better than before, thanks both to Marilyn and to the fact that he was now free to take only subjects of his choice. Of his art majors, which included both historical surveys and practical instruction, he particularly liked painting and design. And at the far end of the spectrum he found his courses in Air ROTC more to his taste than the Naval variety. Except in the fields of mechanics and engineering, which were always his bugbears, he was consistently near the top of his class, and he was eagerly looking forward to actually learning to fly.

There was still climbing, of course: whenever and wherever possible. And when, on Thanksgiving weekend, there was the first chance for a brief honeymoon, it was staged in true Harlin style. Again the scene was Castle Crags Park, in the shadow of Hubris, and again John had hubristic plans for an ambitious ascent. But it was not to be, for a snowstorm struck, and for almost the whole of the time they were confined to their tents. No great hardship on a honeymoon, one would say—except that there were only two tents for seven occupants. As honored bride, Marilyn was awarded the prime sleeping position in the middle of the three-man tent, with John on one side, a fellow SAC member, Paul Scithers, on the other, and herself in the hard wet gap between their two air mattresses. Further, as again the only woman along, it became her privilege to demonstrate the techniques of Thanksgiving turkey roasting in a blizzard.

She too had her toughness: this blonde biologist from the boondocks.

Back home, none the worse for wear, she plunged into work for her final exams. In her spare time she was housewife, houseworker, and vice-president of the Stanford Women Students' Association. And in her spare time from *these* she found an occasional odd moment to consider the fact that she was pregnant.

As a Christmas present, she won her B.S. degree. Then, as the new year of 1956 advanced, and her pregnancy with it, she tapered off her activity. She was still resolved to continue her biological studies, but, with motherhood ahead, had decided to space them out so as to reach her next goal, a master's degree, in June of 1957. This was when John, if all went well, would get his undergraduate degree, and the timing seemed neat and pragmatic.

As of this winter and spring, therefore, the Harlin pace was less strenuous than usual. Even John cut down somewhat on his multifarious projects—though not, to be sure, to the point where he stopped climbing. And while another summer in the Alps was obviously out of the question, he had an eye firmly cocked at more accessible game.

First, however, came the birth of John E. Harlin III, and soon after, with the college year ended, Marilyn and baby moved up to the Milers, near Olympia, Washington. John, his twenty-first birthday behind him, went off for two weeks at Hamilton Air Force Base at San Rafael, California, with the summer training unit of Stanford's Air ROTC; then rejoining his family, had some indoctrination in his new role as paterfamilias. He did not stay put for long, however. With Mount Rainier and other peaks of the Cascades and Olympics virtually in his in-laws' back yard, he spent much of his time on their white slopes, perfecting his snow-and-ice climbing, in which he had thus far had limited experience. When she had regained her strength, Marilyn sometimes joined him, and on one outing they carried baby John, papoose-style, to almost ten thousand feet on Rainier. As always, John exulted in her companionship in the mountains. Of a climb they made in the Olympics he wrote her later: "I was very proud of you. You bore yourself like a man and yet retained your femininity"—which was praise as high as he could bestow. But soon after, leaving wife and baby behind, he was off on a trip to the Canadian Rockies.

This was the first of many times, over many years, of which Marilyn would be asked, "Why did you let him go? Why didn't you stop him?"

74

To which her reply, then and always, was "No one ever stopped John from doing anything."

Nor did she even try. "If I'd tried and was unsuccessful," she has said, "I would have lost him physically. If I'd been successful, I would have lost what he *was*, the man I loved and married. . . . Besides," she would add, "when he was away I could get some studying done."

In any case, off he went. His companions were Jerry Robertson, a student at Arizona State University, whom he had met climbing during the spring; Rick Tidrick, another mountain friend; and a young Stanford faculty couple who were members of the SAC. Making their base in Golden, British Columbia, they climbed in both the Rockies and the neighboring subrange of the Selkirks, and blessed by good weather, made several successful ascents. The easiest was of Mount Victoria, the picture-peak above Lake Louise. Other, harder challenges were on Snowpatch Spire, an almost vertical tower that had been rarely topped, and Mount Sir Donald, on which John, Robertson, and Tidrick set a record for speed. As an added touch, the trio climbed three lesser peaks in a single day, and then the whole group headed homeward, content with a good bag of summits.

For John, however, there remained a final adventure. Dropped off by the others on the outskirts of Olympia, he phoned the Milers to pick him up, and still in his climbing clothes, unkempt and bewhiskered, was waiting at the roadside when two policemen in a cruise car stopped to question him. His answers were not satisfactory, and he was arrested for vagrancy. When, a while later, Marilyn and her father arrived at the scene, they found him holding out his arms and jangling his handcuffs, highly pleased with his pro-tem status as an outlaw.

He was also pleased to be home. And this was to be the case always: however strong his drive to take off for the high and far, his drive homeward at the end was equally so. "I love you excruciatingly," he had written his Mara from Golden; to which she, not to be outdone, had replied, "I love you more and more and more and more." Both meant it. It was so. Now that he was back from his truancy, there was neither pang of conscience for him nor resentment from her. He would be a devoted lover, and at least a passable husband and father—until he next heard the siren song from the far and high.

With the coming of fall they were back in the Stanford orbit, and the first order of business was a change of homes. As a family of three, it was impractical for them to stay on in the Atherton household where they had spent their first year of marriage, and the decision was to move in with the senior Harlins in Los Altos.

On the face of it, it seems a surprising one. Though John's relationship with his mother had improved somewhat, it was still far from easy, and Marilyn's untraditional ways in everything from religion to housekeeping were not calculated to make her the ideal Harlin daughter-in-law. Financially, however, it was a good arrangement. Further, Sue Harlin was both available and happy to baby-sit. With the help of Marilyn's carpenter father an annex was added to the existing house, and the not-so-newlyweds moved in.

Academically, Marilyn resumed her studies, with the emphasis now strongly on marine biology. And John, with only one college year to go, and all dropout thoughts discarded, entered it with a full head of steam. For a course in painting he did five ambitious oils, mostly semi-abstract, with both enthusiasm and talent. In his specialty of dress and costume design (in which individual instruction was provided by the Fine Arts Department) he was awash in patterns, weaves, seams, scallops, taffeta, chambray, tulle and dotted Swiss. And if he tired of these, there was, in his ROTC courses, a contrasting world of altimeter and tachometer, piston and jet, rev and mach. It seems doubtful if anyone else in the history of education has followed quite so schizophrenic a curriculum. But this was John Harlin, and he gloried in it.

In his "third world" of mountaineering his talents were recognized by his election as president of the Stanford Alpine Club; and each weekend, as in earlier years, he was out either on the practice rocks of the Peninsula or in more distant Yosemite. Often Marilyn and John III would go along to Yosemite, and the baby would have his evening bottle by a campfire to the strains of *Jam Crack Joe*. Then, in the morning, wife and papoose would go off for a walk in the valley, while Jam Crack John took to the heights.

Heading the SAC, John was full of projects—and not only for climbs of his own. One was to form a triple partnership between the SAC, the National Park Service, and Walt Disney to make a climbing film in Yosemite. To the Park Service and Disney he wrote: "I want the movie to be about American climbing, about the young people who

76

come to our national parks to enjoy the outdoors through this sport. There is an increasing interest in climbing in the United States, but the general public is almost completely ignorant of the subject. And in no situation has ignorance done any long-term good. I think it is high time the American people recognized climbing by understanding it. It should not be glamorized or approached as a sport for eccentric daredevils." He then went on to describe the type of scenes he thought should be filmed, and ended: "The underlying theme should be that climbing is a sport like any sport, yet one where proper training and techniques are absolutely essential."

This is scarcely the manifesto of an "eccentric daredevil." John Harlin, aged twenty-one, brought a firm set of values along with his animal energy to the mountains he loved. As was to happen so often in his life, however, his initial enthusiasm for a "grand design" bogged down in the subsequent details of implementation, and the project did not materialize.

But another, more personal project did. Early in 1957, as he had long hoped and planned, he became airborne. Provision for flight instruction was made for top-ranking senior students in Stanford's Air ROTC, and John, easily qualifying as such, began his flying in late January at an aviation school near Palo Alto. In a month he was soloing. By early spring he had his private pilot's license. And thereafter he flew as often as time and money allowed.[2] A "natural" from the beginning, he took to the air as he had to the mountains and loved it with almost the same intensity. Soon it had become a hard decision for him whether to spend a free day on a peak or in a cockpit.

Not unconnected with this was another, longer-range decision that presently had to be made: the decision facing every about-to-be-graduated college student in the world—what to do with his life. If he had been a European, it is not unlikely that he would have become a professional mountain guide; but in America it was impossible to make a full-time living in this way. As for dress design, he had stayed with it through two years of study, yet it is hard to say how truly serious he had been about it as a full career. Again there is a plausible *if*. If he had been taken as an apprentice by Balmain or another French

[2] Not "as often," Marilyn amends; "more often."

77

couturier and seen the chance ahead of living and working in Paris, he might very well at least have tried it. But in a job at I. Magnin or such he had no interest, and the thought of him on, say, New York's Seventh Avenue staggers the imagination.

That left what? . . . It left flying . . . flying, which he loved almost, if not quite, as much as climbing, and for which he had had two years of preparation in Air ROTC. He weighed pros and cons long and carefully. He talked with Marilyn and his flying father, but wanted no part of his father's suggestion that he enter either the Air Force or commercial flying as a lifetime vocation. Here and now, however, he did not have to plan all the way ahead. His immediate option with the Air Force was either three years' service without flying or five years' with; and while he didn't much care for the prospect of half a decade in uniform, he liked that of being an earthbound airman even less. There was more thought, more talk. Then John Harlin, mountaineer extraordinary, ex-football-playing dress designer, and amateur pilot of Pipers and Cessnas, made one of the major decisions of his life. He signed on with the Air Force for a five-year hitch.

Yosemite was not quite gone yet.

—And one day, across a valley campground, came the shout "Hey, look who's here!"

It was now three years since John and Gary Hemming had met, but the tall beatnik wanderer from San Diego and way stations was still unmistakably himself. His wanderings, however, had meanwhile expanded considerably. With San Diego State and engineering studies behind him, he had put in eighteen months as an Army paratrooper and, to prove it, now carried his pack on his chest instead of his back. Further, while in the paratroops, he had qualified for admission to the new Air Force Academy at Colorado Springs, and had spent a few months there before it was mutually decided that someone, somehow, had made a mistake. With a little money saved, he had hit the road again—the good road, the high road, to the mountains he loved as much as John Harlin.

"How's to a climb together?"

John was ready, and they climbed.

"And how's to this summer? Some sort of climbing trip?"

John was for that too. And it could be managed, because the Air

Force would not be calling him up until fall. They talked enthusiastically of wheres and whens, and laid their plans.

But first there were final Stanford exams, then graduation, and when the day came he and Marilyn together put on their gowns and mortarboards. She received her master's degree, plus associate membership in Sigma Xi, a national honorary scientific society. He received his bachelor's degree and a reserve commission as second lieutenant in the United States Air Force. They kissed. They received congratulations. They were very happy. Then John went home and oiled his climbing boots.

It was still to be some time before he pulled them on, however, for there was an acute absence of money to finance the planned trip. An old hand at itinerant labor, Gary Hemming had become a pro-tem salesman of the Encyclopaedia Britannica, covering rural areas of northern California and Oregon; and after depositing Marilyn and the baby with her parents near Olympia, John joined him as assistant. To round off an improbable crew, there was also along, as second assistant, a Stanford student from the Fiji Islands, named Naidu.

Richly endowed with the gift of gab, Gary was a good salesman. And Naidu was at least an attention getter. But John was a total loss on the door-to-door trail, failing to sell a single set of books. As a change of pace, he and Naidu got a succession of jobs haying for farmers and laying pipelines, so that he had at least a few dollars in his pocket when he returned to Olympia. Here Gary, too, checked in presently, plus two others who were to go with them on the climbing trip: Henry Kendall, a Stanford physicist, with whom John had done much Yosemite climbing, and a friend of Kendall's named Hobie de Stabler.

Activity began with a climb of Rainier. Then in late July they headed northward, again toward the Selkirk Range of the Canadian Rockies. This time, however, plans were more ambitious than in the previous year, for their objective was the southern section of the Selkirks, which was almost primeval wilderness. Even to reach the base of the peaks they had to bushwhack for days, carrying eighty- to ninety-pound packs; and to compound the difficulties, their maps were inaccurate, the weather was foul, and a plane they had hired to airdrop supplies to them was, because of the weather, unable to do it. Nevertheless, they kept going, and finally succeeded in making several

79

climbs, including a first ascent of the north ridge of a peak called Mount Hallway.

The four both performed and got along well together. But John and Gary tended to compete in tests of skill, strength, and endurance. As serious climbers, dedicated to a code of "pure" mountaineering, both believed that man-to-man rivalry should have no place in the sport. But in both, the competitor was stronger than the philosopher. "I-can-do-it, let's-see-you-do-it" was often the order of the day—and would continue to be through the years of their up-and-down friendship.

When the climbing was over, John worked for a while on a ranch near Pendleton, Oregon. Then it was back to Olympia—and at summer's end to Los Altos. Although the Air Force had definitely accepted him, it took its time calling him up; and he lived at home most of the fall, working for two months as a laborer in a road-building gang. With his earnings he continued his private flying, sometimes taking Marilyn or his parents along as passengers. And as a counterbalance to graders and bulldozers, he kept his hand in at *haute couture*, creating a bouffant cocktail dress that he intended—but never got around to—submitting to I. Magnin.

Then in November the Air Force called, and Second Lieutenant John E. Harlin II took off for a new life. Marilyn stayed behind to have her second baby, which was due early in the new year.

7. Fledgling

"'What sort of nut is this?' I was asking myself. We'd just met in the bar of the Officers' Club, and I ask him will he have whisky or beer, and he says vermouth half and half. Later we get to talking about what we'd done before the Air Force, and he says he was studying dress-making. I damn near flipped."

—Thus one of John's friends-to-be on his early days in the service. Nor was his story unique. John was to flip a lot of people, in and out of the air, during the next few years.

Scene One was at Lackland Air Force Base near San Antonio, Texas, and it scarcely started with a bang. First, he reacted badly to his immunization shots and was briefly hospitalized. When he came out, there was not a plane in sight—at least not for a class of rookie lieutenants—and the ensuing six weeks of basic training were strictly terrestrial. John acquired his uniforms, exchanged his long blond hair for short blond hair, and learned to say "Sir" to persons other than his father. There was not a mountain in hundreds of miles. And it was a lonely Christmas.

As usual, however, he was not exactly quiescent. Appointed physical training officer to a class of GI recruits, he worked out with them on the base obstacle course and led them on a twenty-five-mile hike. On his own, he entered several inter-unit track meets and outran everyone in sight. For mountaineering, he found a bridge across the San Antonio River, and at night, with no police about, clambered around its steel superstructure, using rivets for hand- and footholds.

Soon he had higher heights to contend with. From Lackland's pre-flight training he was assigned to Bartow Air Base near Winter Haven, Florida, and there he began truly to function in his chosen profession. In San Antonio he had been strictly an earthling, except for his bridge-climbing. Here there were planes, and it was his business to fly them.

Or at least to learn to fly them. The function of Bartow was to give what the Air Force calls primary pilot training, and for the next six months John, as one of a class of about fifty, would be schooled in the rudiments of military aviation. The rudiments of flying he of course already knew. The T-34s, in which instruction began, were two-seater, one-engine Beechcrafts, almost identical to the craft he had flown back in California; and from the start he was well out ahead of the rest of his class. Back in the air again, he exulted. What he exulted about less was that now he had to do everything by long check-lists and memorized procedures.

Half of each workday was spent on the flight line; the other half in classes on such subjects as principles of flight, aircraft engineering, navigation and weather. Strictly military activities—drill, inspection, reviews, and the like—were minimal at Bartow. But even that was too much for John's freewheeling tastes. Throughout his Air Force career, his motto was to be "A flier yes, a soldier no."

More than half his class were married men, and those whose wives and families were with them were housed off base. In the beginning he himself lived in the Bachelors Officers' Quarters, rooming with a fellow-trainee, John High. For evenings and weekends, the base was well supplied with facilities, and at intervals there would be junkets to the nearby towns of Winter Haven and Orlando. Here there were movies, restaurants, bars, and for John his copyright vermouths and sometimes beers. No homebody by nature, he enjoyed his pro-tem bachelor status when and where he could. But at the same time he missed his Mara and wrote her often—not duty letters but love letters—with much discussion of the name of their soon-to-come second child.

There was no mountain within two thousand miles. Not even a fair-sized bridge was handy. But as at Lackland, he was active athletically, again serving as physical training officer, and taking the job with enough seriousness to make him persona non grata to less strenuous types. For himself, scouting about, it did not take him long to discover that the surrounding Florida citrus country was full of lakes, and soon, with roommate High—who was an expert—he was going all out for water skiing. Also, it developed, High was accomplished at weight-lifting; and in this too John was soon involved. No beginning at the beginning for him. At the Bartow gymnasium one day, High had just managed to hoist a two-hundred-pound barbell above his head when John confidently stepped in to give it a try. "There was a terrible whomp," High reported. . . . "But after a while he was doing it."

Socially, he was far from "one of the boys." Among the more machine-tooled products of service conformity, he was a sport, a maverick. But non-other-directed John had his own ideas of what was and was not important, and for the judgments of others he gave not a damn.

(Except, perhaps, for two judgments, and in these he was secure. He was both the best athlete and best flier in his class.)

In early February came the word from California that the new baby had been born. It was a girl and she would be called Andréa. Shortly after, a formidable expedition consisting of Marilyn, her two children and her parents drove across the country in the Harlin station wagon plus Miler camper, and John's brief bachelorhood come to an end.

Before their arrival he had gone home-hunting, and now—with the Milers returning westward—he and family moved into a housekeeping motel not far from Bartow. There was a lake at their doorstep, good for swimming, boating, and water skiing, and soon, happily if expensively, they were cruising about in a motor launch of their own. Marilyn was, if possible, even less "service-minded" than John, and they almost totally avoided the more formal aspects of Air Force social life. But, with feminine variations, she was not less active than he, and whenever they could they took off on tours of Florida. There is no record of their having reached its highest point (345 feet above the sea); but they visited the Everglades, the west coast, the east coast, and once even the un-Harlinesque fleshpots of Miami Beach. John gloried in the clear warm waters, perfect for swimming, skiing, and snorkeling. Biologist Marilyn would have preferred rockier coasts, as more productive of specimens, but was entranced by the wildlife of the Everglades.

In flying, John's class moved on from the T-34 to the T-28, simultaneously studying instrument flight in Link trainers. The T-28 was, like its predecessor, a one-engine piston plane, but bigger and more complex than the Beechcraft—roughly equivalent to the standard fighter of World War II. The order of the day was no longer routine flying, with an instructor supervising from the rear seat, but solo aerobatics— each man on his own in the climb, dive and swoop of simulated combat—and here John was in his element as he had never been before. But it was not of a World War II pilot that others thought as they watched him. It was of an earlier breed. "You could almost see him before your eyes," one of his class has said, "wearing the old helmet, goggles, and scarf, like Snoopy in *Peanuts*. It wasn't a T-28 he was climbing into, but a Sopwith Camel. He wasn't just going on a toot around Florida, but out to get that Red Baron or else."

John himself was not unaware of his affinity for those vintage days. Among his books was one called *Red Knight of Germany*, a biography by Floyd Gibbons of World War I's ace of aces, Baron Manfred von Richthofen, and in it he had underscored the lines: "Organization was not inborn with him. He was an individualist. The spirit of the hunter, the stalker, was strong within him, and with it ran pride of conquest, the natural outgrowth of strong competitive and combative senses."

In a still earlier time, one feels sure, John Harlin would have been literally a knight, complete with spear, armor, and caparisoned stallion. A few centuries later, he might well have been a conquistador or privateer. In the actual world into which he was born, the air—along with the mountains that pierced it—was the last frontier of high adventure, and it was for this reason, above all others, that he was a flier. Though he was part of the greatest fighting force on earth, he himself was no fighter in the modern style. Though involved with the most intricate machinery, he was no engineer. Physically, he was endowed with marvelously quick reactions and almost faultless depth perception. But however great his technical skills, he was in essence the old seat-of-the-pants airman: the instinctive flier, the loner, the adventurer. What he loved in flying was its solitude, its freedom, its magic.

Nor, when he flew, did he leave the artist behind. In the air, no less than on the ground, he was acutely conscious of the world that encompassed him; of form, color, texture; of the ambience of earth and sky and wind and cloud and sun. Sometimes—as he was to remember long after on a mountain wall—the sun called to him through the clouds: "I'm here, I'm here. Can't you reach me?" At another time, as he wrote later, "The warmth of the sun through the canopy had a pleasant sting, but it became a bit too much for my eyes, so down came the green-tinted visor. In the same instant I pulled back and to the left on the control stick, rolling the plane in sheer joy of freedom and movement. The aircraft was my body and the sky the dimension of my youth. Whether flying or mountain climbing, the sky had become more than a playground. It was my life."

"Playground," he said. And so it was. Through all his flying days he was half small boy playing the hero, shouting "Look Mom, no hands!" But here, as on earth, there were also the "other Johns," on many levels, perceiving life beyond the playground—pragmatically, esthetically, philosophically. He knew the story of Richthofen, but also the books of Antoine de Sainte-Exupéry—*Night Flight, Wind, Sand and Stars*; and he hoped one day to express, as had Saint-Exupéry, not only the facts but the meaning of flight. Of the moments before take-off, in the workaday world of earthlings, the Frenchman had written, "My footfall rang in a universe that was not theirs." It was John Harlin's universe, however. It was his life. And he cherished it.

Increasingly, in these days, he was a reader. At the core of his library were flying and mountaineering books, but his interests extended beyond them in many directions. He retained his enthusiasm for Conrad. He became deeply involved in T. E. Lawrence's *The Seven Pillars of Wisdom*. He ranged through Hemingway and Steinbeck, Sartre and Camus, Lawrence Durrell and Graham Greene—as far as Bertrand Russell at one end of the line and Ian Fleming on the other. Marilyn, too, loved reading (though she drew the line at James Bond); and one of the best parts of their marriage was their shared enjoyment of talking about books and their ideas.

John throve on ideas. He throve on action. What he did not thrive on was service routine and discipline. At Bartow, as at all Air

Force training schools, the grading of student pilots was based on three categories: flying, academic, and military. And in flying he stayed first in his group. In classwork, however, he tended to get bored and careless, failing a test or two; and militarily, in the domain of spit-and-polish, he was always in trouble. As a consequence, his over-all rating, after four months at Bartow, was no better than fortieth in his class of fifty-odd. But following a visit from his father a spectacular change occurred. It was not the result of paternal lecture; that, if anything, might have had the opposite effect. John I simply reminded him that priority of choice for future Air Force assignments was based entirely on class standing, and that if John II wanted any choice at all, he had better do something about it.

John II did. He stayed awake in class, memorized procedure lists, did his best to approximate the Air Force concept of an-officer-and-a-gentlemen—and in his last two months at Bartow zoomed up as if airborne, from Number Forty to near the top. His next assignment would be to basic pilot training. And his high-choice selection was Vance Air Force Base[1] near Enid, Oklahoma, which if not the garden spot of the Western Hemisphere, was at least nine-tenths of the way from Florida to the Rocky Mountains.

They arrived there in midsummer. The sun boiled down on the prairies. The wind blew. Dust blew. But they were hardened gypsies by now and scarcely noticed discomfort. They found a home and moved in. The children were flourishing. And John flew his first jets.

They were T-33s, known as T-birds; subsonic in speed but marvelously maneuverable, and he liked them the best of all the planes he ever flew. As at Bartow, he went up first with instructors, then solo, finally, for the first time, in formation with other planes. There was parachute jumping, which he greatly liked. There was aerial gunnery, using a target of aluminum foil, called a dart, towed by another plane on a 1500-foot cable. In the classrooms there were all manner of courses, more advanced than at Bartow, paralleling the changes from piston plane to jet and from simple piloting to combat flight.

It was no child's play. There were accidents, fatalities. And though

[1] Bartow, with military training facilities but primarily a civilian installation, is known simply as an Air Base. Vance, entirely military, is an Air Force Base.

John escaped these, he had his share of near misses. On one occasion, while he was flying alone several hundred miles from base, there was a breakdown in his plane's electrical system (which, among other things, controlled the flow of fuel), and he had to glide in, powerless, almost the whole way home. At another time, coming in for landing with almost no fuel left—and therefore no maneuverability—he narrowly escaped collision with a whole formation of T-33s. Over-all, the chief hazard was the jets' great speed, which made everything, including emergencies, happen far more quickly than in prop planes. But once John got the feel of them, he had also control. Soaring, rolling, diving, he was again the Red Baron-chaser of the skyways—at almost five times the speed at which the originals had flown.

The Harlin home in Enid was in conventional suburbia, half a duplex in a row of similar houses. But there was nothing conventional about its interior. In their lives together thus far—in Atherton, Los Altos, Olympia, Bartow—Marilyn and John had had no need to buy furniture of their own. And now they still had not bought any, except a crib. They themselves slept in bedrolls on the floor. They ate sitting on the floor, from a low table built by John. Possessions were hung on hooks or stacked on shelves.

It was not a matter of penury. They had a car. They kept buying books. They had acquired, bit by bit, a hi-fi-stereo complex and a collection of records and tapes. As for furniture, they simply didn't want the usual assortment of budget-priced stereotypes and decided to settle for uncluttered simplicity. "Japanese style," was Marilyn's description. "A home should blend with its environment," said John. (And true enough, the Vance runways and Oklahoma plains were both models of bareness.)

An on-duty Hell's Angel and an off-hours bohemian, John was now learning a third role: that of Father. Johnny III was now past two, Andréa in her second six months. Both were blond, like their parents. Both were healthy, active, and demanding of attention; and while this was fine in essence, it was not quite so fine for John, whose enthusiasms did not include baby feeding and diaper changing. Indeed, he often fudged on paternal duties, but Marilyn took it in stride and, herself, throve on motherhood. Both more patient and more organized than her husband, she had her many jobs in well-departmentalized working order, finding time even to keep up her reading in biology.

Socially, as at Bartow, they saw little of the cocktail circuit or the Officers' Club. But they had their own circle of friends, among them John High, now with wife, who had also moved on to Vance. And as always, they were busy on many fronts. Across the road from their home was a small public golf course, and here John played for the first time, driving for vast distances, if with no great accuracy. At the base, he competed in track meets and, when fall came, organized an intramural football league, captaining one of the teams until, to his disgust, he pulled a leg muscle.

As in Florida, too, he and Marilyn—now often with the children along—explored the surrounding countryside; and here, of course, it was vastly different. On one brief holiday, they drove for long empty miles across former Comanche country—now longhorn grazing land and buffalo refuge—coming at last to a small uplift in southwestern Oklahoma called the Wichita Mountains. "They were roughly equivalent," said John, "to a lesser foothill in California." Also within weekend range was a group of mesa-type formations known as the Glass Mountains, good for camping, hiking, and occasional duck hunting with fellow officers. But to a mountaineer they offered nothing; and the longer, much-hoped-for trip to the Rockies failed to materialize.

Through the weeks, then the months, life was largely base routine and domesticity, and even the first fine thrill of jet flying had begun to wear thin. Again John got the anti-Air Force itch. He behaved as unmilitarily as possible. He talked of leaving the service by hook or crook. He had always wanted to visit Alaska, and when he was out of uniform he would get a job flying for Alaska Airlines, homestead in the Matanuska Valley, and climb every mountain in sight.

By now he was getting really desperate for mountains—and fed up with what was keeping him from them. In his Vance class "yearbook" he wrote under Personal Preferences: *Likes:* climbing. *Dislikes:* Air Force.

Along with the Rockies, however, there was to be no Alaska. He stuck out his six months at Vance. As at Bartow, he finished first in his class in flying and received, along with his pilot's rating, a certificate "for outstanding achievement." In academic work he was close to the top, in military grading close to the bottom. Averaging out the three categories, he was fourth highest in his group and therefore again had a high choice for his next assignment.

He chose to continue with training as a flier of jet fighter-bombers and in January 1959 was posted to Luke Air Force Base near Phoenix, Arizona. He now wore wings on his uniform. Soon he would wear the silver bar of a first lieutenant. The reluctant warrior was moving up in the world—and at least closer to mountains than in Florida or Oklahoma.

8. Skyways

"The sky," he said, "was the dimension of my youth." And now the dimension was broader, higher. The plane was swifter, more powerful. It was the F-100, then the ultimate fighting machine of the U. S. Air Force, and John, in its cockpit, was king of the blue.

Out of the blue, one day, he bore down on the desert. Across the desert was a ribbon of road, and parked off the road among the mesquite, a car. He knew the car would be there, because this was a rendezvous. The car was his, and Marilyn was standing beside it. Down he came, faster than sound, then flattened out and roared toward it, a scant few yards above the mesquite. To Marilyn it almost seemed that the plane was on the ground itself; that in the next instant it would strike the car and atomize it. Even in the hundredth of a second that it took to pass, it seemed to plunge through it, not over it. There was a roar, a scream. Then it was gone: back to nowhere, to the blue. The car's dusty roof had been swept clean by its jet afterburners.

The Air Force took a dim view of buzzing, except in official target areas. Some time after, during a mass flight from Luke, one of the planes in John's training group all but scraped the rooftops of a small town near Phoenix; and except for two pilots who had not been flying, the whole unit was grounded and confined to quarters pending the culprit's confession. Writing to Marilyn, who was away at the time, John said, "Of course you're dying to know, did I do it? Well, guess what. I was one of the two who weren't flying that night. If I had been, I'd have been tried and hung by now, guilty or not."

In some ways he liked the F-100 less than the T-33. It was heavier, harder to maneuver, and was known to its pilots not only by its official name of Super Sabre but also, less admiringly, as the Lead Sled. Its power and speed, however, were enormous, and in short order John had detonated his first sonic boom and was a certificate holder in the Mach Busters' Club. With his pilot's rating already won, his instruction was now largely in fighting techniques—pursuit and evasion; gunnery, strafing, and bombing—and in these, as before in straight flying, he was consistently at the head of his class. "John was an 'at-the-limit man,'" one of his fellow fliers said of him. "Whatever he did in the air, he went as far as you can go."

Domestically, at Phoenix, life was more expansive than at Enid. At higher rent than Marilyn approved, they took a big one-family house in a good neighborhood, complete with carpeting, French windows, air conditioning and appliances. To augment it, they bought, for the first time, a few pieces of furniture, but did not carry the bourgeois trend to the point of beds. For all but Andréa, who was still of crib age, it was bedrolls on the floor.

Around the house—when he came down from the altitudes—John was interested in its esthetics: the form, color, and texture of its furnishings. On occasion, he even went so far as to perform household chores, accomplishing them, according to Marilyn, "with a can of beer in one hand and in the other a book of Saint-Exupéry's from which he reads his favorite passages aloud." In the world roundabout, both were fascinated by the life of the Arizona Indian tribes, and they made trips together to the reservation villages. Another more ambitious excursion was by rented plane, with John piloting, to have an aerial look at the Grand Canyon of the Colorado.

As always in the service, there had been a turnover in friends between posts. John High, for one, had gone elsewhere from Vance, and in his place now, as John's closest companion, was a young F-100 pilot from Texas named Donald Arneson. Also at hand was his old climbing partner Jerry Robertson, still at Arizona State and now a cadet in Air ROTC. And the three, with others sometimes added, saw to it that the intervals between flying were not unduly restful.

As in Florida, there was water skiing, now not on lakes but irrigation canals, with a car on a bordering road supplying the power. Also, of course, Arizona had mountains: neither of the snowy Alpine nor sheer Yosemite type that John would have preferred, but still real mountains, which was a step up from Florida and Oklahoma. Few weekends passed on which he, Jerry, and "Arne" Arneson were not off on one or another of the desert uplifts—Camelback, the Monk, the crags of Box Canyon—and sometimes Marilyn and the children went along too, for camping and hiking. Johnny now moved under his own three-year-old power, Andréa in Harlin-papoose style on her father's or mother's back.

Then came the day when the cast further expanded. Gary Hemming reappeared. Long, loose-limbed and unencumbered, he had spent the past year-and-a-half mostly as a mountain vagabond, climbing in the Rockies, the Sierras, Canada, Mexico, and when necessity demanded, earning a few dollars at casual labor. He had kept track of John, however, and now, staying over for a week, again matched strength and skills with him on the barren peaks of Arizona. In the Harlin home, one gathers, he eyed wife and children, textbooks and uniforms, washing machine and air conditioner—and mused on the prison in which John had enclosed himself. Then, still long, loose-limbed and unencumbered, he hitchhiked off toward the horizon.

Of his two loves, climbing and flying, John was always to feel that flying was the more dangerous. On a mountain, he believed, it was totally a matter of a man and his capabilities, and in his own he had supreme confidence. But in a plane there was always the added factor of what a machine would do, and when a supersonic thunderbolt like an F-100 went out of whack, the odds against its occupant were not encouraging.

On the record at Luke, while he was there, there was little to contradict him. In one period of only two weeks, five planes were lost, and day after day, almost routinely, there were narrow squeaks. John's came without warning when, during a formation flight near base, the fire light on his instrument panel went red, and a moment later he received radioed instructions to bail out from both the control tower and his flight commander. Whether flame and explosion would suddenly engulf him he could not tell for sure. But a quick check convinced him that he could bring the plane down intact. So he stayed with it. And brought it down. On the runway, fire trucks and an ambulance were waiting for him, but he taxied safely to a stop and walked away.

John craved adventure as other men crave food and drink. Trained in parachuting and—with ground mockups—in self-ejection from planes, he greatly wanted the experience of bailing out in earnest. But perhaps he was too good a pilot for his own inclinations; he never made it. "The damn things cost a million dollars apiece," he said of the F-100s, "and at that price per jump you need a pretty good reason."

His very strengths tended sometimes to become his weaknesses, and at Luke, for the first time, he ran into trouble in the purely flying phase of his training. He had been top man of each class he had been in. By now he felt himself the complete pilot: better, in fact, than most of his instructors. And this was an attitude the instructors did not greatly care for. On the basis of two flights with him, one of them, a regular Air Force captain, graded him as careless in certain aspects of performance. John protested this as unwarranted, and a considerable hassle developed. The only immediate result was that his class rating in flying dropped from first to fourth. But the shadow of the affair was to catch up with him more seriously later in his Air Force career.

It had been decided that when the hot weather came to Arizona Marilyn and the children would again go to her parents near Olympia. But John got to the Northwest first, flying up on a quick trip with Jerry Robertson, during which they managed to fit in an ascent of Mount Rainier. It was the first snow-and-ice climbing he had had in almost two years, and for two happy days he was able to forget his private war with the Air Force.

Then, with summer, his family took off, and he moved into the Bachelor Officers' Quarters at Luke. At about the same time he rented a small studio apartment in Phoenix, where for the first time since Stanford he tried his hand at painting. In his letters to Marilyn he spoke of other projects as well: a course in typing, dancing lessons,

94

learning to play the guitar. But little came of any of them, including the painting. If John's actual accomplishments in his brief life are enough to fill a book, his unrealized plans, of every conceivable nature, could fill a library shelf.

One long-range "project" that has to be faced sooner or later was WOMEN. And here there is much disagreement among those who knew John as to what was fact and what was fiction. In Phoenix, it was generally believed by his fellow fliers that the function of his "studio" was only incidentally for painting. And John was not the one to deny this, for he himself was the master builder not only of Harlin achievements but of Harlin myths. Had he, aged nineteen, truly killed a man in Rome? Just what, aged twenty, had he done on the Matterhorn? . . . And now (and for the rest of his life) to what degree was he a philanderer? . . . No one knows for sure. Out of one side of his mouth he talked freely of many affairs; out of the other he denied all but a few. Most are in a sort of limbo between fact and rumor, and the tales told vary greatly with the teller's attitude toward John—and Marilyn.

Two things are certain: that he was no monogamist by either nature or conviction; and that, in spite of this—or at least along with it—his love for Marilyn was deep and enduring. On the one hand, he craved freedom, not only of the sky and peaks but in all of living. On the other, he needed the anchor, the security, even the responsibility, of wife and family. Much as he would sometimes have liked to be, he was no Gary Hemming, built for vagabonding through life without ties or commitments.

He himself was well aware of his conflicts. During his last weeks in Phoenix, with his family in Olympia, he wrote to Marilyn about them, and at this stage of his life, he felt, they centered largely on the children. He loved them, he declared. He truly loved them. But—"When I'm away from the kids, my desire for you, my sex appetite, my personality, everything, changes. With them I have a trapped feeling, and I lose interest in myself, you, even life. I just become a slob. . . . But away, I become a romantic. My whole body starts enjoying life—a breeze—the taste of a drink—the sounds that are all around—music. I become very sensitive, careful of how I speak; more graceful in movement—more interested in sports (and better at them)

95

—just a different person. This person is more me, and it's the way I want to be."

He was not the first nor the last man to resent the shackles of domesticity. But he shook them harder than most. Writing to Marilyn, he made suggestions as to how in future they should make more use of sitters and nurseries, so that they could have more time alone together. Then he burst out: "I miss you till it hurts, and I hope you love me. I miss the kids too when I look at their pictures. That's all, though: *I'm no family man.*"

But he was.

In August 1959 he completed his advanced pilot training at Luke and moved on to Stead Air Force Base near Reno, Nevada. Not without a slight detour, however; for he was well aware that Reno was not far from Yosemite, and with Jerry Robertson as companion, he veered off for a few days of grace in his well-loved Valley of the Sun. Here they were joined by another old climbing partner, physicist Henry Kendall, and with him, John pioneered a route on one of the vertical buttresses of El Capitan. Then, refreshed by the touch of granite and blue air, he went on to Stead.

There was no flying here. Stead was the site of the Air Force "Survival School," at which fliers were trained in how to behave if brought down in combat behind enemy lines. It was designed as a rugged workout. There were races through an obstacle course, simulating the border of a hostile country, complete with trenches, barbed wire, barrages, and machine-gun fire. There was prisoner of war "practice," with rough interrogations, brainwashing and solitary confinement. Finally, there was a week in the bush, during which each man had to get along on his own, with no food or shelter provided. To most of the men it was a once-in-a-lifetime ordeal; but to John, after the rigors of El Capitan, it was all pretty tame. "The physical training part, especially," he wrote to Marilyn, "was ridiculously easy."

From Stead, it was downstate to Las Vegas and the final stage of his training at Nellis Air Force Base. Here again he was airborne. And instruction was in the most advanced techniques of his trades, among them, aerial refueling and nuclear bombing. For off-hours—and a drastic change of pace—there were the pleasure domes of Vegas, and John had his share of *la dolce vita* desert style. But gambling, like drinking, was not his forte, and at the casinos he was strictly a small-change operator. During his early days at Nellis he lived at the BOQ with Arne Arneson. Then Marilyn and the children came down from Washington, and they set up housekeeping in a nearby motel.

His personal war with the Military Establishment continued, and he achieved a signal minor victory on the subject of boots. The Air Force, not unnaturally, had its own style of flying boot and expected it to be used. But John did not like flying boots. He liked climbing boots—and wore them. He was called for it. He presented his case. A combat flier, he averred, had to be physically and psychologically at ease to perform at his best, and he was able to attain this salubrious state only when wearing climbing boots. The powers at Nellis deliberated and reached the decision to be permissive. First Lieutenant John E. Harlin would be allowed to wear climbing boots, if he dyed them black.

Another, and more spectacular, contest ended in what seems to have been a standoff. Here the opponent was not the Establishment but an individual—one Captain John Boyd, a flying veteran and former ace in the Korean War who was now an instructor at Nellis. Along with the rest of his class, John was aware of Boyd's fame and talents as an aerial dogfighter. Further, he was no less aware of his own talents and yearned to match them with the master's in the Nevada skies. To his delight, he was given the chance; the two went up together in an aerial duo; and this time, happily, there was no such aftermath as when he had locked horns with the instructor at Luke.

"It was quite a show," said one of John's classmates, recalling the performance. "Boyd was a real scientist of the air, a whiz with sines and cosines and overshoot angles. John wasn't a scientist at all; he couldn't tell a cosine from a carburetor. He was the artist, using feel and perception, thinking of flying patterns as a sort of abstract painting." In any case, they were evenly matched as they wheeled and swooped through the blue, pursuing and dodging in the struggle to get each other's tails in their gunsights. And when they came down there was neither victor nor vanquished. Snoopy had met the Red Baron at last—or at least a friendly Red Baron—and held his own with him.

This sort of flying was meat and drink to John. He also enjoyed the complex and precise maneuvers of aerial refueling ("—it's like bees after honey"), but simulated bombing with nuclear weapons was far less to his liking. In individual confrontations, as a knight in the jousting lists, he excelled and exulted. For the mass destruction of modern warfare, real or feigned, he had no taste at all, and his aversion was to increase with time and experience.

His one major mishap at Nellis could well have been fatal, but ended instead in broad comedy. Off alone on a cross-country flight, he succumbed—not for the first time—to the temptation of "flatheading": gunning his jet, for kicks, a scant few feet above the ground. There seemed to be no hazard, either physical or disciplinary, for the earth was flat, empty desert, and as he returned to base it was, so far as he knew, from a pleasant and uneventful joyride. That, however, was not to be the status quo for long. No sooner was the plane back at the field than the ground crew discovered strands of chewed-up wire in one of its engines, and it became quickly apparent that he had had an unwitting encounter with Nevada's communications system. Fortunately he had hit telephone lines, not high tension—or there would have been no more John. Also fortunately, in fact astonishingly, the wires had neither sheared off a wing nor, once sucked into the engine, caused fire or explosion. Both John and plane were intact. But there remained the little matter of what the Air Force would say and do. John recalled all too well the furore at Luke when a pilot buzzed a nearby town. And then there had been only sound effects; not actual damage, as now.

He could not only fly fast. He could think fast. Before anyone other than he and his ground crew knew what had happened, he called the Mountain States Telephone and Telegraph Company, announcing who he was, what he had done, and offering to pay for the damage. The strategy paid off handsomely. The company had had lines downed before, but never had a culprit stepped forward to assume the blame. The management sent John a glowing letter of appreciation (along with a bill for two hundred dollars). It also wrote the Air Force command at Nellis, commending its honest and upright young pilot. And for the command, the disciplining of such an honest and upright young pilot posed a delicate problem.

In the upshot, there was no disciplining at all. "But," said John, "I had a big phone bill that month."

Once more while in Nevada he got over to Yosemite. Flying there in a borrowed Piper Cub, he again joined Henry Kendall, plus a latter-day group from the Stanford Alpine Club, in a happy weekend of climbing. Now at last, however, beloved Yosemite was not the be-all and end-all. Even wider horizons were opening before him; mountains greater than El Cap and Half Dome loomed and beckoned ahead. For his fond dream, nursed through two years of Air Force wanderings —through Texas, Florida, Oklahoma, Arizona, Nevada—was now about to come true. With his training almost at an end, and in spite of his sundry brushes with the Establishment, he received notice that his first choice of next assignment had been granted. He was going to Germany, to the Rhineland. And up the Rhine, not too distant, were the Alps.

On the first of December 1959 he left Nellis. For the next few weeks, on leave, he returned with Marilyn and the children to his parents' home in Los Altos. Then, before year's end, they flew eastward: by TWA to New York, thence by MATS toward Europe.

The winter ocean was invisible below. The plane droned through the night. First Lieutenant John E. Harlin, USAF, was off on yet another lap of his journey without end.

On his first trip to Europe he had been ten years old. On the second, nineteen; on the third, twenty. Now he was twenty-four and a half— still of no great age—no longer a high school boy in golden shorts, nor a college boy in a football jersey, but still with golden hair, with an athlete's body, with the strength and drive and high desire of undiminished youth.

In the years since he had last seen Europe he had done much growing, much living. But his essence remained as before. And his contradictions. Now he had been for four years a married man, for three a father, yet he still sought and demanded freedom in every aspect of his life. As a pilot-officer in the Air Force, he had been subjected to rigid training in a vast and powerful organization, yet was still a total and unregenerate individualist. In a plane he was simultaneously the Boy Wonder chasing the Red Baron and an abstract artist weaving his visions into the air. On a mountain he was consumed by the lust to excel, to conquer, but also by the tiny miracle of an Alpine bloom, a flake of snow.

The contradictions were obvious, the essence hidden beneath them. Many who knew John well have said that he seemed a man born out of his time. For in his time, and ours, romance is an anachronism, and he was, above all else, a romantic. . . . "In our lives, Mara, we'll have many adventures," he had said to his wife in the first days of their marriage. Then, musingly, he had added: "One day, perhaps, we'll have *the great adventure* and never come back." . . . And now, in a plane over the Atlantic, he was closer than he knew to just that. Behind him, in darkness, America receded and vanished, and except for one brief visit years later, he would never return.

If this was indeed *the great adventure,* however, it was opening with an off-key overture. In the plane jampacked with service families, the romantic turned paterfamilias held his sleeping son on his lap and shifted from one cramped buttock to another. Marilyn rummaged in a bag, brought out Andréa's baby food, and Andréa drooled it. Johnny, awakening, announced the need for weewee.

9. Hawk (and Dove)

In the beginning there were no Alps. Nor much Europe either. John's assignment was to Hahn Air Base,[1] in a section of the central Rhineland known as Hunsrück, but his initial stay there was little more than a check-in. While Marilyn, with the children, set up housekeeping in a base apartment, he was dispatched for special training to Wheelus Air Base in Libya.

The winter weather at Hahn was miserable for flying. At the very heart of crowded western Europe, it also provided little space for bombing and gunnery practice. But Wheelus, close by the Mediterranean near Tripoli, had year-round sunshine and the whole Sahara behind it, and soon John was cruising high and wide in the African sky. The experience was not as new to him as to most who were sent there. He still had his boyhood memories of Egypt and Ethiopia, and through the books of Saint-Exupéry he had long since ranged in

[1] Here again the military distinction between Air Base and Air Force Base enters in. Since it is in a foreign country and not owned by the Air Force, Hahn is known simply as an Air Base.

imagination along the skyways of the desert. Saint-Exupéry had flown in the fragile crates of aviation's youth. John, at the stick of an F-100, was in an awesome powerhouse of supersonic speed. But the essence of the experience, the encompassing world, were the same, as like the Frenchman before him, he penetrated the vast empty kingdom of wind, sand, and stars.

The American military in overseas stations is notorious in its propensity for being "at home abroad." In their tight, structured domains, many servicemen and their families seem scarcely conscious that they are in foreign lands. John, however, was at the opposite pole. A traveler by choice, not merely by order, he brought with him everywhere intense awareness and interest, and at Wheelus, when off duty, he was up and away into Africa. In a scrounged car or rented bicycle, he toured up and down the coastal road and as far into the desert as their wheels would carry him. He explored the Roman ruins of Leptis Magna. He visited Arab villages and oases, and in letters to Marilyn described the houses, the wells, the palms, and—*couturier redivivus*—the cut and colors of the women's clothing.

If he was John the tourist, however, he was still also John the adventurer. And one of his adventures, if less than heroic, was nevertheless memorable to its witnesses. On a bicycle trip near Wheelus, he and a few friends came to a short stretch of road that had been freshly tarred, and the others dismounted to walk around it. Not John. "Hell, I can make that," he said, and took off, pedaling furiously. "And by God, he almost did," said one of his friends. "But not quite. About ten yards from the end the bike stuck and off he went, flat in the tar: uniform, hands, face, everything. But the worst of it was his hair. Like with his climbing boots, he'd conned the Air Force into letting him wear that blond hair of his longer than regulation—and he was combing tar out of it for the next two weeks."

There was another adventure, too, that almost ended more seriously. Near the base, on the coast, were long beaches, beyond them the Mediterranean, and though the water was cold (and John was anti-cold water), it was marvelously blue and alluring. Furthermore, there was scuba gear available at Wheelus, and the combination was too much to resist. John had never dived before. But he was a powerful swimmer, a veteran snorkeler and water skier, and presto—as in so many other fields, he was an "instant expert" at scuba. Close in to

102

shore, especially at Leptis Magna, were extensive underseas ruins, which he explored in what he called submarine archaeology. Beyond were sea gardens, grottoes, great shoals of fish—a whole hidden world of shimmering mystery—and on successive trips he pushed off into it farther and deeper. In the absorption of adventure he scarcely noticed the coldness of the water, until one day, at his farthest-out point, he realized that he had gone numb. His arms and legs were leaden, almost immovable, and the shore was barely visible in the distance. It was only by discarding his aqualung, and after a desperate hour's struggle, that he at last reached it and collapsed exhausted on the beach.

"I thought I'd had it," he said afterward. "More than ever in a plane or on a mountain, I really thought I'd had it in that sea."

In flying itself, at Wheelus, he kept out of trouble. The mach speeds, the dart gunnery, the bombing and strafing and refueling and formation flying were by now *vieux jeux* to him. Neither he nor his planes suffered any lapses, and when alone in the skies he resisted all impulses to take off for Zanzibar or Timbuktu. In late January, after not quite a month in Africa, he returned to Germany, midwinter, and his family.

But not to Air Force housing at Hahn. He and Marilyn had agreed that, in Europe as in the States, they wanted no part of base living, and even in the brief period before he had left for Wheelus they had found time to look around for an outside home. Their choice had fallen on a house in the Mosel[2] valley town of Bernkastel, and by the time John returned, Marilyn and the children were installed there. Like many things Harlinian, its military acceptability was doubtful. Air Force regulations specified that flying personnel must live no more than fifteen minutes' drive from the base, and Bernkastel, twenty-five hilly and winding kilometers from Hahn, scarcely seemed to pass muster. But the erstwhile speed king of Redwood City and Los Altos had confidence both in himself and his newly purchased Volkswagen. VWs, he was aware, were not noted for hill climbing, but what he lost on the upgrades he would make up on the down.

The contrast between base and town was total. Bernkastel—in its full name Bernkastel-Kues—is a small twin community straddling the Mosel River: medieval in aspect, provincial in outlook, a storybook place of nooks and alleys, gables and turrets, untouched by the shells

[2] Mosel in German, Moselle in French.

and bombs of World War II. Roundabout, on steep hillsides, lie some of the finest vineyards of the Rhineland, and from their new home, on its own hillside in the town's outskirts, the Harlins looked out over miles of them—and to a high and ancient castle across the river. Theirs was a two-story house, neat and new, but without central heating or hot water, and they occupied the upper level. On the lower lived a German engineer and his family, cultured and friendly, but speaking little English; and except for one other resident American couple, the language elsewhere in Bernkastel was exclusively *deutsch*.

They did not mind this. It was what they wanted—especially Marilyn. From the beginning she studied German conscientiously, and was soon doing well with it. The children picked it up automatically. John, who didn't study, lagged behind the rest, but got by when he had to. At the beginning, and for the usual reasons, he had a strong prejudice against Germans. But he learned gradually to judge each on his own, and in the end it was a German who became perhaps the closest of all his friends.

At Hahn, vis-à-vis Bernkastel, there was hardly an echo of Germany. It was like a U.S. air base anywhere: not only in its planes, hangars, and runways, but in its patterns of life. There was the standardized housing. There were the PX, the cafeteria, the movie house. There were the assorted clubs, with slot machines in the lobbies. There were men in dungarees, women in hair curlers, children in Superman shirts (Batman was then yet to come); and the two main thoroughfares for the Fords and Chevies were called Main Street and Broadway. Into this transplanted Middletown, Marilyn came once every two weeks for PX shopping, occasionally for a movie, classes, or to the hospital with the children, and almost never for social events. John of course came every working day, but saw little of the place besides planes and his flight line headquarters.

His assignment was to the 10th Tactical Fighter Squadron of the 50th Tactical Fighter Wing, known less officially and more briefly as the Hahn Hawks. And his service began with a nasty shock. One of the reasons he had wanted to go to Hahn was, of course, its proximity to the Alps. Another was his desire to serve with and under a flier named Cal Davey, one of the most famous fighter pilots in the Air Force, who was currently stationed there. But he was barely to have a chance to shake his hand. Just a day or two after John's arrival, and before he left for Libya, Davey came in for a landing in Hahn's wretched weather, overshot the almost invisible field, and crashed to his death against a stand of trees. Pilot Harlin was by now well aware that crashes and death were part of the game of flying. Yet it was nonetheless unnerving to see a long-standing idol killed almost in the moment of meeting him.

In Europe, it was routine for planes to fly in weather that in Arizona or Nevada would have kept them totally grounded. ("If we'd waited for *their* kind of weather," said John, "we'd have never flown at all.") His training was now theoretically over, and he was a certified graduate fighter pilot. But in practice, in a peacetime military establishment, training never ends. That is all there is for it to do—train— against the day when it may be called to strike in earnest. And so it was at Hahn. Precisely because of the bad weather, much of the training was for bad-weather conditions, specifically instrument flying. There were solo flights, and flights of two, four, and up to seven planes in formation. There was practice in traffic patterns, low-level flying and aerial combat maneuvering.

Here too, close beside the Iron Curtain, there had to be constant readiness for the button that might someday be pushed. Long hours had to be spent on alert at the flight line and in the underground command post, called the Cave. At night, the pilots took turns sleeping within a few yards of their planes, prepared, if the signal was given, to be airborne in three minutes. The Hawks' assignment, come D-day, would be in effect a suicide mission à la Doctor Strangelove: delivering nuclear weapons to their targets with insufficient fuel to return, and bailing out over enemy country to whatever awaited them there. John's target was the city of Prague in Czechoslovakia.

He was still no enthusiast for nuclear bombing. Nor for daily earth-bound routine. But once he took off in his F-100 the thrill of flight was as fresh and magical as ever. Up, up he would soar through the clouds of the Rhineland, with the sun calling "I'm here, I'm here. Can you reach me?" And then he would reach it. He was high, clear, free. His plane was fast, and Europe was small, and in the blue and gold far above it he gloried again in the dimension of his youth. He bore to east and west, to north and south, and to the south were the Alps. He could not fly over ever-neutral Switzerland, but close enough to see its great peaks rising white and radiant above earth and cloud. To see one, in their northern forefront, that was not white but black

—too steep for snow, too awesome for mistaking—and he knew that after almost six years he was looking again at the wall of the Eiger.

Then presently, as he looked, it was no longer black. Evening had come to Europe; the sun was low in the west; and in the last moments of the day it touched the savage face with the gentle fire of alpenglow. It seemed to fill the earth, the sky, the very cockpit of the soaring plane. And then John banked the plane, and it was gone. His fuel was running low. Night was coming. Faster than sound—almost as fast, it seemed, as the waning light itself—he streaked back to the cloud and darkness of the north.

It was not long before he was looking up at the Alps as well as down. Throughout his life with Marilyn he had talked of "a honeymoon in Switzerland," and as soon as the chance offered they were off together in the Volkswagen. It was perforce a short junket, little more than a long weekend. But they managed quick visits to Geneva, Zürich, and Bern, and, most importantly (for John), reached Grindelwald, high in the Bernese Oberland in the very shadow of the Eiger. Neither time nor the winter weather permitted any thought of climbing. But John was already full of plans and projects for his leave during the coming summer.

In that first season they also made brief trips around Germany, and one to Paris—where he was the guide, but she the stronger walker. And in the longer between-times they worked out their pattern of living at Bernkastel. Though they preferred it to life at the base, it was by no means all ideal. The winter coldness of their house and the lack of stateside amenities did not bother them, for they, and the children too, were old hands at Spartan living. But despite its beauty, they found Bernkastel oppressive in its deeply Catholic, *petit-bourgeois* provincialism, and made fewer friends among the locals than they had hoped to. At the other end of the spectrum, they avoided the Hahn cocktail circuit. But from here and there, nevertheless, they assembled a circle of congenial friends.

Among them were old colleague John High and his wife, now stationed at a helicopter base not far away. Later Arne Arneson appeared, assigned to Hahn in the same squadron as John. Of new friends, the closest, particularly to Marilyn, were the other American couple living in Bernkastel, a somewhat older pair—though also with young children—by the name of Roland and Elinor Osgood. "Ladd" Osgood was the civilian education officer at Hahn; his wife taught part-time at the branch of the University of Maryland that had been established in West Germany; and Marilyn found her far more stimulating company than either standard-brand service wives or German *Hausfraus*.

By a trick of circumstance, the senior Harlins were now more in evidence than when John and Marilyn lived back in the States. John I had been transferred in his piloting from the domestic to the overseas division of TWA; his European terminus was often nearby Frankfort; and he made frequent brief visits to Hahn and Bernkastel—sometimes with Sue Harlin, when she flew over with him. Since John had entered the Air Force, he had got on better with his mother than when he was younger. And Marilyn, for her part, was glad to have an occasional one-of-the-family helper in the care of Andréa and Johnny III. One of the things that pleased her most about their present life was that, after the long series of moves, the children now had a home that would presumably endure for a few years. And the children responded by flourishing happily.

Of the four of them, it was John who was flourishing least. The move to Europe had only heightened his conflict between love of flying and dislike of the Air Force, and though he spoke sometimes, and seriously, of "my duty to serve," he grew increasingly restless in its day-to-day fulfillment. One of his senior officers, speaking later of his early days at Hahn, recalled that "he had a huge lust for life. He was aggressive, able, a fine flier, but terribly impatient of routine." And routine, of course, was most of life at the base. Further, the more John thought about it the unhappier he became about his potential role as nuclear bomber—and that when and if the grim day came, his target would be Prague. He recalled Prague from his boyhood visit as one of the loveliest of cities. He remembered its avenues and parks, its castles and bridges, the crowds promenading in Wenceslas Square. . . .

He explored the possibilities of *out*. On his early visit to Zürich he inquired at Swissair about his chances for a pilot's job, but was told that few non-Swiss were hired and there were no current openings. (How, if there had been, he could have got out of the Air Force makes an interesting question, but John seldom let himself be bothered by such technicalities.) Later, he learned to his excitement that a Major William Hackett, an Army officer and well-known mountaineer, was in Munich organizing a joint German-American expedition to the Karakoram subrange of the Himalayas; and he promptly rushed to meet him, in the hope that Hackett would accept him as a member and arrange the necessary leave for him to go. By the time he appeared, however, the team was set and ready to take off, and for John it was back to Hahn in disappointment.

He set his sights for the coming summer and the Alps. To condition himself, he took to gym workouts and road-running, and presently to actual climbing—not on mountains, for there were none available, but on the walls of ancient Rhineland castles. Sometimes he climbed alone, sometimes with John High or others whom he could persuade to join him, and not a few of his ascents up towering battlements were equal to a "Class V" on the cliffs of Yosemite.

Still his restlessness persisted. At home, he would pace the rooms as if about to burst out of them. Then depression would follow. "What I do doesn't make any difference anyhow. Soon we're all going to be blown up," he would say to Marilyn, adding savagely "—and I'm going to be one of the blowers."

According to her, the years at Bernkastel were the most difficult of their life together. Unhappy in his work, he also chafed at domesticity, growing increasingly impatient both with her and the children. There were arguments, fights, recriminations, often ending with his slamming out of the house to walk off his anger in the surrounding hills. The direct fuse for the explosions would be something small and specific, but beneath it were causes far deeper and more subtle. They might, for instance, be at home of an evening, reading; and as so often with them in their interests, the usual male and female roles would be reversed, with Marilyn studying a scientific journal while he scanned a magazine of art or design. Back at Stanford, he had acknowledged this reversal at the gathering of biologists with the wry comment, "I'm a wife." And now, too, he accepted it; indeed was proud of Marilyn's mind and intellectual interests. What he could not abide was that the scientist in her overflowed from her mind into her personality.

She was practical, objective, controlled. He was imaginative, sensitive, volatile. Almost invariably, the pattern of their quarrels was that he would become aroused, whereas she would remain calm, and her calmness goaded him farther. What he wanted and needed was that she get as angry as himself, that there be an emotional climax, then a forgiving embrace. But Marilyn was not built that way. He could not drive her to anger, only in the end to tears; and the tears were the last straw for him, eliciting a shove or a slap and the slamming door. In an hour or so he would be back—if not contrite, at least gentle and tender—and before the night ended, as likely as not, they were making love.

For whatever their trials, this was the core of their relationship: that he loved her and she loved him. "Even after years of marriage," Marilyn has said, "I could not have imagined a better lover. For John, sex was not just a physical thing; it was dance, painting, poetry, music. The surroundings had to be right. The mood just right. What we said and felt; what we wore, or didn't wear. Each time he came to me, it was almost as if it were again for the first time, and he cared as much for my pleasure as for his own."

It was a precious and meaningful thing to a woman. And a thought she clung to when the going was hard.

Plans for the summer solidified when it was learned that Jerry Robertson was coming over. He would graduate from Arizona State in early June and enter the Air Force in September. But in the past year he had become an afficionado of aerial soaring, and during the summer interval he was visiting Europe to compete in an international sail plane meet in Cologne. . . . Would he have time to climb with John in the Alps? Yes, indeed he would.

Preparations were made. So that Marilyn could go along on the trip, it was arranged that Sue Harlin would stay in Bernkastel as sitter-in-residence during the month of John's leave. For so important an expedition, he decided, something more "U" than a Volkswagen was needed, and in its place they acquired a Sunbeam Alpine convertible —small in bulk and capacity, but long on speed, power, and red-painted glamour. They had had it only a week when John, on one of the Hahn-to-Bernkastel curves, met head-on with an Army truck. (No insurance: cost eight hundred dollars.) But neither car nor John was irreparably damaged, and both were back on the road when Robertson arrived.

In fact two Robertsons, for along with Jerry came his younger brother

Gary. First in their program came the soaring at Cologne; and to this John went when he could, not only as spectator but to have his own first experience of engineless flight. Then in mid-June, with the meet over, they were off to the south. There were four of them—the three men and Marilyn—crammed into the tiny Alpine, with arms, legs, and gear protruding. But within John, wedged behind the wheel, there welled a tide of freedom he had not known in years. Before him, at last, were not a mere few days but a whole month in the mountain world, and he split the air with wild yodeling "Y-A-A-A-R-V-O" as he gunned the car toward the promised land.

On this trip, as always, he was the director-general, the planner. And as always, too, the plans were ambitious. Pre-eminent among them, of course, was the Eiger, but as the *pièce-de-résistance* this would come last. First they were going to Chamonix, in the French Alps at the foot of Mont Blanc, and there he and Jerry—with non-climbing Gary and Marilyn as camp followers—would work out on the great galaxy of peaks that comprise the highest massif in western Europe. The domed snow-summit of Mont Blanc proper did not greatly matter; most of the routes to it were of the "tourist" variety. What John had his eye on were its surrounding spires and towers— the famous *aiguilles* (or needles) of Chamonix—offering challenges comparable to that of the Eiger itself.

When they reached Chamonix the weather was fine, and they did not stay long in the town. Ascending to the great glacier called the Mer de Glace, they pitched a tent made of a parachute over a home-made frame, and the next morning John and Jerry set off for the heights. Their objective was the north face of a rock-peak called the Dru, known as one of the steepest and hardest climbs in the Alps. But they were barely able to come to grips with it. Though the weather was still brilliant, recent early-summer storms had left great accumulations of snow on the almost vertical walls, and after floundering about for a while in crumbling whiteness they had to beat a retreat.

Next, they tried another famous pinnacle, the long needle of the Grépon. Here, taking a route over the crest of the neighboring Aiguille du Roc, they found less snow, and with John leading throughout, climbed high on the sheer but solid granite. When they were just short of the top, however, sunshine gave way to cloud, wind, and lightning; and John, though he took most perils in stride, was never one to argue with the weather. Roping down the Grépon, they returned to their parachute tent, and the next day, in continuing bad weather, all hands descended to Chamonix.

Home here was a campground in the town's outskirts, frequented by climbers and hikers from all over Europe, and there were lively times in a babel of languages. Ever the scientist, Marilyn took to botanizing in the adjoining forests. And for John and Jerry there were cliffs nearby, on which practice climbs could be made even in poor weather.

After a few days, Gary Robertson had to take off for home. Then, with clearing skies, Harlins-plus-Jerry again moved upward, now toward a spire called the Aiguille du Plan. But again there was frustration, when an avalanche roaring down from near its base gave warning of perils ahead. After some discussion, Marilyn and Jerry descended toward the hut where they had spent the previous night. John continued on for a while, to scout the situation for a try the next day. Then he too returned to the hut—and a loud explosion.

"It was really fantastic," said Marilyn later. "There in the hut, Jerry and I had somehow got to talking about John and girls; to what extent he'd strayed since we'd been married, and how much was just talk and rumor. It was almost as if John were psychic. As if he knew what we'd been saying and had decided to reverse things." In any case, he burst into the hut burning with suspicion and jealousy. They had turned back early, he declared, so they could be alone in the hut. They were having an affair. He was through with both of them. He wanted a divorce.

Marilyn tried to calm him. Jerry assured him he had never dreamed of touching his wife.

To which John, in a fine non-sequitur, responded, "Oh, she's not attractive enough, is that it?" Then he stomped up the ladder to the hut's sleeping loft.

When, later, he came down, he had changed totally. He told Marilyn he was sorry. He told Jerry he was sorry. And he was crying. It was the first and last time Marilyn was to see him cry. It was the first time he had done so, he told her afterward, since, as a boy, he had shot the dik-dik in Ethiopia. For the rest of the evening, as they ate supper and prepared for sleep, there was not much conversation. Like the storms of the Alps, John's came and went quickly. In the majestic stillness of the mountain night, this particular one must have seemed, in retrospect, more than a little ludicrous, and in the morning he and Jerry set out to climb again as if nothing had happened.

The Plan still looked like a bad bet, however, and they moved over to the Aiguille du Midi, directly above Chamonix. The route they chose was called the Éperon (spur) de Rébuffat, named after the famous Chamonix guide, Gaston Rébuffat, who had led its first ascent. His party, however, and the few others who had followed, had made the climb with artificial aids, and it was John's ambition to be the first up by free climbing, using pitons only for protection, not for holds and stances. It was a bold project, and he and Jerry almost made it. Indeed, *did* make it in all but the most literal sense, for every difficulty of the sheer face was beneath them when at last they called a halt because of darkness. Instead of continuing to the very summit of the peak, less than fifty feet above, they traversed to the nearby Aiguille du Midi station of the Mont Blanc aerial cable-car line, thus scoring a technical near miss. But it had nevertheless been a satisfying accomplishment—and a topflight climb in any alpinist's book.

The rest of the Chamonix campaign, like its beginning, was disappointing. Next on John's list was the Grand Capucin, another jagged rock-and-ice spire, rising close to Mont Blanc and not far from the Italian border. But again weather was the enemy. No sooner had they reached the foot of the peak than it vanished in cloud and spindrift, and they were barely able to grope their way back across vast snowfields to the shelter of a hut.

Finally they returned to the Dru, for what, in prospect, was their most ambitious venture of all. This time it was not the north face but the even more difficult west face they were after, and with them—as companions, not for pay—went two of the best of the younger Chamonix guides, Georges Payot and Marc Martinetti. Things started promisingly. In clear, sunny stillness they ascended glacier and snowslope to the foot of the huge precipice and passed a hopeful night encamped there. But the Alps, in that early summer, seemed incapable of putting together two fair days in a row. With morning came the usual debacle of wind and snow, and they retreated to the accompaniment of lightning flashes and a sinister buzzing of their steel ax-heads.

That was the end of the climbing in the range of Mont Blanc.

John's leave was running out; if there was to be an Eiger attempt, it must come quickly; and so he, Jerry, and Marilyn moved over to the Oberland and the Kleine Scheidegg. He was not optimistic. It now seemed obvious that the Alps were in for a summer of bad weather, and the wall of the Eiger, in its exposed northern position, was notorious for the worst weather of all. Also, he had come to feel that Jerry, though a competent climber and good companion, was not a strong and experienced enough partner for this most murderous of mountains. Still, it was for him also the most alluring of mountains, and he had at least to come, to see, if not to conquer. By that summer of 1960 its north wall had been climbed seventeen times by a total of forty-seven men—with a matching seventeen deaths. But it had yet to be scaled, or even seriously challenged, by a single Briton or American.

John ached to be Number One. But it was not to be; not yet. As in the Mont Blanc range, the weather pattern was one fair day followed by two or three of storm, and the best that could be done was a bit of reconnoitering. With Jerry, he ascended some distance above the base, but not much farther than he had with Tenzing six years earlier. Further, they made use of one of the Eiger's unique features: the mountain railway line that cuts through its core on its way from Kleine Scheidegg to the nearby Jungfraujoch. About a third of the way up the face there is a row of windows in an opening in the rock beside the line; and riding up, they clambered out and explored the wall for a short stretch above. This, however, was all they could accomplish. The precipices were plastered with snow and ice. The weather broke, and broke again. After a few more days of waiting and frustration, they were back in the Sunbeam Alpine, bound north toward Germany.

In results achieved it had been a disappointing campaign. But there were mitigations. As far as the Eiger went, no one at all was to climb its north wall during the whole of that summer. And in the Mont Blanc range, though only one summit had been reached, there had been at least two fine climbs and much high adventure. Too, there would be more summers, more climbs ahead, and John was ever the one to look forward, not back. "One thing about the mountains," he wrote soon after to a friend, "is that they are always waiting for us poor fleas to return. And successful or unsuccessful, you've enjoyed every moment and learned a little more to use in the next engagement."

Significantly, he did not even look back with discomfort at the contretemps with Jerry and Marilyn. Rather, he seemed wholly to have forgotten it, as he bade Jerry a warm goodbye and turned his attention to other things.

One of them, in his spare time, was soaring. He had greatly liked his few flights with Jerry at Cologne, and soon after his return home he began going up on his own from a nearby field. As with so many of his activities, it seems to have appealed to him on two levels. On one, he was, in effect, still the small boy, saying "If Jerry can do it, I can do it." On the other, he was the artist, the esthetician, enthralled by the graceful magic of silent flight.

Then, with early fall, came something else that was new, and that for a while changed the pattern of his service life. Like many American bases in Europe, Hahn had a football team—called the Hawks—and John became both its fullback and coach. In the first role, he enjoyed playing again after the lapse of years and succeeded in going through a rough season without injury. As for the second, it proved so demanding that for the length of the season it became virtually his full-time job—with only the requirement that he put in enough time in the air to maintain his pilot's rating. This was fine with him: flying without ground duty. And it was fine too to be boss man of a football team instead of a struggling aspirant on the Stanford jayvees. The Hahn Hawks did not become the champions of Europe, but they didn't do badly either, and at season's end he was warmly praised by the base commander.

At season's end, too, came another, more meaningful change in his service status. In Hahn Air Base Bulletin Number A-1717 announcement was made that *1st Lt John E. Harlin A03083857, 50th Tactical Fighter Wing, this station, is appointed Instructor Pilot and Instrument Flight Examiner in T-33A type aircraft, effective 4 November 1960. Auth: AFR 60-4 and USAFE Reg 51-6.*

The change was at his own request. After almost a year at Hahn and three in the service, he had taken the extraordinary step of going on record, through official channels, that he was morally opposed to nuclear bombing, and therefore wished to be relieved of his duties as

114

a fighter bomber. What disposition would be made of this—and him—was, for a while, a question mark. There had been interviews and deliberations. In the end, however, his superiors not only granted his wish but, in his assignment as instructor, put their seal on him as a flier of the first rank.

As so often with John, there has been disagreement among those who knew him about his real motives in this switch of duties. What might be called the pro-John faction has accepted his stated reason as wholly true and sincere, whereas the anti-Johns point out that by changing jobs he put himself in a position where he could get more and longer leaves for mountaineering. This last would seem to be true. And it is true, too, that he would do almost anything to clear his path to a mountain. But—once again—he was not a simple man. If he was selfish, he was also an idealist. If he was an adventurer, he was also a crusader. If he was a Hawk, he was also a Dove.[8]

Far more than most men, John Harlin wanted to be a hero. But on his own terms, not someone else's.

[8] This was before the words came into general use in the Vietnam war. But John in himself was already both.

10. The Rover Boys

"Are you there? Are you there?"

This time it was not John speaking to the sun but the ground speaking to John. He and his plane were lost over the mountains in night and storm.

During the Thanksgiving weekend he and Marilyn had visited Copenhagen, returning to Hahn-Bernkastel in an all-night drive. And the next morning, in his new role of instructor pilot, he had taken off with a student on an out-and-back mission in a T-33 trainer. The "out" part of it was to a base in northern Italy, and though John was slightly the worse for wear from lack of sleep, it had gone routinely. The "back" phase, however, an exercise in night navigation, was in trouble from the start.

It began soon after takeoff, amid rain and lightning, when John, in the instructor's rear seat, saw that the plane's heading indicator was differing from the magnetic compass at an increasing rate; and at the same time ground control notified him that they were drifting off course. As he tried to rectify this, the cockpit lights dimmed and the electrical system went out. The emergency system, he soon found, was out too. The only working instruments were altimeter and radio. But radar contact with the ground was gone, and though control could still talk with him, it could no longer tell where he was. Nor, in the cloud and storm, could he. What he did know, however, was that there were mountains close by—the jagged peaks of the Italian Dolomites—and he quickly got permission from control to climb from his authorized six thousand feet to twenty thousand.

Yet he was still lost. Even at this height there was no visibility, and for some time he maneuvered, trying to break out of the storm. At intervals came a squawk from below: "Are you there? Are you there?" Yes, he was still there, he told them. But he obviously could not stay there, flying blindly, forever. Circling widely, the plane probably crossed the Yugoslavian frontier into forbidden air space, but since no one could see it, no one shot at it. Then control, still struggling to find him by radar, suggested he descend to fifteen thousand feet; and he tried to. But with the plane lurching and careening in the turbulence, the altimeter, too, was gyrating wildly. After more desperate minutes had passed, control put him on a bearing that it believed would take him out over the Adriatic Sea, and told him that if necessary he should prepare for ejection.

John did not want to bail out. The plane carried no water survival equipment, and not long before, a pilot friend of his had been lost in just such a jump. . . . So the broken dialogue continued. . . . For a time there was an especially bad interlude when a second ground station broke in, garbling the instructions of the first. But presently the two were coordinating, and it was apparent that the plane had been picked up, at least faintly, by radar. With the ground's assurance, and his own prayer, that he was clear of mountains, John nosed it on downward and at last broke out of the weather at about twenty-five hundred feet. For the first time since taking off he could see the earth. And with the radar now fully operative, he was guided on until he could see the airfield. The rain was still torrential. His landing light did not work, and when he touched the runway his brakes barely functioned. Yet there was no crash. He made it. He still had not lost a plane or himself—but it was the closest shave he was to have during his years in the Air Force.

That was in late November 1960. Soon after, he was sent on a brief assignment to an RAF base in England, and with the Christmas season approaching, Marilyn and the children accompanied him. Ironically, his job was the instruction of British fighter pilots in nuclear bombing techniques. But he raised no formal objection. A compensating factor may have been that his duties were light; and from his station at Malcolm Air Base, in Norfolk, he and family were able to tour about widely.

They got down to London. They drove through Scotland, the Lake District, Wales. At a small mountain inn in the northern Welsh highlands they stopped for what was theoretically to be one night. But when John discovered it was a holiday headquarters for top British alpinists the one night expanded into three, while he climbed by day and talked climbs by evening firelight. Among others, he met Sir Charles Evans and Joe Brown, respectively stars of the older and middle generation of English mountaineers. And, more importantly for the future, he also became acquainted with a wealthy young sportsman called Beverly Clark, who was to become a close friend and associate of later days.

Toward the end of January 1961, it was back to Hahn and Bernkastel. To his assignments as instructor pilot and instrument flight examiner there was now added that of assistant flying safety officer, and from now on he was to be not only individually but professionally involved in his unit's mishaps and disasters. One of them, unforeseeable and freakish, occurred soon after he had taken on his new duties. During the course of a routine flight, the cockpit canopy of one of the planes, carrying two men, loosened and tore off, and the man in the rear seat, caught in the torrent of the slipstream, was strangled to death by his own scarf.

In a plane, as on a mountain, there are many ways of coming to grief. But John's own luck was still holding. His only accident during his Air Force career—and the only broken bone of his lifetime—was suffered not in a plane, nor even at Hahn, but on a quiet Easter Sunday in Bernkastel. Hunting for painted eggs with Johnny and Andréa, he kicked what he thought was an egg but turned out to be a stone, broke a toe, and limped shoeless for a while thereafter.

Like any home with small children, the Harlin house was a lively place. Johnny was now in a local kindergarten, Andréa at nursery school, and both chattered bilingually. Two Siamese cats had been acquired and named Kuzma and Maus. Marilyn, in an effort to catch up with her son and daughter, was now taking German courses at the nearest branch of the University of Maryland, and John, in his off-hours, was writing an account of their past summer's adventures, called *The Roving Alpine*, which he hoped to sell to a magazine. To work off excess energy, he still ran, did calisthenics and climbed castle walls (now often with a new friend, a Hahn flight surgeon named Leon Canapary); and when these proved not enough, he took to water skiing on the Mosel and private flying with the Hahn Aero Club.

In spite of all this, plus his change of jobs, he remained restless and dissatisfied. His mind's eye ranged out past Rhineland horizons to the Alps, the Himalayas, even for a while, surprisingly, to the jungles of the Amazon, where the highest mountains are, literally, anthills. Meanwhile, on a less exotic level, he had become interested in the idea of establishing, somewhere in Europe, a new American school to be run on unconventional lines, and had many talks of this with neighbors Ladd and Elli Osgood, who were both professional educators. But for the time at least, school, mountains and jungles were all equally pipe dreams. He was still a prisoner of the Air Force, and his only escape—ironically, thanks to the Air Force—was in his soaring flights across the skies of Europe.

Tension at home increased. Door slammings and solitary walks increased. From the prison of Hahn he returned to what he now felt was the prison of Bernkastel, where Marilyn presided as warden and the children as turnkeys. And Marilyn, for her part, felt he was making ever more impossible demands on her. "All John wanted of a wife," she has said, speaking of those days, "was that she be a Balmain model, an Eiger climber and a perfect housekeeper, have shining hair (without curlers), get a Ph.D. (in her spare time), be a devoted mother (with invisible children), plus a reader, mixer, camp director, secretary-treasurer, and (also in her spare time) do anything else she wants."

Sometimes she too took a walk—not down roads and through forests but to the nearby Osgoods. John would come after her. He would tell her he needed and loved her. But though this was true and she knew it, their troubles continued. Grew worse.

—Until presently, perhaps inevitably, the "other woman" appeared.

120

She was the wife of another Hahn pilot, unhappy both with her husband and with service life, and from soon after their meeting she and John made no secret of their involvement. His earlier strayings had occurred during Marilyn's back-home absences, wreathed in rumor and denial. But this one was authentic and acknowledged. John was in love, he declared: no longer with Marilyn but with Mary X. He wanted a divorce. He would marry Mary. As soon as he could get out of the Air Force they would go away: not to mountains or jungles—and certainly not to a school—but to a South Sea Island. (The fact that Mary X, like himself, had two children made things no easier, he conceded, but ways and means would be found.)

This was not the straying of a wolf but of a romantic; of a romantic's ego that could not bear to be taken for granted. And in fairness to John it must be said that, now as always, he seemed rather less pursuer than pursued. In his strength, his "blond god" handsomeness, his palpable aura of adventure, he was vastly attractive to many women, and not a few let him know it. Assuredly, Mary X let him know it. And he, for his part, found in her and their affair an excitement hard to come by in a five-year-old marriage. Here was no "other John," a philandering playboy John, suddenly showing his face. He was of the same piece as John the flier, John the climber, hell-bent for the heights wherever he found them.

Marilyn understood this. She strove to be calm and self-possessed, and in large measure succeeded; but as on previous occasions, this drove John still farther. In emotional crises her "scientific mind" was anathema to him, and with other women, what he sought, in reaction, were certified "non-scientists," as imaginative and impulsive as himself. Mary X, from all evidence, was far from a trollop or pushover: on the contrary, a sensitive and intelligent person with standards and a conscience. Marilyn, who could hardly be expected to be an admirer, found her "an arts-and-drama type—and of course a live-for-the-moment type." But she could understand, if not endorse, her allure for her husband. "She was good for his ego," she said philosophically (or scientifically). And as for Mary's side of it: "After all, he *was* an awfully attractive man, if you didn't have to live with him every day."

Still, the Air Force remained and the South Seas were distant. No one left home. No one filed for divorce. For some time the situation continued in delicate balance, and when finally the climax came, it

121

was from an unexpected source. At home alone one night, in deep depression, Mary's husband, John's fellow pilot, downed a bottle of whisky and a handful of sleeping pills, and was found unconscious by John and Mary. Rushed by them to the base hospital, he recovered. But, though the lovers continued to see each other for a while thereafter, this was the beginning of the end for them. Shock and remorse, one gathers, played a part, but the passage of time an even greater one. "Time was in my favor," said Marilyn, "and I knew it. As soon as any woman—or man, or child—began to interfere with John's freedom, they were done for. She would make that mistake. She did." . . . And John retreated. . . . Life in the house at Bernkastel continued much as before.

Briefly, at least.

Then enter a new protagonist.

The prologue had come the previous fall with John's receipt of a letter. It had begun, "You crazy gung-ho bastard"—and ended—"Yours, and more a bum than ever." And the signature, of course, had been Gary Hemming's. In the two years since he had appeared in Phoenix, Gary had been, among other things, a private detective in New York and a mate on a fishing boat based in Tampa, Florida. Now, in another change of venue, he was a student at the University of Grenoble, whence he had tracked John down through a series of APO addresses. And early in 1961 he appeared in person on the Harlin doorstep.

He was not long in making his mark on both their home and Bernkastel. On his first night in residence, Frau Hoffmann, the wife of the engineer who lived in the downstairs apartment, was startled to find a tall, long-haired, bearded figure asleep on the stairway. (Gary said he was comfortable there.) Not long after, a passerby called an alarm when he saw the same figure hanging from an upstairs window. (Gary was practicing climbing.) In exchange for his keep he washed dishes, did odd chores, and allowed the children to pull his whiskers. But for John he did more than that—and received much in return— for the two had a vast talent for reciprocal stimulation. First, last, and between times, of course, they talked mountains. It was not by happenstance that Gary had lighted in Grenoble, but precisely because it was next door to the Alps; and now he and John spieled the nights away on plans for what they would soon be doing there together.

In fact they did more than plan. They acted. Wangling a short leave, John accompanied Gary down to Chamonix, where they put in a few days doing winter practice climbs and mapping more ambitious ones for the summer to come. The only fly in their ointment was that, at about this time, word came from the Bernese Oberland that a German-Austrian team of climbers had just made the first winter ascent of the north wall of the Eiger. It was one of the great feats of modern Alpine mountaineering: one that John, in particular, would have dearly loved to have done himself. "When he came back to Bernkastel," Marilyn wrote to a friend, "he was groaning with envy."

Vis-à-vis the Harlins as a couple, Gary's influence, though less spectacular, was no less unsettling than Mary X's. And it lasted longer. He was a loner and wanderer not only by nature but by philosophic conviction, and it baffled and annoyed him that a man like John had mortgaged his freedom to marriage and domesticity. Though they had their brushes, it was not Marilyn individually whom he considered the enemy. It was the institution of wedlock in general—and in particular, the Great American Boss-Wife, whom he regarded with a special horror. Nor was he averse to speaking his mind. In matters matrimonial, John's or otherwise, he was the devil's advocate and proud of it; and with John forever straining for freedom, he seemed to have good material to work with.

—Up to a point, yes. But beyond it, no. When John, as he so often did, told Marilyn that he loved and needed her (as now, after his brief lapse, he did again) it was perhaps truer than he himself was aware. Their marriage had weathered the Mary X storm, and it would weather Gary.

During the spring of 1961 he shuttled back and forth between Grenoble and Bernkastel. When he and John were not together, they were corresponding, further developing their plans, until their summer program was plotted out like a military campaign. First they would do practice climbs of increasing severity; then several classic routes of the "extreme" variety; then some new routes of their own, even more ambitious; and finally, of course, there would be the north wall of the Eiger. As they planned, their anticipation grew until it almost burst. "Johnny, you old (Garyism)," G.H. wrote from Grenoble, "this is going to be our year to *romp!*"

It was an outsize project, by far the biggest of their climbing careers. But now, typically, in the very midst of its preparation, another even bigger one developed. During the year since he had missed out on Major Hackett's expedition to the Karakoram, John's thoughts had kept moving out past the Alps to the greater heights of distant Asia; and putting two and two (i.e., mountaineering and the Air Force) together, he had come up with an idea that dazzled his imagination. When told of it, Gary was dazzled too. And so, with one eye still on the Alps, they turned the other toward the Himalayas and set to work to make things happen.

They called the project HASL—for High Altitude Space Laboratory. And its goal was no less than that the United States Air Force establish such a laboratory, for the training of astronauts, among the Karakoram peaks of Pakistan. The venture, as they conceived it, would begin the following year with an expedition to K2, highest peak of the range and second highest in the world; and in its purely mountaineering aspects the two of them would be in charge. There would also, however, be scientific personnel involved, and the scientists, using the climbers as their first guinea pigs, would then go on to organize a longer-range program of high altitude research and experiment.

On the face of it, they seemed an unlikely pair to make much impression on the Air Force establishment. John was a mere lieutenant with a record of scrapes and eccentricities, and Gary, the professional non-conformist, was as remote from a proper service type as could be imagined. But their enthusiasm was vast and their labors prodigious. Together, with Gary holed up at Bernkastel, they secured and studied much of the existing literature on high altitude studies, and wrote a presentation arguing that their project would be a great forward step in preparing men for landings on the moon and the planets. They cited references, suggested procedures, recommended equipment. They prepared a timetable, a roster of team members, and opened a correspondence with the Pakistani government. On the European front, John made contact with a variety of senior Air Force officers whose support was essential; and on a still higher plane his father was called into service. Along with his TWA career, John Senior had, since World War II, maintained his naval reserve status and risen high in it.

He was now both a rear-admiral and national president of the Reserve Officers' Association, and thus in a position to open important doors back home.

For a while, there were quick and promising developments. A high-ranking space physiologist, attached to the Air Force in Europe, warmly endorsed the plan. So did the base commander at Hahn and others with influence. Letters of recommendation went off to the Air Force Office of Bioastronautics in Washington, and John was hoping soon to take off himself, to see generals, chiefs of staff, perhaps even Defense Secretary Robert S. McNamara.

But the crest of the wave had been passed. No quick summons came from Washington. And on their end, John and Gary were running into trouble with the more detailed presentations they had been asked to prepare. Each had his own idea of how to do it; each fancied himself as an articulate and persuasive writer; and the stimulation they drew from each other when they were in agreement easily turned to irritation when they weren't. John felt that Gary niggled at details. Gary felt that John was bemused by Napoleonic grand designs and didn't know a detail when he saw one. But late spring HASL had become largely hassle, and with no further encouragement coming from upper echelons, it gradually faded away.

The Alps, however, were still *there*. They loomed and beckoned. And the two old friends had no intention of letting their argument spoil their climbing. By the beginning of summer, with hatchets buried in favor of ice axes, they were ready to romp. Gary was wholly new to the Alps. John had had only a single full campaign there, and that a disappointing one. By the standards of top European climbers, mostly professional guides, they were little more than novices; but they had a few things going for them nonetheless. Both were young, strong, and immensely ambitious. Both had undertaken, and achieved, some of the hardest climbs in North America, and if they were still rather in-experienced in ice and snow work, they had, in Yosemite, made pure rock climbs equal to anything, anywhere. Not least importantly, they were equipped with certain Yosemite-developed techniques and gear, both for attack and safety, that were unquestionably the best in the world. On practice climbs near Grenoble with some of the best French mountaineers, Gary had been amazed at the primitive hardware[1] that had been used, and appalled at the lack of proper safety precautions.

They were out to "romp," yes. But they were deeply serious climbers —Gary no less than John—and this last was a fact that it took some a while to recognize in the tall, eccentric loner from San Diego. In his everyday life he was the very archetype of the beat: in his hair, beard and clothing; in his full vocabulary and empty pockets; in his non-commitment to conventional society's rules of the road. But with mountain rock beneath his feet he was a different person. Not only in appearance, with boots and parka, helmet and goggles. But inwardly. For here his commitment was total. His love of climbing was total. As a mountain rose before him it became the focus, the very meaning, of all the life that was in him, and as with John, its climbing was an adventure less of the flesh than of the mind and spirit.

Mind and spirit, however, are one thing; the facts of life another. And one basic fact this summer was that John was not able to take a full month's solid leave, as he had the previous year. The schedule had to be adapted to this—plus the weather—with much commuting between Hahn and Alps; and in the upshot he was to spend almost as much energy on cross-country dashes and all-night drives as on the mountains themselves.

In a reversal of the timetable, their first visit was to the Eiger: not, however, for a serious attempt but simply a weekend reconnaissance. Accompanied by John's castle-climbing friend, Flight Surgeon Leon Canapary, they did not even venture onto the north face itself (which in late June was still clogged with loose snow), contenting themselves with scouting it from the bordering west ridge. This was the "routine" way up the peak, and for John and Gary routine climbing. But the inexperienced doctor had his troubles, and presently elected to stop and wait until the others returned. Soon, however, loneliness and cold got at him. He began to descend alone, slipped, and when John and Gary came down they found a furrow in the snow that indicated he might have fallen to his death. He hadn't. When they caught up with him it was to find him not even injured. But the Eiger had shown that even its "easy" route was no place for a novice.

That same night, it was back to Hahn for John and Canapary, and

[1] Pitons, carabiners, and the like.

126

to Grenoble for Gary. Then the next weekend, minus the doctor but plus Marilyn and a French Hemming girl friend, there was a rendez-vous for a longer campaign in the Mont Blanc area. This time, how-ever, the base of operations was not Chamonix but Courmayeur, on the Italian side of the range, for most of their climbing objectives were in that sector. Also, for the Harlins, there was a Courmayeur sub-project: the investigation of a property which they believed might make a good site for the school they hoped to start when John left the Air Force.

Spaced over a few weeks, with another return to home grounds intervening, he and Gary made three difficult and successful climbs. One was of Mont Blanc itself, by the long and demanding route of the Brenva ridge. Another was the ascent—made only twice before—of the north face of the Col de Peuterey, on Mont Blanc's southern flank. The third, involving three days' climbing and two bivouacs, was the forging of a new direct route on one of the buttress-ridges of the Grandes Jorasses. In the process, they had their share of hazard and hardship. On one ascent, Gary had a long fall before he was held by a belayed rope; on another, a falling stone cracked John's plastic helmet but spared his skull. Yet as it developed, none of them was to be their major adventure. This came in mid-July when, unexpectedly, almost accidentally, they became involved in one of the worst storms —and worst tragedies—of Alpine history.

It began while they were waiting out a spell of weather at the Courmayeur campground. Several days before, in the mountains, they had met another young pair of climbers, a French-Swiss named Henri Briquet and a German named Konrad Kirch; and now these two were long overdue in the valley. As successive days brought more wind and rain—which meant blizzard above—John and Gary became seriously concerned for them, and at last decided to go up on a search. They tried to find a second team to go with them. The terrain south of Mont Blanc, where Briquet and Kirch were lost, is perhaps the wildest in all the Alps, and its glacial crevasses, now hidden by fresh snow, could be lethal traps for a mere twosome. They could find no one, however. So they set out alone.

Their first destination was a hut called the Gamba, about 8500 feet up amid the ridges and glaciers. And this they reached in the late afternoon, in heavy wind, rain and fog. Soon after, there appeared a corps of about a dozen Courmayeur guides, then a group of five

Frenchmen, and John and Gary learned that the two they were after were not the only ones lost in the storm. Almost a week before, a combined team of four Frenchmen and three Italians had set off to challenge the Central Pillar of Frêney, a southern buttress of Mont Blanc that was perhaps the outstanding unclimbed route in the Alps. And they had not been heard of since. Adding extra drama to the emergency was the fact that they were all accomplished and well-known climbers, topped by the great Italian guide, Walter Bonatti, who was one of the two or three most famous in the world.

With the arrival of the official rescue teams, John and Gary found themselves in an uncomfortable position: outsiders among insiders, amateurs among professionals. But even more, they were angrily astonished at the professionals' dearth of equipment, poor organization, and casual attitude toward the job at hand. In any case, with darkness coming, there was nothing anyone could do. Jammed in the tiny hut, all hands ate, then slept. And in the early morning, with the weather better, but still unsettled, the rescue parties started out. The five Frenchmen and most of the Italians headed up toward the base of the Frêney in search of their compatriots. Three of the Italians bore eastward toward the area where Briquet and Kirch were lost. But John and Gary noted that they were moving downward, not up, and the custodian of the hut said that they were merely going to a good lookout point where they could scan the heights through binoculars.

More furious than ever, John and Gary started off on their own. The one chance of the Swiss and German's being still alive, they had reasoned, was that they had holed up in a tiny shelter called the Craveri Refuge, high on the Peuterey Ridge. And this was their objective. Between them and even the base of the Peuterey, however, were a huge intervening ridge called l'Innominata, and beyond it the Frêney Glacier, both smothered in snow from the long days of storm; and to make things worse, as they moved on, the storm began again. The only conceivable route across the first barrier was by a lofty cleft known as the Col de l'Innominata, and toward this they fought their way, hour after hour, through vast drifts of old snow and howling gusts of new.

"The last hundred and fifty feet," Gary noted, "are nearly impossible. The snow is either waist and shoulder depth or it treacherously covers

128

the rotten rock of the ever-narrowing couloir which we are ascending. The wind is increasing now, and the snow is falling steadily and heavily. With only sixty feet left to reach the col we very nearly turn back. But John forces a way up a passage that was quite beyond my abilities to lead, and on reaching the crest of the col yells 'Off belay' to me. Here he gets two answers: one from me and another from behind him, somewhere out in the fog!"

So their quarry was alive. But where?

"For thirty minutes," Gary continued, "we yell and call out questions in French, German, and English as to their whereabouts and condition. Nothing comes back but an occasional OOOOHH-AAAAHH groanlike response, sometimes near, sometimes far, depending on the wind." Able to hear nothing intelligible—only the groans—they concluded that the two lost men were at the Craveri Refuge and by now close to death. But they knew that to go on farther would mean almost certain death for themselves. If, as was highly likely, one of them fell into a hidden crevasse on the Frêney Glacier, the other alone would be unable to get him out. The only course was to retreat to the Gamba Hut and come back with reinforcements.

On the descent, they left one of their two ropes fixed at the steepest part of the couloir, to ease the way on their return. Then they struggled on down to the Gamba, reaching it in midafternoon after seven hours out. Here they found that the professional rescue teams had already called it a day. The main group that had gone up toward the Frêney Pillar had found no trace of Bonatti and his six Italian and French companions. But the three who had gone down with binoculars had at least *seen* something: two tiny figures, that had to be Briquet and Kirch, descending from the Peuterey Ridge toward the Frêney Glacier. . . . John and Gary were excited and heartened. So at least they had not died at the Craveri. Now the next step was to go out with a strong team and help them across the glacier. . . . But none of the guides would go. They had done their day's work, they said, and further rescue attempts would have to wait until tomorrow. Again seething with anger and frustration, John and Gary debated what to do, meanwhile preparing themselves some much-needed food and drink.

As it turned out, they did not have to do anything. Stepping outside the hut, John saw two figures following his and Gary's trail down the nearby slopes, and in a few minutes Briquet and Kirch had arrived. They were cold, hungry and close to exhaustion. But not to death. They were basically all right. Having weathered the worst of the storm at the Craveri Refuge, they had today descended from the Peuterey, threaded their way through the honeycomb of the Frêney Glacier, and on the Col de l'Innominata made good use of the rope left by John and Gary. . . . Then what of the groans their would-be rescuers had heard, that had made it sound as if they were *in extremis?* . . . They had not groaned, they said. They had shouted that they had left the Craveri and were descending. Obviously, wind, fog and distance had distorted both sets of voices. All they had heard of John and Gary's multilingual calls had been similar oooohhs and aaaahhs, as if from mountain ghosts.

They ate, drank, and warmed themselves. Then, with a few hours of daylight remaining, they began the descent to Courmayeur. John and Gary intended to stay on at the Gamba, to help in the next day's attempts to rescue the French-Italian party. But all the bunks in the hut were now occupied. More importantly, and hurtfully, the guides again made it clear that they wanted no help from amateur outsiders. So John and Gary left too. As a final indignity, the custodian of the hut presented them with a carefully itemized bill for services rendered.

It was not until late the next day, down in the valley, that they learned of the dreadful dénouement up above. Several hours after their departure, in the dead of the night, Walter Bonatti and one of his Italian companions had staggered into the Gamba.[2] Several days before, their group had all but reached the top of the Frêney Pillar when the storm engulfed them, and their subsequent bivouac and descent had been a nightmare. Now four of the others were scattered over the heights in varying states of collapse, and the fifth—Pierre Mazeaud, the strongest of the Frenchmen—had stayed behind to do what he could. With this, the corps of guides in the hut at last went into action. During the rest of the night and the next morning, following Bonatti's directions, they pushed up and found the others—too late. Mazeaud was all right, or at least alive. But the remaining four, three Frenchmen and one Italian, had died of exposure and exhaustion.

[2] They too, on their descent, had used the rope left by John and Gary on the Col de l'Innominata.

130

For some time thereafter, newspapers roundabout praised the work of the Courmayeur rescue team who had "risked their lives" to go after them. But John Harlin and Gary Hemming held a different opinion.

John was manipulating his Air Force leaves like a master magician. From the Frêney disaster he returned to Hahn-Bernkastel, with Konrad Kirch accompanying him part of the way. Then, with the required flight credits under his belt, it was back to the Alps and Gary—and almost at once they were on the fringe of another disaster. This was the summer in which a French military plane, flying close in to the peaks, cut the cable of the aerial tramway that carries tourists across the massif of Mont Blanc, plunging several cars into the great central snowfield called the Vallée Blanche. John and Gary were nearby at the time, in a high mountain camp, and were among the first at the scene. In and around the smashed cars were six dead and many injured, and they spent a grim day doing what they could, until Chamonix guides and French mountain troops arrived en masse.

Then they turned to their next climb, the Grand Capucin. Though on the far side of the range, near the Italian border, this peak is of the same order as the Aiguilles of Chamonix, a huge needle of rock thrusting vertically skyward. Indeed, on one of its sides, its east face, it is more than vertical; through much of its three-thousand-foot sweep it leans outward. After several unsuccessful attempts, it had been first mastered in 1951 by Walter Bonatti and a companion, in a struggle lasting four days and three nights. And now, ten years later, John and Gary were out to match their talents against the great Italian's.

True, a route once climbed is no longer as formidable as it was when virginal; but still the Capucin's east face was an awesome affair. One menace was absent: with its succession of overhangs, rocks falling from above whizzed harmlessly through thin air. But the steepness and exposure were unrelenting. Virtually the whole ascent had to be "nailed" up the wall with hammer and piton, and often the only possible stance was in *étriers*, or rope stirrups, attached to the pitons by carabiners. This in itself did not bother them. They were used to heights, depths, and "artificial" Grade VI climbing. What did concern them was that, as they ascended, the weather was again deteriorating, and that they had both begun to suffer from dehydration and nausea.

Still they kept on. At least there was no full storm, and knowing the best route from Bonatti's description, they moved faster than he had. By dusk they reached a point about two-thirds of the way up the peak, where the east face was seamed by one of its very few ledges, and here, pitoning themselves in, they spent the night. Then at dawn it was up again. "Now every succeeding pitch overhung a little more," John recorded, "and at the top of each was a big overhang—a roof. All the wall below was tucked away under us, so that we were out beyond the base of the climb. Clouds covered the glacier, where we had started, and we were sealed in our own world of overhanging slabs and roofs."

Sometimes they worked their way around the roofs, sometimes up over them. Once John fell, but was held by the rope and a piton. Once a flake of rock came loose as Gary clung to it, but he managed to swing away to a piton off to one side. Close to the top of the Capucin they came to the worst roof-overhang of all: the great triangular hood, like a monk's, that has given the Capucin its name. But they surmounted this too. In the early afternoon of the second day they stood on the summit. Then they roped down the merely vertical north face of the peak to the valley—and storm.

Storm. Always more storm. John wrote to Marilyn, who had returned to Bernkastel: "It looks like the weather has sunk us on the Eiger."

And he was right. Leaving the Mont Blanc area, he and Gary crossed over to the Oberland and Kleine Scheidegg to examine the peak that was to have been the grand climax of their campaign. As in 1960, it had not been climbed once during the summer, and it seemed unlikely that it would be; for the north wall was choked with snow, and it appeared that still more was coming. For the third time, John, now with a new partner, explored its lower reaches, but went little higher than with Tenzing and Jerry Robertson. He did not like the look of things, and Gary liked it even less. Indeed, Gary was by now pretty well climbed out. For a newcomer to the Alps, he had done well in their campaign, but not so well as either he or John had hoped, and at this stage of the game they both knew that he was not up to the Eiger. Besides, as in the later stages of the HASL project, friction had begun to grow between them; and John, for his part, had to return to Hahn again, and this time stay there. Summer was ending. The Rover Boys parted and went their separate ways.

132

No sooner was John back in Germany than the Alpine weather cleared wondrously. During September 1961 the north wall of the Eiger was scaled by five parties totaling sixteen men: Swiss, German, Austrian, Czech, and Polish.[3] But again he could only groan and look to the future.

For him, the Eiger still waited. As he had said, "The mountains are always waiting for us poor fleas to return."

[3] There was also one late-summer fatality, when an Austrian, making a try at a first solo ascent, fell to his death.

11. Heights (and Valleys)

Marilyn's mother, Gertrude Miler, came to visit, and the two of them, with the children, went off on a camping tour through Italy and France. For the trip, a second car, an Opel, was acquired, leaving John with the Sunbeam Alpine to use on the Hahn-Bernkastel milk run. Though he fought no more losing skirmishes with Army trucks, he left his share of skid marks on the winding roads.

At the base, he still held the dual job of safety officer and instructor pilot, as he would continue to for the rest of his Air Force service. Also, as in the previous fall, he played football with the Hahn Hawks, but now no longer coached, so that less time was involved in it. During Marilyn's absence, his parents made one of their periodic visits. His father, granted a year's leave by TWA, was this time touring military installations in Europe in his capacity as rear-admiral and president of the Reserve Officers' Association, and among his engagements was a talk at Hahn.

In October came a satisfying and prideful few days when John went to Trento, in northern Italy, to attend its annual festival of films on mountaineering and exploration. Though he himself had made no film, he was invited as an honored guest in recognition of his climbs of the past summer; and Marilyn interrupted her mother-and-children junket to join him briefly. The Trento Festival traditionally attracts the top climbers of Europe. There he met Walter Bonatti and Pierre Mazeaud, with whose destinies he had been so closely involved (though without meeting them) a few months before, as well as many others known to fame in the world of the peaks. One of the youngest men at the gathering, he was also the only American; and his presence was tangible evidence that he had begun to make his mark in European mountaineering.

In interesting counterpoint was a letter he received not long afterward from Gary Hemming. For its tone was far different from that of the erstwhile Rover Boy who was ready to romp. "Let me tell you, and very seriously," he wrote, "how sorry I am about last summer. Looking back, I can see how badly I let you down. Certainly, if there was ever anyone ready for the big climbs, it was you . . . if you had only had a seasoned partner." Continuing, he said that he hoped the two of them would climb again, but with himself only as a sort of auxiliary. For a full and equal teammate, he felt, John should have a climber of greater experience.

In the light of their joint accomplishments, it would seem that Gary was eating more humble pie than was called for. Still, there was some truth in what he said. Both with Gary that past summer and with Jerry Robertson in 1960, John had been teamed with climbers who were not wholly on a par with him, and he would unquestionably have done even better if it had been otherwise. He himself was aware of this. In fact, he was already in correspondence with Konrad Kirch, with whom he had formed a quick and warm friendship, discussing plans for future climbs together. Though only twenty-four, a year younger than John, Kirch had already compiled a formidable mountain record, and John had been greatly impressed by the way he had handled himself in the crisis above Courmayeur.

In mid-autumn, however, climbing was still well in the future. John was, for a while, a full-time pilot. Air Force regulations required of him a minimum of one hundred flying hours a year, but he consistently flew more than twice that, averaging about twenty a month on ten to

136

a dozen flights. Some were, of necessity, routine. Others, however, were anything but, and he had developed to a fine art the knack of getting to places he wanted to visit. While Marilyn, with her mother and children, were in southern Italy, he appeared, with Leon Canapary as passenger for an out-of-the-blue hello. He got to London (for lunch), to Rome (for the opera), and to bases as distant as Spain, Greece, and Turkey. Following a brief bout with pnuemonia, he wangled a re-assignment to Wheelus, in Libya, to reap the benefit of the sunshine. In a small L-20 trainer, he flew to Grenoble to see Gary and, while there (with no Air Force brass on hand to rule otherwise) gave Gary's French girl a ride in the plane.

On solo flights near the frontiers of East Germany and Czecho-slovakia, he enjoyed "testing the line" as closely as possible. Though so opposed to nuclear bombing that he had resigned as a fighter pilot, he would have liked nothing better than a man-to-man duel with a Red Baron in a MIG. (None materialized.) Once or twice, flying at thirty thousand feet or so, he experimentally turned off his oxygen supply to see if he would black out. (He didn't.) Best of all routine-relievers, however, was Alp watching, and this he continued to do through all his Hahn service with undiminished gusto. If he could not get to them week in and week out, he could at least see them, feast his eyes on them, as he counted the days to the time of return.

The wait, as it developed, was not too long. For in the early months of 1962 he managed, by hook, crook and marathon driving, to get in his first European winter climbing. His companion, as planned, was now Konrad Kirch, and the locales of their first ventures were, for John, new territory. One was the Austrian Alps, where they made several difficult ascents on routes first blazed by the late great Tyrolean climber, Hermann Buhl. The other was the Dolomites, in northeastern Italy, whose jagged towers and spires call for the utmost in technical cragsmanship.[1] Both ranges, though formidable, are lower than the western Alps, with resultingly less severe winters. When the weather did close in too heavily for climbing, the two new partners skied together,

[1] Most notable of their completed climbs were: in Austria, the east face of the Scharnitzspitze and the Buhl Pillar, both on the massif of the Wetterstein; in the Dolomites, the Cassin route of the Piccolissima. A challenge that failed—because Kirch's fingers began to freeze—was on the most famous and difficult of all Dolomite routes, the north face of the Cima Grande di Lavaredo.

in John's first go at the sport since his "instant" debut long before in California.

The better acquainted they became, the stronger was the rapport between them, and John was forced into some drastic renovations of his prejudices against Germans. Indeed, Konrad Kirch was a total antithesis of the "kraut" stereotype. Physically he was lithe and slender, with a fine-boned, almost ascetic face, often bridged by steel-rimmed glasses, and even in climbing gear he looked every inch the student— as in fact he was. The son of a prosperous engineer, he was north-German by birth, but now lived in Munich, where he was a law student at the university and president of its prestigious climbing club, the *Akademische Alpenverein*. Serious and conservative in his tastes, he had no trace in him of Gary Hemming's flamboyant bohemianism, nor did he share John's role as rebel and maverick. Yet he was broadly cosmopolitan in training and outlook, speaking English and French almost as fluently as his native German. As a mountaineer he lacked, both bodily and inwardly, John's brute power and drive. But in skill, judgment, and determination—and in his love of the heights for their own sake—he was fully a match for the man who was now his ropemate.

Hahn—Austria. Hahn—Dolomites. It was a schedule that would have frazzled most men to a standstill. Yet, in the very midst of it, John was laying the groundwork for a bigger project: a try at the first winter ascent of the Walker Spur of the Grandes Jorasses.

He had been on the Jorasses the previous summer with Gary. But the route they had climbed was only one—and a lesser one—of many. As its plural name indicates, the mountain, close by Mont Blanc on the French-Italian border, is less a single peak than a long jagged ridge of many peaks, and of all the routes leading to its crest, the Walker is the most formidable and famous. Indeed, it has been listed by Gaston Rébuffat, in his book *Starlight and Storm*, as one of *the* great north walls of the Alps—the others being those of the Eiger, the Matterhorn, the Dru, the Cima Grande di Lavaredo, and the Piz Badile in the Engadine. All had been first scaled, in the summer, during the surge of modern climbing in the 1930s—the Walker by an Italian party led by Riccardo Cassin. But this was the only one that, by now, had not also been ascended in winter, and its accomplishment would be another notable *first* in the Alpine ledger.

John himself, of course, was no stranger to the Big Six. Discounting

138

the clouded saga of his early Matterhorn venture, he had had at least peripheral experience with all the rest except the Piz Badile. To the Eiger he had already gone four times. In 1960, with Jerry Robertson, he had made two passes at the Dru; and with Konrad he had just been on the Cima Grande. But he had not yet achieved an ascent of one of the classics. To do so on the Walker, and in winter to boot, would put a brilliant feather in his mountaineer's cap.

It was too big a project, he felt, for him and Konrad alone. As additional teammates he signed up Gary (again ready for the wars) and a top Yugoslavian climber named Aleš Kunaver, whom he had met in Trento. Also invited was Pierre Mazeaud, who was unable to accept. But even without him it was to be a good-sized venture: more in the nature of a small expedition than of the simple two-man teams he was used to. Further, it would be international in membership, and this pleased him greatly, for it was one of his strongest convictions that mountaineering should break the barriers of country and language. The work of organization and preparation (food, gear, and all the rest) was immense, but he accomplished most of it himself; and though there was to be no official leader on the climb, it was he, in the event, who made the plans and decisions. On any project in which John was involved, that was the way it was.

In early March the foursome assembled in Chamonix, and from there went on to set up a camp on the Leschaux Glacier at the foot of the Grandes Jorasses. With them, as a semi-participant, went a young American named Jim Bjorken, a physicist friend of Henry Kendall's, who had volunteered to serve in support. They were prepared, if necessary, to spend several days on the mountain, and had with them items of equipment that were innovations in Alpine climbing. One was a set of walkie-talkies, to maintain contact with base and receive relayed weather reports that Bjorken would pick up on a standard portable radio. Another was an assortment of newly developed American pitons—made of a chrome-molybdenum alloy and called "chromollies" or "mollies"—so pliable that they could work their way into rock cracks and crevices that would wholly defy a more rigid old-style spike. "The planning and the gear," said the impressed Bjorken, "were really tremendous." He was only to learn by degrees that John, the detail hater, was inclined to forget things like forks and toilet paper.

139

In any case, man proposes. . . .

After skiing down to Chamonix and returning to base with a second load of supplies, the four actual climbers began the siege of the Walker Spur. On the first day, in cold but clear weather, they attached fixed ropes to its lower pitches, reaching a point some fifteen hundred feet up, or about a third of the way to the top. At day's end they roped down to base. So far, so good. But the second morning it was good no longer. During the night snow had fallen—not in a true storm but enough to plaster the mountain—and its solid flanks of rock and ice were now sheathed in crumbling whiteness. Even worse, the weather forecast was bad; general storm was predicted. And John, with his Air Force meteorological training, took forecasts seriously.

Gary, Konrad, and Kunaver were more hopeful. Still in sunshine, the four started up again. But even with fixed ropes, the new powder snow made the going hard, and soon, sure enough, came wind, cloud and snowfall. Added to this, presently, there was a still more ominous portent: they could tell from the lack of sensation that their toes had begun to freeze. So down they went again. The next day there was full storm. And the next. And then, with almost a week gone, the time had come when John had to return to Hahn. Like so many mountain ventures, with all their hope and labor of preparation, this one ended in anticlimax and frustration. Turning their backs on the peak, the team floundered down to Chamonix through the snowdrifts, and that, for them, was the end of the Walker in winter.[2]

John's toes *were* slightly frozen. They turned color, they hurt—and they smelled. To defeat had been added indignity, but fortunately there were no serious developments, and back on duty, as usual, his chief problem was to find enough outlets for his energy. His work as safety officer had become too routine for his tastes, but he was resolved never to go back to fighter-bombers and their lethal loads. Casting about for an alternative, he applied for parachute training (of which he had already had some in the States), but was not assigned to it. On the Alpine front there were no prospects until summer. The HASL project was dead. From Aleš Kunaver came an invitation to join a planned Yugoslavian

[2] Its first winter ascent was made the following year by Walter Bonatti and an Italian companion.

140

expedition to Nepal; but this died on the vine almost before he could start wondering about how to get leave for it.

A momentary fillip was provided when he was held up one evening on the drive from Hahn to Bernkastel. Picking up a hitchhiker—a dark-skinned, French-speaking man whom he took for a Moroccan—he had not gone far when he was told to stop the car and felt a gun at his ribs. Presumably, memories of another holdup went through his mind; of what had, or hadn't, happened on a night in Rome eight years before. But this time he resorted neither to violence nor mythmaking. He talked. Apparently he talked well. For after several minutes, according to John, the man opened the door and took off minus loot—either to mend his ways or seek easier prey. When John arrived home, Marilyn reported, he was in high good humor; there was nothing he liked better than a crisis, of any sort. But the euphoria soon passed. There was not a holdup a day to keep boredom away.

With the climber inactive and the flier on a treadmill, the "other Johns" now surfaced. Prime among his non-mountain projects, and now more serious than ever, was that of following up his Air Force career by the foundation of a new school in Europe, and into its conception he put his most cherished ideas and ideals. For one thing, it would not be an American but a truly international institution, both in its students and its curriculum. For another, it would embody many of the principles of the British "Outward Bound" projects, stressing "character building through adventure"—with the emphasis, of course, on mountaineering. The Courmayeur property he had previously investigated was no longer available; and where, in any case, the money would come from was a total mystery. But John was vastly unconcerned about money. It would come from somewhere: a foundation, a beneficent tycoon, the United Nations. What he was interested in was the idea, the ideal, and he worked at it.

Neighbors Ladd and Elli Osgood, with whom he had first developed the plan, were taking off for the States and therefore temporarily out of the picture. But in their place, now, was an Air Force medical officer named Roy Brown, who had become a close friend of John's and shared many of his enthusiasms. Further, Brown had a brother-in-law who was about to received a Ph.D. in educational administration at Harvard, and who he was sure would be interested. John wrote him, and yes he was. John wrote again, urging him to come over as soon as he had his degree. But he temporized. . . . Why? asked John. Because things still seemed vague. That would not be for long. . . . Was there money? Not yet. Then he would have to wait. . . . He had no faith, no ideals, said John. Yes, he had both, but also a family to support.

The school project hung fire.

John was also involved in more immediate affairs. He had not painted or drawn for several years, nor did he recommence now, but he started an art course at Hahn for such servicemen and their families as were interested. Also, his thoughts were turning increasingly to writing, and he met frequently with others at the base who had similar leanings. Most interesting among them, he found, was a young Negro draftee who in his off-hours was a serious poet, and he did what he could to help and encourage him.

Tentatively, he was taking stabs at writing himself. *The Roving Alpine*, his account of 1960's summer adventure, had been published by a house organ of the Sunbeam company in England. Now, trying fiction for the first time, he wrote two short stories—one called *Sewer Escape* (laid in East-West Berlin), and the other *The Slave* (with an Amazon setting)—and to his encouragement, the first won a prize from a service magazine. Also, ranging widely, he submitted a brief essay, *What Can I Do for Freedom?* (it was not bombing) to the Freedom Foundation of Valley Forge, and a discourse on Siamese cats to the Cat Fanciers' Association of Eatontown, New Jersey. In sundry stages of planning were more ambitious efforts: stories of his climbing and flying experiences, in which he hoped to present not merely the externals but the inwardness of high adventure. But little of these got down on paper. Though highly articulate and bursting with things to say, he was weak in what the Germans call *Sitzfleisch*, the ability to apply the seat of the pants to the seat of a chair.

Up he would jump. Off he would go. For a walk, a run, a game of squash, a bout of conditioning exercises in the Hahn gymnasium. All this before, between, or after a full day of Air Force duties. And in the evening, when other men were yawning and heading for bed, he was still going strong. As his new friend, Roy Brown, described one night and morning after:

"We had sat up very late at John's house, talking and drinking more than our share of cool Mosel wine, so we decided it would be simpler for me to stay over rather than drive home. I went up to the attic spare room and there, while preparing for bed, found an amazing assortment of equipment piled in disarray around the room. There were boots, ropes, jackets, pitons, helmets, cooking gear, and all sorts of clothing scattered about. I poked around for a time, and then with daylight not far away finally went to bed.

"At six in the morning John burst into the room, threw a sweat suit and sneakers at me in bed, and announced that we would be going for a short run before breakfast. With the mood from the previous evening still with me, I agreed, although somewhat foggy from too much wine and too little sleep. We started by climbing over the wire fence around the rear of the house and then running up the hillside of the vineyard behind. I had never run up such a steep hill before, and although in fairly good condition, I was close to exhaustion upon reaching the top long after John. Assuming we were going to sit down for a break, I prepared to enjoy the breather, when John started off.

"Since I didn't want to disappoint him—which very often was the case with myself and others who knew him—I followed along and soon caught my second and third winds, as we ran for nearly two hours through the woods and fields on the plateau above Bernkastel, finally winding our way down and around the other side of the mountain. We paused midway and sat down on the ground to rest and talk. The early-morning sky and the birds and small game about created a peaceful atmosphere of rural Germany, as we discussed the fate of the world, a world blindly intent on creating enough hydrogen bombs to destroy civilization. John told me what he would do if the bomb were to fall— how he and his family would meet and prepare to face an altered situation, assuming they survived intact. The grim thoughts were vastly in contrast to the surrounding peacefulness, but then, rarely did we find ourselves talking of, or doing, the customary."

Another Roy Brown story is of a time when he and John were on a cross-country ski tour in the Austrian Alps. After an arduous day, capped by a long uphill climb, they stopped for the night at a mountain cabin, and Roy, rummaging in his pack, found at the bottom two large and heavy stones. He was astonished. He swore. Then he looked at John, and John nodded calmly. Yes, he admitted, he had put the stones there, because the heavier the loads Roy carried, the sooner he would be in top shape for even harder going. "One couldn't be angry," said his friend, "after such a confession. It hadn't been a joke, but a real concern for my conditioning; and besides, I knew that his own pack was the heavier by far."

One questions if everyone would have been as tolerant. But John had to be taken at his own values, or not at all. As another of his friends has said: "He had an absolute compulsion not only to demand the most of himself, but to make others demand it of *themselves*." To some, it was an exciting challenge. For the rest, who felt they could do without carrying stones or running miles before breakfast, the only course was to keep away from him. And many did. By now, because of his multiple activities—especially football—he was perhaps the best known junior officer at Hahn; but for every one who was drawn into his orbit, there were many more who avoided it. If he had become (as his friends said) a living legend at the base, he was also (said the non-friends) "some sort of nut." Roy Brown noted that "his motivations and activities were simply beyond the comprehension of the average officer in the U.S. military." Said Leon Canapary: "He shattered conventional types."

—Which was precisely what John wanted to do.

Home was scarcely conventional either. Beneath the Ali Baba cave of the attic, the rest of the house—thanks largely to Danish excursions—had more furnishings than some Harlin stateside domiciles; but there were still no chairs. Seating was on scattered cushions, in competition with cats Kuzma and Maus, and corners were apt to be occupied by visiting firemen's sleeping bags. The children, too, lent their touches of individuality. Son Johnny, now going on six, had learned the climbing technique of the rappel and, to his mother's dismay, took to disappearing from windows on a rope. Home from their Bernkastel classes, where they were the only non-German pupils, he and Andréa did their chattering in a brisk bilingual goulash.

As for John's role in the household, he was by his own admission no star as a father. Like most of the breed, he had a weakness for his daughter, and Andréa—blonde, elfin, and flirtatious—knew how to exploit it. But his span of interest was short. Much of the time the children either bored or distracted him, and it was in their company that he was most conscious of the prison bars of domesticity. Between himself and Marilyn the going continued to be intermittently rocky. There were still arguments, exits, walks in the night (though now none as far as to

144

[1] Ireland 1945.

[2] California 1953.

[3] Coutourier.

[4] Halfback.

[5] Husband.

[6] Cragsman (with Marilyn).

[7] F-100.

[8] Pilot.

[9] Castle climbing.

[10] Bernkastel Christmas—with Sue Harlin.

[11] Among the *aiguilles*.

[12] Grand Capucin.

[13] John, Claude Guerre-Gentons and Gary Hemming in the Vallée Blanche of Mont Blanc, at the time of the telepherique disaster of 1961.

[14] Floral tribute to Gary's beard from Andréa and Johnny.

[15] Grandes Jorasses; the Walker Spur is the main buttress farthest to the left.
The Shroud is wall of ice to the left of the Walker.

[16] Eiger—the "vertical stage" above Kleine Scheidegg.

[17] Konrad and John (in that order) on the Second Icefield of the Eiger.

[18] After Eiger·1962. John, Nik Rafanowitsch, Hans Hauer, Konrad Kirch.

19] "Gypsy Camp" 1963. In foreground: Gary, John, Konrad.

[20] John, Marilyn, Konrad.

[21] John.

[22] Aiguille du Fou, showing route of ascent.

[23] Climbing the Fou: In order: Frost, Fulton, Harlin, Hemming.

[24] Before the Fou (l. to r.) Stewart Fulton, John, Gary Hemming.

[25] John atop the Fou.

[26] Italian Face of Mont Blanc—with Freney Pillars at center, Brouillard Pillars at left.

[27] Instructing at ISMM.

[28] Retreat to the Calanques.

[29] Rock—air—rope.

[30] John in bivouac on the Dru.

[31] Mönch—North Face in winter.

GREAT ROOF

STONE

[32] Petit Dru with *diretissima* route.

[33] John.

[34 & 35] Other Johns.

[36] Still another.

[37] Andréa, Marilyn, Johnny.

8] *En famille* at Chalet Pollux.

[39] The Oberland in winter.

[40] Helicopter reconnaissance.
This picture and those following
are from the Eiger climb of 1966.

[41] Studying the route—John, Dougal, Layton.

[42] Eiger: north wall, normal route, *direttissima*.

1. First Pillar
2. Shattered Pillar
3. Difficult Crack
4. Hinterstoisser Traverse
5. Swallows' Nest
6. Ice Hose
7. First Icefield
8. Second Icefield
9. Flatiron
10. Death Bivouac
11. Third Icefield
12. Ramp
13. Traverse of the Gods
14. Spider
15. Exit Cracks
16. Summit Icefield
17. Summit of the Eiger

A. Foot of Fixed Ropes
B. First Ice Caves
C. First Band
D. Second Band
E. Central Pillar
F. Where John Fell
G. Fly

• • • • • Normal Route

————— Direct Route

//////// German Route,
Where It Varies

[43] Eiger ice—Eiger cloud.

[44] The wherewithal—plus Layton, Dougal, John.

[45] Eiger rock.

[46] Layton prusiking. It was on a fixed rope such as this that John was killed.

[47] John with radio in Death Bivouac.

[48] John's last letter.

SCHEIDEGG HOTELS

Death Bivouac
March ?

Dear Mom & kids,

I'm coming up on our 7th bivouac. I'm certainly hoping that Treato (Topolino) was enjoyable — also that the exams were not too miserable.

We are hoping to make the top in a few days but we are being very safe so don't worry. Love you all very, very much.

Dad

[49] After thirteen days on the wall: Dougal and John.

[50] Triumph on the Eiger: (l. to r.) Lehne, Strobel, Votteler, Haston, Hupfauer.

[51] Burial at Leysin: John's parents at extreme left; Konrad Kirch between Johnny and Marilyn; Bev Clark and wife behind Andréa.

another Mary X). As with others—and as always—he demanded much of her: if not quite everything in her Eiger-to-Balmain list, at least a fair share thereof. He had strong opinions about her clothes, her hair, her speech, her friends, her activities; and he was insistent that she keep herself in the physical pink. There is no record that he ever put stones in her pack, or pocketbook, but he often urged her to run with him. And she did.

She wanted to do, to be, what he desired. She loved him. And she knew that he loved her. He still—except when he was angry—called her Mara. He still made love to her with ardor and imagination. When they were alone together, away from children, household, distractions, responsibilities, their relationship was as satisfying and exciting as ever. "Whatever happened," she said, "life was always an *adventure*." And no matter what went wrong, she never wavered in her belief that he was one man in a million. "John has always wanted to write," she told her parents during one of the lowest periods of their marriage. "He can, too, when he tries. He can do almost anything he wants to. He has overwhelming unused talent."

Not many women, one feels, could have coped with John's pace. But Marilyn had energies of her own. She had talents and interests, and more than most wives, she nurtured them. With her jobs as wife and mother, it was impossible for her to make full-scale progress toward her Ph.D. in biology; but it was a goal she never lost sight of, and to such degree as was possible she kept up her reading and research. When she could, she took University of Maryland courses, and at Bernkastel she was interested and active in the local school system. As a long-range project, she was no less enthusiastic than John about the school of his own he hoped to found, and it was understood from the beginning that she would be an integral part of it.

After two years in the Rhineland, her German, unlike John's, was now fluent. When need arose, he grappled with it. She studied it—as she also studied the histories and cultures of the countries they visited. John traveled for his projects and rejected the role of tourist. She was every inch the tourist: on their trips together; on her tour with her mother and the children; now, in the spring of 1962, on an excursion to Holland, as the only outsider in a group of German women from Bernkastel. Aged almost twenty-eight, she was young for her years. In spite of her wide traveling, she was still very much the wide-eyed girl from the Thoreau-

145

vian family in the rural Northwest, perpetually stimulated and delighted by what she encountered. "I am forever being frustrated," she wrote an old friend, "as I find places and people I fall in love with, realizing I could not possibly get the flavor without staying on a year, and then having to move on. So many wonderful places exist in this world. Oh to have several lives, simultaneously or consecutively!"

This does not sound like—nor was it—a woman about to submerge in the storms of wedlock.

Spring passed. Summer came. And summertime was mountain time. Again John cleared out the attic, loaded the Sunbeam Alpine and roared off toward the south. Again he drove through Friday night, climbed all day Saturday and Sunday, and on Sunday night drove back home again. "I am utterly exhausted," Marilyn wrote after accompanying him on one trip, just for the ride, not the climb, "and do not know how John can keep up the pace weekend after weekend. His answer is, life is short. Lost days will never come back."

As during the winter, Item A was a series of workouts with Konrad Kirch in the Austrian Alps and Dolomites. On one outing they were joined by Gary Hemming, and on another by John's old friend Paul Revak, who had first introduced him to climbing back at Stanford. Now a U. S. Navy flier, as well a long-time German scholar, Paul had been assigned to the faculty at Annapolis for the coming school year and as a summer prelude was brushing up at the University of Marburg. Reunion with John followed quickly. But he had now done no serious climbing in some time and left the bigger game to John and Konrad. In Austria, on this particular campaign, their main objective was the peaks of the Kaisergebirge, near Innsbruck, one of which bears the ominous name of the Totenkirchl—"the Chapel of Death." Peering up at its vertical crags, Paul was ominous too. *"Tot mit Kirch am Totenkirchl,"* was his prophecy for John, as he and Konrad set out for its summit. But the two made it all right. They came back intact. It remained for Paul himself to get involved in the chanciest climb of the trip.

This occurred when he and John, after leaving Konrad, found themselves at night beside an ancient castle, dramatically lighted as a tourist attraction. For them it was an attraction too—if in a special fashion— and presently, joined by a rope, they were clambering high on its

146

craggy walls. In their careers as climbers and fliers, they had met many emergencies, but now came a new one. The lights went out. They stayed out. At hand were neither moon, stars nor flashlight. After what seemed hours of blind groping and clinging they made their way to the ground; but for a while *Tot* had been closer than at any time on the Totenkirchl.

In the Dolomites, as well as the Kaisergebirge, John and Konrad made some stiff summer climbs.[3] But here again the most dramatic event was an unforeseen one—another of John's recurrent brushes with violence. The scene was a mountain hut, where Konrad's Munich club, the *Akademische Alpenverein*, was having a weekend gathering; and John was there as a guest. So too was a big and powerful young German, the friend of another club member, and during the evening he and John, as the two premier musclemen present, got into a friendly bout of horseplay wrestling. . . . Or at least it started as such. . . . Then, suddenly it was no longer friendly but angry and rough, and the others in the hut pulled the two apart. "He's lucky I didn't kill him," said John, seething, to Konrad, but loud enough for his antagonist to hear. And the antagonist rose to the bait. Seizing an ax from a corner—not an ice ax but a heavy woodchopper—he raised it and came at John across the room. "It happened so quickly," said Konrad, "that everyone froze. And so did John. But differently. Magnificently. As the fellow came at him, he just stood there, not moving an inch. He just stared at him—stared him down." Then quietly, fully in control, he talked him down—as he had talked down the holdup man on the road from Hahn to Bernkastel. "Put down that ax," he said. "Get away from me," he said. And presently, saying nothing, the man obeyed. He lowered the ax, put it down, turned away. John turned away. The episode was over.

To some climbers, the true cragsmen, the Dolomites, like the walls of Yosemite, are the ultimate challenge and delight. But John was no great lover—nor, for that matter, a top master—of pure vertical rock. As when younger, he still preferred Class V climbs (free, with pitons only as protection) to Class VIs (which could be done only with the

[3] For the record, their ascents were: in the Kaisergebirge, the west face of the Totenkirchl, the east face of the Fleischbank, the west face of the Mauk, and the southeast face of the Schusslkarspitze; in the Dolomites, the Piccolo di Vael and the Yellow Edge.

direct aid of hardware); and his chief interest in the highly technical Dolomite ascents was for practice and conditioning. What he liked best were "mixed" mountains, a blend of rock, ice, and snow, and along with the Eiger—which never left his thoughts—these were best found in the "many-sided toy" of the great range of Mont Blanc. Besides, he and Konrad still had unfinished business with the Walker Spur of the Grandes Jorasses. After the workouts in Austria and Italy, they went again to Chamonix.

But again, in Chamonix, there was weather. They waited. And John, as usual, had a spate of unscheduled adventures. In the Café National, one night, he was an innocent—though fight-loving—neutral in a brawl between French and British climbers. (Neutrality seems, with an effort, to have been preserved.) Still later at night, on Chamonix' main thoroughfare, he was to be found climbing the façade of Snell's *Magasin pour le Sport*; then for unknown reasons (presumably not incompetence, and certainly not liquor) descending in an entanglement with the sidewalk awning. But the awning was a good cushion, Monsieur Snell a good friend, and no harm came of the fall save perhaps to John's dignity.

With the foul weather continuing, he took off for the French Riviera. Not, to be sure, for the guidebook Riviera: the realm of villas, casinos, and *grand luxe*. For him it was the mountaineer's Riviera, a stretch of coast called the Calanques, near the town of Cassis, where steep cliffs and spires rimming deep inlets provide, in effect, a climber's home-away-from-home. Konrad did not accompany him. But Marilyn and the children came down from Germany, Gary and Paul again rallied round, and for a few days the three men romped on the Calanques. There were no glaciers here; no snow or wind or murderous storm. When they fell from their perches on the rocky headlands it was into the soft blue waters of the Mediterranean, whence they were promptly "rescued" by Johnny and Andréa. During the outing, too, John met another mountaineer he had often heard of but never encountered: Royal Robbins, of California, who in the past several years, through climbs in Yosemite and elsewhere, had won the reputation of America's foremost rock climber. As of 1962 in the Calanques, John and Robbins did only a few scrambles together, but it was the beginning of a relationship that was to become both close and thorny.

Still, the familiar pattern continued, like a rerun movie. From the

Riviera, John and Marilyn returned to Germany. John got in his flying. He returned to Chamonix. With the skies finally clearing, he climbed up again toward the Grandes Jorasses, but this time only with Konrad; for Aleš Kunaver was in Yugoslavia, Pierre Mazeaud and other likely partners were busy elsewhere, and Gary had specifically asked to be counted out. One reason he gave to others was that John was "a Jonah with the weather." But one suspects that there were other, more personal reasons—among them, that he was still unhappy about his performance the previous summer. Though both old friends decried competitiveness in climbing, both *were* competitive, especially against each other. And Gary wanted to be sure that he was fully John's equal before they again did a major climb together.

So it was this time only a John-Konrad duo that set up a camp on the Leschaux Glacier beneath the Walker Spur. Theirs was no hopeless cause, for the ascent required less of an expedition now than in winter; indeed, had been made some twenty times in summer, and often by twosomes, since its first achievement in 1938. Still, it was no "easy day for a lady." It was, at best, two days and a night for the strongest of climbers. And the flip of the coin, as always, was in the hand of the weather.

To begin with, it was kind. For only two climbers, there was no question of a slow up-and-down siege with fixed ropes. But working smoothly together, in almost perfect conditions, John and Konrad made good progress up the sheer buttress, and by midafternoon were above the high point of their winter effort. A few hours later, when dusk came, they estimated that they were halfway to the top—a fine day's going. But now their troubles started, when they were unable to find a good site for a bivouac. The best they could manage was on a tiny ledge, midway on a vast near-vertical slab, and here they tied themselves in with rope and "chromolly" pitons, their feet dangling loose over two thousand feet of space.

This, however, was not to be the worst of it. For with darkness, the weather broke. Soon the wind was lashing them, snow was driving, and from the heights above, more snow cascaded on their unprotected roost. Then, even more dangerously, rocks began to fall. Luckily, neither of them was hit. But a whizzing stone struck and broke one of their securing ropes, so that they had to hang directly onto their pitons to keep from being swept away. Later, while the storm still raged, John,

149

in his bivouac sack, lighted a candle—and burned a hole in the sack. The wind tore through it, chilling his bones, caking his face and clothing with frozen rime.

By morning the storm had passed. The sun rose and beamed. But now it was a mockery, for they were too done in to go farther; and besides, the sheer walls above were unclimbable in their fresh sheath of sliding whiteness. It would be hard enough to get down. But they had to—or else—and through that whole second day they drove their stiff and battered bodies to the effort. With half-frozen fingers they fumbled with ropes and pitons. Rappel followed rappel, into gulfs of thin air, and much of the time they couldn't tell if their rope would run out before they reached a landing place, leaving them hanging in nothingness. Mountaineers are habitually tight-lipped about their most harrowing experiences, but John was less so than most. "We were fighting for our lives," he said later. And so they were. And they won the struggle. It had taken them ten hours the day before to reach their bivouac point. Now the descent—usually a far faster affair—took them eleven. But they made it. Twice in four months the Walker Spur had turned them back, but both times, at least, allowed them to live.

—And to go on to the Eiger.

12. Victory

There it was: black, gigantic, waiting.

And the two fleas peered up at it.

For the flea called Harlin it was the fifth time at its base. Three times he had been on its north wall, twice on its west ridge, studying the wall. Never had he come even close to climbing it; indeed, his forays had been more reconnaissances than actual attempts. But in dreams he had scaled it a hundred, a thousand times. Supreme among all mountains, this was his goal, his heart's desire.

The flea called Kirch was less emotionally involved. For any top-flight climber the Eiger was an ultimate challenge, and he was un-questionably topflight. He and John made a formidable team, and they wanted a formidable antagonist. But for Konrad, unlike John, what rose before them was no magic mountain. If anything, it was repellent, sinister; and he was well aware that, for the twenty-seven times it had now been climbed, it had exacted a total of twenty-one lives.[1] Four of

[1] In German, in fact, there has long been an alternative name, grimly punning, for the face of the Eiger. Instead of *Nordwand* (north wall) it is called *Mordwand* (murder wall).

the ascents and two of the deaths had been in this summer of 1962, and the odds on anyone at grips with the wall were obviously only for gamblers. Konrad was a confident and ambitious man. He was also, however, thoughtful and realistic, and he had not let his parents know (he had no wife) that he was going for the Eiger.

John, on the other hand, had sent a wire to Marilyn, who had just returned to Bernkastel from another visit to Denmark. It had been their long-standing agreement that he would always let her know what he was doing in the mountains.

They had come up on the train to Kleine Scheidegg, and on the afternoon of August 18 pitched their tent in the meadows of Alpiglen near the base of their peak. At the time there was thick fog; the heights above were invisible. But the weather forecast had been favorable, and they knew that the Eiger—*for* the Eiger—was in good condition, with few accumulations of loose snow. In their tent, and piled beside it, were their clothing, gear, and carefully selected food. How long they would be on the wall they had no way of knowing. Once, only once, it had been climbed in a single day, but other successful assaults had taken up to a week. Their hope for themselves was two or three days. But they had enough food to keep them going for longer.

On the first day they wanted as early a start as possible, and at exactly midnight they were out of their tent. The cheering forecast had been right. The fog was gone. In its place were stars and a late-rising moon, and ahead the mountain loomed bold and black against the softer blackness of the night. For an hour their movement was mere walking, first over meadow and boulders, then up the hard-packed snow that covered a small glacier. At the head of the glacier was a bergschrund, the usual deep crevasse that separates a mountain from its skirt of ice; and John, leading, found a narrow bridge and balanced his way across it. At the far end he touched the rock of the Eiger.

Directly above them now was the wilderness of the north wall—six thousand vertical feet from base to summit. But though it was wilderness, it was not unknown to them. Konrad had never entered it; John had barely scouted it. But through reading, the study of photographs and long hours with binoculars, they knew its principal features as if they had lived their lives among them. They knew the route they would

152

take: the now classical route that almost all climbers had followed since the first attempt on the wall in the year of John's birth. To them, as to every mountaineer who ever dreamed of the Eiger, the names of its successive landmarks were like an ancient litany.[2]

. . . First Pillar . . . Shattered Pillar . . . Difficult Crack . . . Red Flue . . . Hinterstoisser Traverse . . . Swallows' Nest . . . First Icefield . . . Ice Hose . . . Second Icefield . . . Flatiron . . . Death Bivouac . . . Third Icefield . . . Ramp . . . Traverse of the Gods . . . Spider . . . Exit Cracks . . . Summit Icefield . . . then. . . .

Then they began to climb.

"To the left," John reported, "I found some free holds. After nervously glancing down into the throat of the bergschrund, I told Konrad to secure me well, and I made my move. It was all arms for about ten feet. This earned a cautionary rebuke: early reliance on arm strength alone would sap my reserves long before reaching the summit." To help himself find stances, he switched on his headlamp. What first appeared in its beam, however, was not a stance, nor rock at all, but a cluster of alpine flowers hanging from a ledge. For a characteristic moment John the climber was gone, with one of the "other Johns" in his place, bending to admire and touch them. "I found them so beautiful and out of place," he said, "that it took an impatient yell from Konrad to get me moving again."

Their course, in the darkness, led up to the right of the tall buttress called the First Pillar; then diagonally over rotten cracks and ledges, laced with ice, in what Konrad called "dangerous hiking." It was not to be "hiking" for long, however, for as they neared the base of a second buttress—this the Shattered Pillar—the wall veered upward, sheathed with ice like boiler plate. Using clefts and bulges, they slowly forced a passage. And on the way they first heard the sound they had been waiting for: "the siren scream of the air above compressing as a huge stone winged its way down from the heights." Of all the perils of the Eiger, this—its enormous rockfall—was probably the worst. John had estimated that, of all its climbers, fifty percent had been hit by rocks and five percent killed by them, with even more casualties caused indirectly by their fall. He and Konrad were of course wearing plastic helmets, and they tried at all times to keep clear of the most obvious

[2] For a photo diagram of the Eiger and its routes, see insert following page 144.

avalanche troughs. But the whole way up it would be chancy going, with their luck, or lack of it, largely beyond their control.

The first projectile did not have their names on it. Nor did others that followed, falling to the side and behind them. Skirting the Shattered Pillar, they traversed around and up to its top, and now ahead was a hundred feet of sheer rock, seamed by a narrow slit called the Difficult Crack. As they drew nearer, the darkness was thinning, and they could see a length of rope hanging down it: presumably one used in the recovery of the body of Barry Brewster, an English climber who had been killed on the mountain just a week before. Behind and beneath them, too, the dawn was spreading. As the valley lights dimmed, fields and houses emerged. Then, closer below, they saw something else, something moving: two figures in red parkas and white helmets ascending toward them from the base of the wall. Faint voices reached them. They were not alone on the Eiger.

Above the Shattered Pillar was a rock rib, steep but negotiable; then a delicate traverse, on which John had to shatter the ice with his ax to find purchase for hands and feet on the rock beneath. This brought them to the foot of the Difficult Crack, and here for the first time Konrad took over the lead. The rope already fixed in the crack was of course of some help; but there were many overhangs, and Konrad's pack was awkwardly heavy. Presently, by various contortions, he removed and lowered it, and now began to move faster, while John belayed from below. Meanwhile, looking down, John again spied the two men who were following them. Indeed, they were much closer now, climbing swiftly, and it seemed dangerously, on a very long rope. Suddenly the danger showed its teeth. The leader slipped and fell several feet before he was held by belay and piton, and assorted German curses floated up through the still air. From his perch above, Konrad announced he could tell by the accents that the climbers were Austrians.

Soon he had reached the end of the Difficult Crack. John came after. But they did not linger at the top, for it was exposed to violent stonefall from the Red Flue, straight above. For a breather, they had four easy rope lengths on a diagonal up to the left. Then they came to one of the most famous stretches on the Wall of the Ogre—the Hinterstoisser Traverse.

Andreas Hinterstoisser had been one of the four-man German-Austrian team which, in 1936, had challenged the still unclimbed face and perished in the worst disaster of the mountain's history. On the ascent, at the point where John and Konrad now stood, it had been he who took the lead, forging a way with rope and piton across 130 feet of bulging slabs that offer scarcely a single natural hold for hand or foot. It was a magnificent feat, but at the end of the traverse he and his companions made a fatal mistake. They removed the rope he had affixed; and later, when, with one climber injured, they tried to descend, they were unable to effect the crossing in reverse. Searching for another route, Hinterstoisser fell to his death, and the three others died on the wall—one of them, Toni Kurz, after three days of agony, at the end of which he was within a hairsbreadth of rescue.[3]

Now, many years and many climbs later, there were two ropes strung across the Hinterstoisser Traverse. But both had been damaged by stonefall, and John and Konrad, as they inched across, had to take their own precautions. Against falling, at least. About further stonefall there was nothing they could do except hope—and move as quickly as possible. While they were midway in the passage a large block of ice crashed into the rock above them, scattering fragments "the size of bowling balls"; but Konrad was untouched and only one small sub-fragment struck John's helmet. Safely across the aerial catwalk, they rested briefly in a small niche in the wall that is known in Eiger topography as the Swallows' Nest.

In the world into which they had entered, however, "safely" was a transient and illusory word. At the point they had now reached (at seven in the morning) they were about two thousand feet up the wall, a third of the way to the top. But the Hinterstoisser Traverse was known as merely the gateway to the *real* climbing, and progress from here on would be slower and stickier.

Indeed, the "stickiness" showed almost the instant they were past the Swallows' Nest. Beyond it was the steep white tilt of the First Icefield —"and once I had got to it," said John, "I wished I hadn't, for the rock and ice falls were continuous. Every second was a gamble, and the odds were heavily in favor of the house. But I found a stance on a bit of solid rock and brought Konrad up. He took one look, said 'Oh my God!' and

[3] For a detailed history of Eiger climbing (through 1961), see *The White Spider*, by Heinrich Harrer. A book by Toni Hiebeler, called in its original German *Eigerwand*, and in French *Combats pour l'Eiger*, carries the story through later years, but is not available in English.

began to lead toward a sheltered position. He had just disappeared around a corner of ice when I went numb and my sight dimmed. A stone had caught me on the side of my jaw just below the ear. Shell-shocked, I fairly ran to Konrad's belay to recuperate."

If it wasn't one thing it was another. Skirting the icefield, they had first to contend with a tricky overhang, then with what John described as the most rotten and dangerous rock he had ever encountered. Konrad, now leading again, kept muttering that he hated the damn mountain and wished he were back on the good firm granite of the Walker Spur. But when a change came, it was scarcely what he had in mind. Above them now rose a sheer, frozen waterfall known, graphically, as the Ice Hose, and in its complex toils they labored for almost two hours. About halfway up, they had a crisis of sorts when the rope jammed between them. During the time that it took to reach the jam and loosen it, they had no effective belay, and a slip by either could have meant disaster. Then, up toward the top of the Hose, the ice gave way to more rotten rock, which refused to hold protective pitons. Konrad, again leading, took a long time here, moving, John reported, "with cautious disdain, like a cat in wet grass. When my turn came, I found out why. One had the sensation of climbing on roller skates with no protection at all."

After the Ice Hose came the Second Icefield. "Field" is a misleading word for these white patches on the Eiger, for they are tilted at ferocious angles—this one at about fifty-five degrees, and with a surface like burnished steel. The two strapped on their crampons, and John took the lead (as he usually did on such stretches, for he had had greater experience in ice work). But he was almost at once in difficulty. Carelessly, he now realized, he had not had his crampons sharpened since the beginning of the summer, and their points slipped and slithered when they should have dug in. This meant the hacking of many more steps than would otherwise have been necessary: hundreds of them in great zigzags up the length of the slope. Progress was agonizingly slow. But worse was yet to come, for, about three-quarters of the way to the top, the strap on his ice ax broke and the ax got away from him. "I lunged for it, missed, and nearly came off," he said; "then watched it slide down the ice and disappear from sight."

It was a demoralizing mishap. One ax between them on the Eiger wall was not a happy situation. But there was nothing for it. After a shouted conference Konrad came up and took the lead, moving more securely and swiftly with his own ax and sharper crampons. By mid-afternoon they had reached the upper edge of the icefield, and there rested in a cleft between ice and rock. From their perch, looking down, they saw that the two climbers they had spied earlier were now close behind them, using the steps they had cut up the long slope. Then, presently, they arrived and there were greetings and questions. Their names were Hans Hauer and Nikolaus Rafanowitsch, and as Konrad had guessed, they were Austrians.

Both teams decided independently to go no farther that day. They had been climbing since the earliest hours of the morning; and besides, the stretch of wall just beyond them was a rockfall area, now at its most dangerous in the afternoon thaw. As it was, it took them until after dark to select and excavate two bivouac sites, barely large enough to sit on with feet dangling downward. Now it was Konrad's turn for a mishap. Taking food and gear from his pack, he dropped both their tea supply and miniature stove, and the two went tumbling off into space. As an emergency measure they impaled a burning fuel tablet on a piton, held a cup of snow about it, and eventually had a warmish brew of melted chocolate.

If some of their luck was bad, some was good. All day, and now all night, the weather held. Above, the stars blazed; and below, in clear blackness, "the lights of Grindelwald, then Thun, and far out, even those of the city of Bern, were all serpentine strings of jewels." Snug and tight in their bivouac sacks, lashed to the rock by rope and piton, they were almost two-thirds of the way up their mountain.

They dozed, woke, dozed again. And soon after dawn, before the Austrians, they were climbing again. Next of the way stations on the classic route was a jutting buttress called the Flatiron, and beyond it a niche in the wall that bore the ominous name of Death Bivouac. It had been exactly that, too. In the summer of 1935, a few months after John's birth, the first climbers ever to challenge the *Eigerwand*, two Germans named Karl Mehringer and Max Sedlmayer, spent the last days and nights of their lives there, marooned in storm, before dying in a manner that will never be fully known.[4]

[4] Sedlmayer's body was found by later climbers at the bivouac; Mehringer's not until 1962—the very year of John's climb—on the Second Icefield.

Now for John and Konrad, twenty-seven years later, it was merely a place for a brief rest, a bite to eat. For them, the sun still shone. . . . How long it would go on shining was, however, the great and over-riding question. For storm, not sunshine, was the norm here, and a whole ascent under bright skies was almost too much to dream of. . . . Even in the crystalline air, they were now so high that the details of the earth below were losing their definition, withdrawing and leaving them sealed in their own private world of rock and ice.

—Then another look down. And with it, astonishment. For their private world was that no longer. They of course knew that the two Austrians, Hans and Nik, were close beneath them, but what they saw now was not merely two figures but six more—"a whole army of them," said John—following the steps they had cut the previous day up the Second Icefield. Along with surprise came dismay; for while much of Eiger-climbing may be misery, it is not the sort that loves company. On the contrary, in all mountaineering it is the very essence of both the struggle and the prize that it not be a wholesale affair. And whereas two teams of two was tolerable, even companionable, a group of ten was—an army.[5]

Still, there it was: the army was coming. As had happened before on the Eiger, a spell of good weather had brought out the aspirants in force, and for John and Konrad there was nothing to do but go about their own job. A few rope's lengths beyond Death Bivouac they came to the Third Icefield, even steeper than those below, at a tilt of about sixty degrees. Using their one remaining ax, John set to work chopping another stairway. But the ice was iron-hard; neither ax nor piton would bite in well, and progress was slow and precarious. "I thought a lot about falling," John reported succinctly. In their labor and absorption, it made no difference if behind them there were a dozen other climbers or a hundred.

Then the Third Icefield was beneath them.

And above was the Ramp.

Because of the Eiger's size, they said later, each of its many sections seemed to them like a complete climb on a lesser mountain. After

[5] What they could not see or know was that there were still another six men, in two teams, below the ones who were visible. These last challengers later turned back. But as of that morning of August 20, 1962, there were a total of sixteen men on the north wall—the most that have ever been there at one time.

negotiating one of its great obstacles, known to them for years by name and fame, they felt as if they had reached not merely a way station but a summit; then pulled in their belts and recharged themselves for the next "summit," and the next. Now it was the Ramp. And it was a terror. Some of the world's top climbers—Gaston Rébuffat, Hermann Buhl, Lionel Terray—had found it the most formidable pitch on the wall; and for John and Konrad it was to be the antagonist for the rest of that day.

The word "ramp" is a misnomer. In structure it is like the Ice Hose, only more so: a thousand-foot chimney cutting a vertical sometimes more-than-vertical face, and lined with ice for most of its length. Two of its principal features are called—this time appropriately—the Overhanging Waterfall (frozen, of course) and the Ice Bulge, and with these, in sequence they did battle for hours. As usual, the ice itself was brittle, the underlying rock rotten, making pitons largely ineffective. Some dropped out and were lost. Others could scarcely sustain a rope's weight, let alone a man's. But still they inched on: hammering, grasping, improvising, contorting. At the crux of the Waterfall, John, hanging from not much of anything, had laboriously to pack ice chips around three pitons to make them hold. Later, on the Bulge, he was confronted by a cannonade of ice and rock roaring down its center, and had to move out to the farthest rim of the cleft in an airy detour. It was grim work. Much of the time he too was grim, in a total output of effort and concentration. But he was still John Harlin—still the man who reaped more joy than pain from supreme endeavor—and in the very midst of his struggles he found himself repeating lines from *Jam Crack Joe,* the song he had sung so often back in Stanford days in Yosemite:

. . . *With his fingers jammed in crannies and his legs a-dangling free, And a thousand feet of nothing down below . . .*

Only here, he noted, it was not a thousand but more than four thousand feet of nothing. And in that knowledge he exulted, for it meant they were closing in on the goal.

Still, on this day they were to get no farther than the top of the Ramp. By the time they reached it daylight was beginning to fade; and worse —far worse—gathering mist and cloud gave notice that their two days of fine weather were coming to an end. They found a place of sorts for their second bivouac. Since it was impossible to place pitons, they looped a protective rope around the block of rock on which they were perched, only to find that the block itself moved under pressure. But there was no other choice. The best they could do was try not to cause pressure. Huddled together, making every move cautiously, they had a bit to eat and drink, and then tried to rest.

With darkness, the mist lifted—but not for the better. In the ensuing clarity of night they could see huge clouds building to the north and west, and at midnight, when they peered from their bivouac sacks, it was to confront a full storm. "I do not know when I have ever seen such a sight," John wrote of those moments. "From one end of the horizon to the other the sky was lit with distant lightning. The line of storm was approaching so fast that you could see cloud movement in the light of the flashes. I told Konrad that we had about four hours before our mountain would be enveloped. Melodramatic as it may seem in retrospect, I strongly felt that if this was going to be the beginning of the end I wanted to absorb all the visual stimulus I could esthetically enjoy. So I kept watching as the storm advanced. Soon we could hear distant thunder and see the glows becoming bolts of lightning. Then the intricate flashes would lace the dark bulbous forms of cloud. The cities began to disappear: first Bern, then Thun, Interlaken, finally Grindelwald. Then it was upon us. . . ."

Luckily, however, not quite in full fury. The heart of the storm, with its electrical discharges, hit the mountainside below, and at their level there was only snow and windblown cloud. When dawn came, conditions around them were bad, but not so bad that they could not move from their bivouac. Among Eiger climbers it had been long agreed that the Ramp was the mountain's point of no return. If storm or accident struck below it, you tried to descend; if above it, you went on, as best you could, toward the summit. On this third morning on the wall, as they struggled into packs and crampons, John and Konrad were well aware of this rule of thumb. They did not even discuss it. They moved upward.

Next on their route was the Traverse of the Gods. Like the Hinterstoisser, this was an exposed catwalk, cutting more or less horizontally across the face of the mountain; and while it required less technical maneuvering, its exposure, at twice the Hinterstoisser's height, was huge and awesome. Also, to be sure, the scudding mist and snow did not make its crossing easier. But it was nothing compared to what greeted them when, at its far end, they reached the foot of the Spider.

Other features are landmarks on the Eiger. The Spider—or White Spider, as Heinrich Harrer has called it—is virtually the Eiger's trademark: a steep icefield high up on its north wall that, with its long strands of snow-filled gullies radiating from it, looks from the distance like a mythic monster at the center of its web. To John and Konrad, however, it simply looked like white hell. "When I saw it," said John, "I was speechless. Konrad, ahead, was belaying from the last rock before we reached it, and all I could see beyond him was the blurred image of tons of falling snow. Finally I called out, 'Does it ever stop?' Konrad could not hear me. When I reached the belay I yelled again into his ear, and he answered simply, 'No.' I felt completely beaten, a man without an acceptable alternative."

After five minutes, however, the flow of the avalanche slackened. Smaller slides still descended the slope, but John thought he could withstand these, and with Konrad again belaying, he moved out into the maw of the Spider. His first objective was a rib of ice running down its center, above the avalanche level, where he would sink a piton. And speed was of the essence, for if another heavy flow came before he got there, it would peel him off into space. In the deep, shifting powder his progress was less like climbing than swimming. But he made the rib and fixed the piton just as the next big slide roared down around him. During the next lull Konrad joined him, then took the lead as they began the ascent of the rib. They estimated that it would take them four 150-foot rope lengths to gain the top of the Spider.

During the past hour or so the fresh snowfall had stopped. But as they advanced it began again, heavily, and they suspected that this would bring more big avalanches in short order. They were right. From a stance some eighty feet below Konrad, John looked up to see him desperately banging a piton, while a great wave of whiteness descended upon him. Then his companion was gone. Everything was gone but the wave, and John braced himself and covered his face. "In the next second," he said, "there was only whiteness and choking—but the pressure was not too great. Best of all, there was no falling body from above." Soon they were climbing again, and though more avalanches followed, none dislodged them. By late morning they were back on rock, with the Spider beneath them.

—Or at least the Spider's body. Above, now, was the upper part of its web: a maze of gullies and fissures known to climbers as the Exit Cracks, leading up toward the final stretch of the Summit Icefield. They knew that the best of the cracks was over toward the left. But from below all were equally evil looking—"sculptured glass funnels, each different in form, but all spewing out snow at high pressure and varying intervals." Before making their choice, they paused and looked back into the cauldron of the Spider—and woke again to the realization that they were not alone on the mountain. They could see vague forms through the fog and snow. When they shouted, answering shouts came back in German. But they could not tell who the climbers were, nor how many. Selecting one of the cracks above, they clambered on to a spot that gave some protection and waited for the others to come up.

When they arrived, they proved to be, if not an army, at least a brigade—of six. The Austrians, Hans and Nik, were not among them. These were the group John and Konrad had seen lower down the previous day, and consisted of two other Austrians and four Swiss, who had joined forces near the start of the climb. They had not seen Hans and Nik since the evening before, when they had stopped to bivouac near the foot of the Ramp; but at that time the two had been all right.

This information given, there was a pause.

So now what?

A few minutes ago John and Konrad had been two men on a mountain. Now they were two of eight, huddled close together in a narrow gully. Above them the gully continued, no less narrow, and there was obviously little choice of routes. From here on, willy-nilly, the eight men would not be three or two teams, but a single unit, and John was quick to recognize and accept this. To a degree, of course, it was disappointing, for he and Konrad had hoped to climb the whole wall on their own. But considered differently, a joint finish was not only inevitable; it had one great attraction. He had long been a proponent of international climbing teams, and this one would be truly so—Swiss, Austrian, German, American. Very well, so be it. He was proud and pleased with the thought.

The others agreed to a pooling of efforts and offered to go in the lead. All the way up the mountain, they pointed out, they had followed the tracks of John and Konrad, profiting by their labors, and now it was only fair that they should take some of the brunt. John and Konrad agreed to the plan. It was only noon; and though a column of eight climbers would move far more slowly than two, they were confident that they would reach the top of the Eiger well before dark. . . . "Bereit? Ready?" "Ja. All ready." They started off. . . . When on the next few pitches, steep but easy, they made good progress, their confidence increased. But beyond these, suddenly, the procession came to a halt—and they were presently to learn that they had made a mistake in judgment.

Above, filling the crack, was a huge, jagged overhang that they knew had given a hard time to many earlier climbers. One of the Swiss, a specialist in rock work, went first, but since the rock was ice-sheathed he retained his crampons. Foot by foot, then inch by inch, he worked his way upward to the apex of the bulge; then reached a point where he could move no farther, hanging on with one hand, and with the other reaching futilely for non-existent holds. When a small avalanche came over the bulge, he came with it. A belay from below broke his fall, and he was not badly hurt. But after an hour of effort and final defeat, he was exhausted and shaken.

Now one of the Austrians tried his luck, and another hour went by. In the end he made it, disappearing above the overhang, and using his belay from above, the other Austrian and one of the Swiss followed. Then, however, a bad blunder was made. To haul up a pack, the one rope leading over the bulge was released from its securing pitons and carabiners, with the result that there was now no upper protection for the men still to come. And what ensued brought the whole party to the brink of disaster.

One of the remaining three Swiss—a youngster named Josef, and called Sepp by his companions—went next, and John noted from the start that he seemed in poor control of himself. Reaching the crux of the overhang, he was unable to surmount it and cried "Zug! Zug!" ("Pull! Pull!") to the men above. But the rope was in no position either to lift or even hold him, and after a few moments of frantic scrabbling he fell, like his companion, thirty feet to a ledge below. Like him, too, he was not hurt. He tried again. And fell again. Then began to climb for the third time. Though still physically uninjured, he was now close to panic, and both his own voice and those of his teammates were edged with hysteria as they shouted back and forth to one another. "It was an incredible performance," said John "—like watching some ghastly burlesque melodrama, the consequences of which have a bearing on your own life."

Inevitably, Sepp fell again. And this time the Eiger rock was not so gentle. He lay where he had landed, moaning that his ankle was broken and that he could not move.

If this was so, burlesque melodrama was over and something grimmer lay ahead. Sepp's distraught partners first spoke of hauling him on to the summit; but on a wall like the Eiger's this was manifestly impossible. If he was unable to climb, John said, the only conceivable course was to leave him—with or without a companion—go full tilt for the top, and descending the west ridge, return as quickly as they could with a full-scale rescue team. They were, he pointed out, less than a thousand feet from the summit. At a spot nearby, in 1957, the Italian, Claudio Corti, had had to be left in similar circumstances, and had subsequently been pulled up by cable in the most famous rescue of Eiger history.

Sepp had no desire to be another Corti. Even as John was speaking he struggled to his feet, and though his ankle was sore, it was obviously, and providentially, not broken. The almost shattered group prepared to move on. But this time it was not Sepp who made the next move; it was Konrad. Hammering pitons as he went, and with John belaying from below, he moved cautiously up the crack, outflanked the overhang, and emerged on the shelf above. With a rope now properly secured, the others followed him up. That particular horror was over.

But—again—what now? With every instinct of self-preservation, John and Konrad wanted to break away from the others, to be once more on their own. But they couldn't. For one thing, there was virtually no room for independent movement; and for another—perhaps more important—they were committed. "Now we were all responsible for one another," was the way John put it, "and whatever the consequences had to stay together."

What those consequences would be was becoming a large and ominous question. Beyond the overhang the going was less severe, but still the file of eight moved slowly. Furthermore, hours had passed during their Battle of the Bulge; daylight was fading; and it was clear that they were not going to make the summit before dark. This was more than a disappointment. It could be the difference between success and failure, life and death. After the long wait at the overhang, all were beginning to feel the warnings of frostbite, and a third night out on the wall could well finish them off. Still moving on, slowly, doggedly, "we began," said John, "to have that old feeling of doubt. You know, that slow realization that maybe the road you are on is a one-way street in the wrong direction. No panic, not even fear; just the strong impression of high odds against you—an unfair twist of luck after winning so much."

In their ragged procession, the Austrians were first, the Swiss next, John and Konrad last. And before them, the gully climbed endlessly on. For a while it was angled at about seventy degrees, plastered with ice and loose snow. Then it steepened to ninety; then eased off again to seventy; but this was even worse than the vertical, for now the funneling walls became an avalanche chute. For perhaps an hour they struggled on into thickening dusk. Then a call came down from the others that they could no longer see and were stopping for the night. They had found no bivouac site, not even a place to sit; but they were stopping anyhow—they had to—and would wait out the darkness standing, holding on.

John and Konrad could not see either. Konrad's headlamp had gone out, and John's was only a feeble flicker. Realizing that they too would have to stop, they searched for cracks in the rock that would take protective pitons. But they could find nothing.

Snow fell. Night fell. The wind rose and howled.

Finally, they at least found a place to sit. Or rather excavated one from snow and ice, using their lone ax to clear a sloping ledge. There was no pitoned rope to hold them onto it. With their feet dangling in space, they were unable to cover them, but they managed to get a bivouac sack over their heads. Even in their acute discomfort, they were so tired they could scarcely keep awake; but they had to, for to sleep would be to fall a vertical mile. As a precaution they took turns holding a lighted candle, with the hand up close to the wick and its reservoir of hot wax, so that if the holder nodded, the tipping would spill the wax and rouse him. To keep the blood flowing in their now freezing toes, they wriggled them to a count rhythm . . . by the hundred . . . then the thousand. . . .

As the night dragged on it grew colder. And that was bad. But cold meant clear. And that was good. Through the sack they could hear and feel that the wind was down. When they peered out, the snow had stopped and they could see the stars.

Then the stars were fading in dawnlight. And again they were climbing. Stiff, half-frozen, battered—but climbing. From above, word came down that the two Austrians had already started for the top, but the four Swiss were still there where they had spent the night. Apparently they had been badly frostbitten, for when they began to move it was awkwardly, fumblingly. Yet move they did. And John and Konrad moved after them. At one point, on an icy pitch, Konrad took a short fall—their first on the mountain—but was not hurt. A little later, John, waiting his turn to climb, fell asleep on his feet and had to be awakened by a jerk of the rope. But still they kept going. The Swiss kept going. An hour passed. Another. And at last the endless gully ended. The exit crack from the Spider was beneath them, and the mountainside opened up into the smooth steep whiteness of the Summit Icefield. Here John and Konrad roped up with the Swiss. No one talked. They simply rested a bit, joined ropes, went on climbing. The footing was now on downward-sloping slabs coated with ice and powder snow, and much care was needed. But gradually the slope was easing—easing—as for another hour they crept on. . . .

Then incredible things were happening. They were no longer on the icefield but on a rim above it; no longer on the north face of the Eiger but on its east ridge, called the Mittellegi, and beyond it was the far side of the mountain and the morning sun. They were climbing the ridge, and though their feet were leaden, their eyes were lifted, and where before, inside of John, there had been the yearning for sleep, there was now, instead, a mighty pounding of the heart. Around and beneath them the world shone in splendor. "Clouds completely undercast the landscape," he wrote, remembering, "with only mountain masses penetrating the blanket. The sun was still low, giving relief, yet more intense because of the reflecting layer below. Thus, the snow ridge leading to the summit cornice had the fantastic brilliance of a jewel lit from within. Chips of ice from ax blows were caught in the air and gleamed in the sun against an impeccable blue."

They stepped up, up, up. Then stepped no farther, no higher, for there was nowhere higher to go. Six of them stood together between the white of snow and blue of sky—then eight, for the two Austrians who had gone ahead were waiting—and the sun flashed golden in their goggled eyes.

"*Bergheil,* Konrad!"

"*Bergheil,* John!"

13. Farewell to Arms

There was to be one more brush with disaster before the great day was done. By evening they were down the west ridge and at the fine old hotel at Kleine Scheidegg. They filled themselves with beer and fondue. They wallowed in hot baths.

After John had been in his tub for more than a half hour, Konrad entered and found him asleep. Wakening him, he returned to the bedroom. But when after another half hour there was still no John, he went back and found him again asleep, this time with nose and mouth a scant inch above the level of the water.

"I didn't think he should drown on the day he'd climbed the Eiger," said Konrad. So he pulled the plug.

Then the Ogre receded. From the Oberland they drove to Chamonix, to see old friends and perhaps (being human) to take a few bows. From there, the epic ended, they went their separate ways: Konrad to Munich and law school, John to Bernkastel and Hahn.

The mountain had not let him off scot free. His toes were discolored and painful, and he spent four days at the base hospital under treatment for frostbite. But he had fared far better than most of his Eiger companions. Of the four Swiss and two Austrians who had been with him at the summit, all lost either toes or fingers or both. The other two Austrians, Hauer and Rafanowitsch, who had gained the top a day later, were hospitalized for weeks. Of a total of ten men, only Konrad had emerged unscathed.

In the European press, the climb was duly noted and applauded. Along with the others, John was again invited to the autumn festival at Trento: now not merely as an honored tyro, but as an Eiger climber, one of the Alpine peerage. Still, the luster of the feat had inevitably been somewhat dimmed by its wholesale accomplishment. Not only had there been their own "army" on the north wall. By the time the summer of 1962 was over, it had been scaled by no less than fourteen groups totaling forty-four climbers, which was far-and-away the record for any one year. In the process there had been five deaths —also a record—and it was these, of course, rather than the successes, that attracted the most public attention.

For John, moreover, there was special and ironic disappointment. However often the Eiger had been climbed, he was the first and only American to do it; yet his fellow Americans, in general, could not have cared less. In the stateside press his climb was barely mentioned. Even at Hahn, not one in a dozen men had so much as heard of the Eiger. During those early fall days, the sports-minded were concentrating on the Yankee-Giant World Series and how Paul Hornung was shaping up for the Green Bay Packers. John was of course aware that mountaineering held nowhere near the same status in the States that it did in Europe. But the awareness was cold comfort. Men like Walter Bonatti in Italy, Lionel Terray in France, and comparable climbers elsewhere on the Continent, were public figures, national heroes. For him, on the contrary, it was only in foreign milieus that his achievements were recognized. To most of his compatriots who had heard of him at all, he was simply "some sort of nut" who enjoyed torturing himself by climbing mountains.

Compounding the situation was an irony within an irony. By all the rules of mountaineering decorum (as established by the English gentry of the nineteenth century) climbers are expected to shun publicity, indeed to treat it as anathema. But while self-effacement is genuine among some of the breed—especially British and Americans— for others it is not; and it certainly was not for John Harlin. This is not to imply that he climbed mountains primarily for fame and fortune. First, last, and always, he climbed because he loved to climb. But he *was* ambitious. He *was* competitive. As much as any man who ever lived, he wanted, fiercely, to excel in what he did, and wanted his excellence to be known. . . . Among Europeans, by 1962, it was known. Among Americans it was not.

This, along with his strong internationalism and his dream of starting a school, was one of the principal reasons why he was planning to remain in Europe after leaving the Air Force. And Marilyn was all for staying too—for the second two reasons, if not the first. The five-year term for which he had joined the service was now drawing to a close; by year's end he was due to become a civilian. Yet he took what at first sight—in view of his non-love of the military—seems the contradictory step of requesting, and getting, a six months' extension of duty. His motive, however, was realistic. Whether for new mountain ventures, the new school, or both, June seemed a far more propitious time for beginnings than December.

At Hahn, meanwhile, he continued as safety officer and instructor pilot. He put in his flying time and still loved it. He put in his ground time and didn't. With other things on his mind, he did not, this fall, participate in football either as player or coach, and in fact limited his base activities exclusively to what was required of him. For its part, the Air Force presently gave him the back of its hand when, after his five years of service, it failed to promote him from first lieutenant to captain. No reason, of course, was given; he was simply passed over. But it is safe to guess that one contributory cause was his unprecedented request for transfer from his original duties. Further, he had had the bad luck to be followed to Hahn by the officer with whom he had had a run-in while in training in Arizona. And presumably he, even more than his colleagues, had John ticketed as a non-promotional type.

John didn't care. In his mind's eye he was already out of the Air Force, a civilian again, and he was now giving immense time and effort to his cherished school project. The fact that he had neither money nor experience in the field still bothered him not a whit. He was reading up, investigating, corresponding in all directions, and was confident that by sheer enthusiasm and idealism he could put the pieces together. The name he had chosen for his now two-year-old brainchild was the International Institute at Mont Blanc.

For prestige and fund-raising purposes, he was trying to line up a board of directors, and with people as with mountains, he always shot high. One of his prospects was none other than ex-President Dwight D. Eisenhower, who was at the time touring Europe. Indeed, after much correspondence, he was under the impression that he had secured an interview with Eisenhower during the latter's visit to Cologne. When he got there, however, his quarry had already left for Paris; and when he followed him to Paris, he had already left *there*. Frustrated but not daunted, John returned home and continued writing to assorted statesmen, ambassadors, corporate executives, and college presidents.

He could fight for other goals than mountaintops.

In the realm of mountaintops, writing was in process too. Witness a vignette of the Eiger ascent:

"Calling together for the thirty-seventh time my last reserves of stamina and will power, I examined the route ahead. Ignoring the fifty-knot gale that threatened to blow me into the abyss, I looked upward at the face, shielding my eyes from the occasional avalanches of house-sized blocks of stone mixed with tons of snow, gravel, ice, dirt, mud, water and climbers. Flexing my toes, which I hadn't felt since a week ago Thursday, I began to climb. . . ."

The author thereof did not happen to be John. It was Paul Revak, as self-appointed alter ego, marveling at "this Frankenstein I created when I first took John climbing back at Stanford." But John, too, was writing the Eiger story—and for a while had high hopes that it would be taken by either *Life* or *Sports Illustrated*. As of that time, however, this did not materialize. Its only stateside publication during his lifetime would be in the *American Alpine Journal*, an annual highly esteemed by mountaineers but almost totally unknown to the general public.[1]

So much for the log of the past.

But what of the future?

[1] With more than a touch of irony, *Sports Illustrated* reprinted it after his death in 1966. Indeed it was not until then that he received any recognition to speak of in the American press.

In a letter to her friend and ex-neighbor, Elli Osgood, Marilyn wrote: "I have checked the Eiger off my list of things to be done in this lifetime. Even the immortal *Freiherr* reveals the possibility of its being the last climb for him." (Whether she—or John—clung to this thought for two, five, or ten minutes is not recorded.)

Granted, his ascent of the north wall had brought problems along with satisfaction. For years the Eiger had been his dream; now the dream had been realized, and the overriding question was: What next? What could top the Eiger? . . . For some the problem might have been insoluble. But not for John. He already had the answer, and it was *the Eiger itself.* . . . It had now, of course, long since been climbed from all sides: by the west and Mittellegi ridges; by the northwest face and various southern approaches; finally, and now frequently, by the once "impossible" north wall. Yet one route still remained. A route within a route. A new "impossible" that had not yet been proved otherwise. This was the Eiger Direct—the north wall *direttissima*— not in a meandering zigzag course, as always before; not by the "classic" trail, already so often followed; but by a brand-new one, untouched and virginal, straight up the mighty peak from base to top. Among the world's best Alpinists, a *direttissima* was now regarded as the foremost of all mountaineering challenges, and its accomplishment even on lesser peaks was a rare and prized occurrence. To achieve it on the unholiest of holies, the Eiger, would be the ultimate of ultimates.

—Thus John's thoughts, after those two (or five, or ten) minutes in which he had (or Marilyn thought he had) considered giving up climbing. And soon he was not only thinking but planning. Early in the fall of 1962 he received a letter from his old climbing partner, physicist Henry Kendall, who, it developed, had been in the Mont Blanc area while John was on the Eiger. There he had climbed with Gary Hemming, and the two had made a successful ascent of the Walker Spur of the Grandes Jorasses, which had twice repulsed John earlier in the year. He congratulated John on the Eiger. John, in return, congratulated him on the Walker. Then—"Would you consider," he wrote, "joining me and two others next on an Eiger *direttissima?*" Some details followed. After which he concluded: "I can't hide the danger from you. There will be more risk than one is usually forced to accept in the mountains. But I'm game; how about you?"

He wrote also to Konrad and Gary. And Gary, for one, was interested. As a climber he had had a good summer, making not only the Walker with Kendall but a notable "first" on the west face of the Dru with Royal Robbins, and as a result had regained the confidence he had lost in his first brush with the Alps in the previous year. Also, it transpired, he had had other adventures. After his two big climbs he had been accepted as a student guide by the *Compagnie des Guides de Chamonix*, a signal honor from that august trade union of professionals. But after three weeks the project had come to grief on the issue of his beard and shoulder-length hair. "If they'd told me at the start they didn't like them," said Gary, "I just might have done something about it. But they wait for three weeks, for Christ's sake, and then tell me to get them cut, and by that time it's a moral issue." So he and the *Compagnie des Guides* had parted company.

That, for a while, had been the end of Chamonix, but not of the Hemming saga. Still comfortably hirsute, he had hitchhiked to Paris and there been promptly jailed for sleeping at high noon on the bank of the Seine. Thence the trail led to England—and more trouble with uniforms, when Immigration took a dim view of him both esthetically and financially and ordered him back on the cross-Channel ferry. At this, Gary was less angered than pleased; for he recalled that "my hero Henry Miller had had the same treatment by the English thirty years ago, so it made me feel most humble that an identical honor should be bestowed on me." As it turned out, however, he was not, like Miller, actually deported. In a weak moment he phoned a solvent friend, who underwrote him, and he was allowed to stay on. At the time of writing John he was (1) climbing in the Lake District, (2) earning beer and skittles by ditchdigging, and (3) planning, after another go at the Alps, to take off for Australia to avoid The Bomb.

By Air Force standards John may have been a wild non-conformist, but alongside Gary he was the All-American Square. He supported his wife and children. He punched the time clock at Hahn. He prepared to weather another winter of discontent, while counting the days toward civilianhood and freedom.

Then, as always, something happened. Or rather—as always—he made it happen; and it was a lot better than getting a captaincy. Through military channels, a call was made for candidates for the combined

U. S. Armed Forces ski team, and he forthwith applied. Except for sporadic outings with a few friends, he had had little practice in the sport for several years. But again, as in California, he became an "instant skier" and was accepted as a member of the interservice training squad. In December he was transferred from Hahn to a tour of duty at Garmisch, in the Bavarian Alps.

"Duty" was scarcely the word, for it was a dream assignment. Not only was he being paid and receiving full military credits for doing something he loved, but he was also, at Garmisch, wholly out from under the service atmosphere he so cordially hated. Housing was in a pleasant mountain inn, surrounded by civilians. Ski and sports clothes supplanted uniforms, and there was no brass in sight. The ranking officer on the premises was a young infantry lieutenant, a lover of both skiing and mountaineering, who was soon to become one of John's closest friends.

The end objective of the Garmisch training was competition in what is known in Europe as CISM—*Championnat International Militaire de Ski*—which was held in late February in Chamonix. And the events there would be downhill slalom and cross-country. For the slalom, with its split-second timing and complex techniques, John was not remotely qualified. But for the cross-country—despite his lack of experience—he was a natural: in his strength, in his superb conditioning, above all in his love of pushing himself to the utmost in tests that for others were only ordeals. Further, the military version of the event included rifle marksmanship at targets en route. And though here again he was short of practice, John's shooting eye was still as sharp as in long-gone boyhood days in Ireland and Ethiopia. Exultantly, he fairly devoured the white countryside of the Bavarian Alps, and presently was the U. S. Armed Forces champion in overland skiing.

Besides his *raison d'être* for being there, Garmisch offered a wealth of fringe benefits. Marilyn and the children came down for the Christmas holidays and other visits, and in no time at all, much to his father's pride, six-year-old Johnny was whizzing about like a veteran. Then, with Marilyn back in Bernkastel, there was a multi-national assortment of snow bunnies on hand to enliven the hours of *après ski*. As back in Phoenix—as anywhere and everywhere with John—there were stories of extracurricular adventures, with the protagonist almost simultaneously propagating and denying them. But whatever the balance of fact and myth, the Harlin seven-year-itch, which was now upon him, seems to have been no more acute than earlier itches; and there was at least no talk of divorce and South Seas.

Also satisfying (and non-controversial) was the male companionship at Garmisch. For here, unlike Hahn, everyone spoke John's language of the mountains. Augmenting the regulars, several of his old friends appeared for visits, among them Roy Brown, Leon Canapary, Gary Hemming, Konrad Kirch; and with Konrad he had, along with skiing, a few good bouts of winter climbing. Closest to him during these days, however, was his fellow officer, Harthon—known as Sandy—Bill. Not only was Bill in charge of the ski training and himself a member of the slalom team; he was also a mountaineer of parts and longed to emulate John in his climbing achievements. Best of all, he was strictly non-military, non-service, in temperament and outlook—like John, an unregenerate, freewheeling romantic. And soon the two, as they skied and climbed together, were building plans for the future—including (need it be said?) a *direttissima* on the Eiger.

They were to have one brief look at it that winter, as in mid-February they made the trip from Garmisch toward Chamonix. Then it was on to the slopes of Mont Blanc and the CISM championship meet. With competing teams from sixteen countries, ranging from Scandinavia to South Korea, this was the climax, the grand finale, of the military skiing season, and it may be presumed that visions of glory danced through John's head. But that, alas, was not to be the way the cards were dealt. Instead of glory, he was headed for one of his periodic debacles.

The villain was a bug. Or perhaps two bugs—for no sooner did he reach Chamonix than he was hit simultaneously by both flu and diarrhea. John being John, however, he brooked no thought of being sidelined, and on the day of the cross-country race appeared at the starting line at the head of the four-man American team. Whereupon his troubles started. More specifically, his diarrhea. There being no better refuge available, he took to the woods; but with skis, boots, and layers of clothing to contend with, the requisite speed was impossible, and the upshot was—in a word—disaster. What followed was disaster compounded, with overtones of a Marx Brothers production (under lax

176

censorship). After a struggle he succeeded in divesting himself of his woolen underpants, but the consequence was acute refrigeration of his private parts. What to do? He came up with the answer. Or rather down with the answer—removing his woolen ski cap and stuffing it in his pants around the afflicted sector. In a few minutes he was back on the starting line. He was off in the race. For more than half of its fifteen-mile course he kept doggedly going: uphill and down, across valleys and ridges, laboring mightily with ski and pole, pausing to aim and shoot at the marksmanship targets along the way. But the price was a stiff one. His displaced cap kept sliding down his trouser legs. His unprotected ears began to freeze, and when two of his teammates encountered him they saw that they had gone dead white. They urged him to quit the race, but John refused. Then they insisted he quit, and at last he gave in.

An irreverent bard wrote later:

> *No champion he*
> *At Chamonix*

—and that was the end, for John, of the *Championnat International Militaire de Ski*—though, happily, not of his ears or his privates.

Hahn: He counted months, weeks, days.
Bernkastel: He took stock.

Not of the skiing fiasco: that was past. Not even, for the moment, of climbing plans. What demanded immediate attention was the course to be set when he left the Air Force in June.

What he wanted most to do was start his school, but the bald fact of the case was that little progress had been made. There had been long discussions, vast correspondence. There had been many expressions—some from high places—of interest and enthusiasm. But of solid support, no. Like the Space Laboratory project of two years before, the thing had reached a certain promising level and begun to wither away. There was no site for the school, no faculty, no pupils, no money.

John was far from ready to give up his dream. But he was realist enough to have anticipated delays, and he and Marilyn had talked much of alternatives. By far the best, they had agreed, was for them both, if possible, to take jobs in an already existing school in Europe, either American or international. And to this end Marilyn had for months been writing to a whole spate of institutions—in England, France, Germany, Switzerland, Italy. Some had replied with a simple turndown. Others had shown tentative interest. With all, the principal problem was that neither she nor John had any teaching experience to speak of. To rectify this, Marilyn had during the past fall conducted an evening biology course at Hahn; and now John, after a lapse, resumed his art course. But he had a fair idea that if a school took him on, it would be for his athletic rather than his artistic talents.

And if no school did, for any reason?

That was a hard one.

The opportunity presented itself for him to stay in the service and go to Alaska, for training with full-time ski troops. But he did not want that. Then applications were circulated among Hahn pilots of training as NASA astronauts. But among the requirements was a degree in physical sciences and engineering (plus, one would say, a tolerance for bodily confinement that John was far from possessing). His father, still a frequent Hahn-Bernkastel visitor, would have liked to see him follow his own course as a commercial pilot. But though he had once, on his own, investigated a job with Swissair, he now considered this too routine for his tastes.

In his casting about, sundry Johns surfaced briefly. He secured and filled out, but did not submit, an application as a Peace Corps staff member (with assignment preferably to Nepal). His eye again roved, with unspecified aims, toward the Andes and Amazon in South America. For a while, as a result of his art classes, his old affinity for design revived, with thoughts of returning to couture or becoming an interior decorator. And finally, most persistently, there was his urge toward writing. In its current phase, this involved planned collaboration with Roy Brown (who shared the urge), and the proposed program, marvelously Johnian, was to buy a Volkswagen Microbus, tour Europe while writing, and end up in Paris when publication was indicated.

(Instead, Roy, out of the Air Force and separated from his wife, went off to Peru on the medical mission ship *Hope*. His son Jeff became, for a time, a member of the Harlin household. And though John's writing plans continued to simmer and bubble, he still could not muster the *Sitzfleisch* to sit long at a desk.)

One great thing that he had going for him, now as always, was Marilyn's total belief in his abilities. Writing to her parents about plans and prospects, she repeated the theme she had stated so often before: *"There is nothing John cannot do!"* Nor had the trials of their marriage, including seven-year-itch, dimmed the glow within her. For now she also wrote: "I am happier than I have ever known myself —fulfilled, re-created, complete—anticipating an exciting future and terribly glad to have what I have. The core of my happiness, of course, is being so very much in love."

Her brief moment of delusion that the Eiger would be John's last big climb was long since over, and she was well aware that whatever else the "exciting future" might hold, it would include mountaineering. Indeed, as spring now moved on toward summer, his next Alpine campaign loomed ever larger in his thought and talk. One prospective partner was suddenly, almost tragically eliminated. Word came from Ulm, in Bavaria, that his new friend Sandy Bill had been critically injured in a fall from a small practice cliff and now lay in hospital with a shattered spine and multiple broken bones. Meanwhile, however, correspondence was in process with other, older climbing colleagues— among them Konrad, Gary, Henry Kendall, Pierre Mazeaud. On home grounds, he worked out in the gymnasium and ran through the hills with long-time companions Arne Arneson and Leon Canapary. And to these was presently added a new convert to Harlinism, a young Air Force dental officer and aspiring climber named Cleveland McCarty.

Also during the spring there reappeared the oldest of all his friends— his quondam high school classmate, Bob Rosenaur, who was touring Europe with his wife. Almost alone of John's intimates over the years, he had been a confirmed non-athlete, impervious to the Harlin creed of the strenuous life; and now, a successful and portly businessman, he was more so than ever. There was no gym, hill, or mountain in their reunion. Only food, wine, and talk—of old times and new. And it was during one of their talks, in the house at Bernkastel, that John said to Bob, "I once killed a man."

As his friend heard what followed, it was his impression that it had taken place in the recent past, during John's Air Force career. But it was the same story John had told Marilyn soon after he met her in 1954: the night in Rome, the footpad, the confrontation, the climax.

Bob and Marilyn never mentioned it to each other. As far as can be ascertained, John had told the story to no one else between 1954 and 1963. There it was—a twice-told tale with a nine-year interlude—and after that one evening's talk Bob Rosenaur asked and heard no more about it.

Why John chose to tell it when he did, he doesn't know. Whether there was more, or less, to it than he was told, he doesn't know. Nor does anyone.

The past was for an old friend in the nighttime. The future came in the morning by the hand of the mailman. The postmark was of the Swiss town of Leysin, in the canton of Vaud, near the eastern end of Lake Geneva. The letterhead was of the Leysin American School. The content was that the school stood ready to employ John Harlin as athletic director and Marilyn Harlin as biology and chemistry instructor for the academic year beginning in September.

They talked it over.

They said yes.

And in the second week of June, John's five and a half years in the United States Air Force came to an end.

Much as he wanted out, it was not altogether an easy step to take. More than most occupations, the service offered an assured future, financial security; whereas at the school there would be no tenure and the salaries, though twofold, would be negligible—with Marilyn receiving the larger share. Nevertheless, his mind was made up, and on the most serious level. Shortly before leaving Hahn and Bernkastel he wrote a letter to old friend and Navy flier Paul Revak, and concluded: "You might ask me and even yourself how we could give up military flying. My answer would be this. It has been a great experience that I wouldn't trade, but when you consider the twenty-four hours in a day and 365 days in a year, there appears a question of values. Air-to-air combat is going, gone, and the rest of flying somehow lacks, if you have to prostitute the rest of your life to it. The meadows and mountains of a lifetime clock make pushing throttles a little insignificant."

Then again he was off to the south—for perhaps the fiftieth time in three and a half years. But this time it was for good; this time with wife, children, possessions, and a one-way routing. He was two weeks short of his twenty-eighth birthday. Above him, as he drove across the Mosel and out of Bernkastel, an F-100 soared up from Hahn, skyward, into the dimension of his youth. Then the clock ticked on toward the meadows and mountains, and the dimension of the future.

14. Free

Outwardly, at least, the dimension was familiar. Ahead, the Alps rose white and shining in the summer sky, and soon they were among them, following the well-known roads through valleys and passes.

The trail took them first to Leysin, their home-to-be. But this, their initial visit, was merely a check-in and look-around, for duties at the American School would not begin until fall. In short order they were off again: first to Chamonix, for a brief rendezvous with Konrad Kirch; then to the town of Grindelwald, near the foot of the Eiger.

The immediate objective was not the mountain, but a meeting at one of Grindelwald's hotels. Since his Eiger ascent of the previous summer, John's name had become better known to mountaineers in the United States. His story of the climb had appeared in the *American Alpine Journal*. He had received and accepted an invitation to join the American Alpine Club. Further, the then president of the club, Carlton P. Fuller, had written him, saying he would be in Switzerland that summer and suggesting a meeting; and it was for this that the expatriate "mystery climber" now came to Grindelwald.

183

It was a great success. John spoke of his doings and plans, and particularly of his hope, later in the summer, to return to the Eiger and climb it *direttissima*. It would, he said, be not only an ambitious venture but an expensive one, and he wondered if the AAC might be able to defray some of the cost. Fuller replied that at the time there were no club funds available for such a purpose; but he was so taken with John, and impressed by his "grand designs," that he forthwith gave him a personal check to help the cause along. This marked the beginning of a relationship in which the older man was to become, in effect, John's mountaineering godfather. And it was to mean much to John, both practically and psychologically, for it gave him his first solid tie with the mountaineering world of his own country, from which he had so long been an exile.

As usual, the Eiger was to be saved for the climax of the season's campaign. From Grindelwald, he and family doubled back to Chamonix, and there again set up tent-housekeeping in the campground outside the town. Meanwhile, Konrad had had to return to Munich for law studies and examinations, but others were on hand, by prearrangement, to fill the gap. One was Gary Hemming, again full of confidence and ready to romp. Another was Stewart Fulton, an accomplished young Scottish climber whom John had met earlier in the year at Garmisch, where he had been wintering as a combination ski bum and custodian of a chair lift. And as a top-drawer fourth for an Alpine team, there was Californian Tom Frost, by profession an engineer, by avocation one of America's foremost Yosemite cragsmen.

Their choice—meaning John's choice—as first objective was the Aiguille du Fou, one of the most formidable of the Chamonix Needles. And, of course, not the Fou by any old route, but by its precipitous south face: one of the few remaining walls in the Alps that had never been scaled. He and Gary had studied it yearningly during their 1961 campaign, but had regretfully agreed that as of that stage of their experience, it was too much of a challenge. Earlier this same summer, he and Konrad had reconnoitered its lower reaches, before being driven down by storm and avalanche. Now, however, he felt that time and team were both right. Midsummer had arrived. For such an ascent—which would require much stringing of fixed ropes—a foursome would be far more effective than a duo. In addition to his cragsman's skills, Tom Frost had brought with him a superb assortment of Californian "chromolly" pitons, the ideal weaponry against the sheer rock of an *aiguille*.

Still, the Battle of the Fou was to consume almost a month, in four successive attacks. The first, little more than another reconnaissance, was made by John and Stew Fulton and ended in storm and oncoming darkness. But in the process John believed he had discovered a route that would prove not only feasible but deeply satisfying. Such a route, said the esthetician of the mountains, as "would not merely taste the face but savor and devour it."

On the next attempt—the first real one—all four went up, affixing ropes as they climbed and taking turns in the lead. At the most difficult pitches, however, Frost, the "artificial" expert, moved up ahead. To surmount one jutting overhang, he had to hammer in no less than twenty-six pitons, and when at last he was up, the rope that he lowered hung more than ten yards out from the wall beneath it. Sixth degree climbing such as this was of course painfully slow, and by the time they were about halfway up the face darkness dictated a bivouac. There being no ledges wide enough to hold a man, they slung two hammocks from pitons in the rock. But when John and Stew climbed into theirs it promptly ripped apart. Since they themselves were also roped to the mountain, they did not fall far; but the upshot was that they had to spend the night standing in improvised stirrups. To add to their misery, darkness brought heavy rainfall. And in the morning, soaked, stiff and bedraggled, they rappeled down to their base camp.

Full storm came. And they waited.

On their third try at the face, climbing the fixed ropes by the prusik method,[1] they gained height quickly. But up on virgin rock Stew took a nasty fall. Soon rain came again. And they descended.

Then—after more storm, more waiting—came their fourth and final attack. This time, Tom and Stew went up ahead, again made swift progress to the top of the fixed ropes, and from there on, using a vast variety of "mollies," engineered a route still higher. Almost every bit of the way now had to be done artificially. On one overhang, even worse than that encountered below, Tom had to whack in twenty-eight pitons, ranging from tiny two-centimeter slivers to bulky four-inch spikes, called "bongs." Still they made headway—by a foot, ten feet,

[1] See Glossary.

a hundred, five hundred—and when dusk came they had their reward by finding a ledge that, though narrow and sloping, would hold a bivouac for four. Using the lines the others had strung, John and Gary prusiked up after them, carrying supplies. And by nightfall all were roped into their eyrie, some two-thirds of the way up the vertical wall.

A climb is not only a contest of men against natural obstacles. It is also the interrelationship of the men involved—"the penetration," as John has said, "of one life into another." The four on the Fou had now been together for many days, much of the time under stress, and though the work accomplished had been magnificent, the "penetration" had begun to show, and cause lesions. Not all mountain partners found John the easiest man to climb with, and Stew Fulton was one of them. Small in stature, but toughly fibered and assertive, the Scotsman did not greatly take to his driving, take-charge propensities, and he occasionally let him know it—less often in anger than by burred and caustic wit. Also, John and Gary's long-standing antagonisms emerged again, in repeated and heated arguments about routes and procedures. Quiet, controlled, and objective, Tom Frost was the only one who stayed clear of dissension, though he conceded later that the John-Gary conflicts "took away much of the joy of such a fine route." Then he added, "It is a mystery to me why, with all their disagreements, they continued to climb together."

In that high bivouac on the Fou, however, there were to be more pressing problems than personalities. During much of the day bad weather had threatened, and now as they prepared for the night, said John, "the sky tore open and a storm broke. Lightning was all about, striking the Fou and lacing the darkness with incandescent whiteness." As in their earlier bivouac, the hours were wet and miserable, and when dawn came, though the storm was over, they were wrapped in an opaque grayness of cloud. This time, however, there was no turning back. It was now or never for the peak of the Fou, and with John and Gary leading, they began fighting their way up the top third of the precipice.

Steepness and smoothness were unrelenting. Again pitons had to be hammered, hour after hour, in a veritable stairway up the granite wall. But as morning moved on toward noon, the clouds around them began to break, and to right and left they could glimpse fantastic landscapes of soaring rock and ice. As always when he led a climb, and when the goal was near, John, in the midst of his labors, felt a surge of strength and exultation. "Life effervesced within me," he said. And as always, too—when the goal was finally won—the fighter in him subsided and the "other John" emerged.

"At last," he wrote, "we pulled ourselves onto the summit slabs. Here the top of the Fou floated in the clouds, and the towering cumulus all around at our level reminded me of many similar moments while flying. However, here one could actually feel the elements and be part of them. These sculptured forms, ever-changing like life itself, made mockery of our Fou. Its south face was perhaps the hardest climb in the western Alps, yet it could not compare to a soaring cliff of vapor with cracks and chimneys of translucent crystals never to feel a human hand."

It would be nice to leave him on his mountaintop, in triumph and revery. But that, alas, was not the way the Fou climb ended. Leaving the hard-won summit, they began their descent by an easier, but still precipitous route, and in short order, trouble—real trouble—broke out between John and Gary. It began with John's shouting up to Gary, higher on the rope, that he was being careless in dislodging loose stones. Gary hotly denied the charge. The shouting continued. And soon—incredibly, on the almost vertical wall—the two were maneuvering toward each other to have it out nose to nose. Providentially, Stew Fulton was on the rope between them. In size, he was not much of a barrier: a bantam compared to the two men who were converging toward him. But he was a tough bantam. He had a pungent Scottish vocabulary. With a Glaswegian variant of "a plague on both your houses," he kept the would-be combatants apart and prevented what could have been the most fantastic fight ever staged outside a Bond-Flint-Batman movie scenario.

The fracas on the Fou was, unhappily, to be a milestone in John and Gary's relationship. They never again took part together in a major climb. But at least neither knocked the other three thousand feet off a precipice. Though there were subsequent rumbles and flashes, the descent continued, and at the foot of the peak there was no chance to resume hostilities. Their conquest of the Fou's south face had been a major feat, an authentic "first" in Alpine annals. Reporters and cameramen were on hand to greet the returning heroes. And John and Gary, recalling the rules of *noblesse oblige*, managed to refrain from public fisticuffs.

Theirs, it developed, had not been the only adventure of the two days just past. Marilyn Harlin had had hers too. During the Fou campaign she had spent most of her time at the campground in Chamonix, caring for Johnny and Andréa and boning up on textbooks in preparation for her teaching at Leysin. At the start of the final climb, however, she had gone up into the mountains, and on the morning when John and Gary set off after Tom Frost and Stew Fulton, had been one of several camp followers who accompanied them on the approach. The Fou, from the south, is a well-hidden peak. The route to its base cut across the lower cliffs of the neighboring Aiguille de Blaitière, itself a formidable climb for a girl who had done no real mountaineering since her days at Stanford. But she was well aware of how much her coming along pleased John, and for her part, had total confidence when tied to him on a rope. As they moved up through the bright morning, her thoughts went back to another morning, years before, when she had followed the boy she loved up a peak called Hubris in the Castle Crags.

Presently, however, there had come the time for parting. John and Gary went on toward the Fou, while the others stopped to turn back. And here the trouble started. For the descent, her companions were two young climbers, one English, one American; or perhaps "semi-climbers" was the better word for them, for she soon discovered that they were no John Harlins. On the steep rock there was much fumbling, slipping and indecision about routes. One of the men was hit on the head and partially stunned by a falling stone. With a 2 P.M. start, it took them the rest of the afternoon to reach the foot of the Blaitière, and ahead was still a long stretch of steep and deeply crevassed glacier. Dusk came—then night—and worst of all, storm: the same storm that struck John and his partners in their bivouac high above. And for more hours they groped and stumbled downward, expecting momentarily either to be struck by lightning or plunge into a hidden chasm in the ice.

Neither happened. At 11:30 at night, after some twenty hours out, they reached the refuge of a high mountain cabin; and the next evening, greeting John on his descent from the Fou, Marilyn was able to report that she was none the worse for wear. Her adventure on the Blaitière, however, was to be her first, last and only in high Alpine mountaineering. In her own way, she loved the mountains no less than John. With a part of her, she would have loved to be the companion of the heights that he so wanted her to be. But with another part, she knew by now that ambitious climbing, even of a modified female variety, was not for her. And with *all* of her she felt an obligation to her children that at least one of their parents keep a grip on terra firma. She and John rarely spoke of the hazards implicit in the life he led. Knowing and loving him for what he was, she did not want to change him; and even if she had so wanted, she had not forgotten that "No one ever stopped John from doing anything." Nevertheless, she was thoroughly aware of the risk in most of his "anythings." And if she was, of necessity, a fatalist about him, and even herself, she saw no reason to expose Johnny and Andréa to double jeopardy.

Meanwhile, John's climbing star was rising high. No sooner had he come down from the Fou than he was offered membership in the prestigious French climbing club, *Groupe de Haute Montagne*—only the third American so honored. And immediately thereafter, he and Tom Frost were designated by cable from Carlton Fuller as representatives of the American Alpine Club at an upcoming mountain conclave in Chamonix. Known as the *Rassamblement International D'Alpinisme*, this was a gathering of expert climbers, during which various participating teams attempted ascents of the greatest difficulty; and John and Tom, fresh from one virgin climb, forthwith set their caps for another. This was the westernmost of the three great pillars supporting the Italian, or Fréney, face of Mont Blanc—to which the two Americans were to give the name of the Hidden Pillar of Fréney.

To John, this was familiar territory. Bordering their route was Fréncy's Central Pillar, the scene of the French-Italian tragedy of 1961, during which he and Gary had been close below.[2] But he had never been on any of the pillars; nor had anyone yet scaled the nearby "hidden" one, at which he and Tom now launched themselves.

Along with the Fou, this was to be one of his finest successes. Perhaps the most ominous part of the climb was its prologue, during which they worked their way up through the wilderness of glaciers and ridges to the base of the pillar; for here, every foot of the way, they were conscious of the successive disasters that had overtaken the French and Italians in their 1961 descent. But once on the Hidden

[2] The Central Pillar had been first climbed, almost simultaneously by two parties, later in the summer of 1961.

Pillar, they were in a world of their own. The weather, for them, was merciful. And they made a strong and harmonious team, plagued by none of the bickering that had marred the ascent of the Fou. "We were as one, in thought and action," Tom Frost was to say later; "so in tune with each other that little was said, particularly in the way of orders or directions, during the entire climb." Then he added: "John was a strong leader, and I was proud to be along."

Actually, they took turns out front—with Tom, as on the Fou, leading the "artificial" pitches and John the "free" sectors. And their progress was steady, with no mishaps. The most dubious moments came during their one halfway bivouac, when the night turned freezing under a deteriorating sky. But John, mindful of past tragedy, counseled that "Safety is up, not down"; and in the morning, up it was, straight up, toward the top.

On this second day they encountered the most difficult going, notably on a 500-foot precipice—half vertical, half overhanging—called the Red Wall. But with piton and stirrup, muscle and balance, they overcame it, to emerge at last at the crest of their pillar. Here, besides victory, a special bonus awaited them. For there was no need to make their descent down the fearsome Frêney. From its top a sequence of easy snow-ridges led on up to the dome of Mont Blanc; and following them, they reached the summit, crossed it, and descended by a conventional route to Chamonix—effecting their second triumphal entry in little more than a week.

Tom Frost was not much of a one for triumphs; he kept in the background. But John's cup was running over. A few months earlier, in that spring of 1963, an expedition from the United States had climbed Mount Everest, both by an old route and a new one, thus establishing Americans in the front rank of Himalayan climbers. Now, with two successive and brilliant "firsts," a comparable feat had been performed in the Alps—with himself as architect and prime mover—and his already considerable fame in Europe (though not, still ironically, in his own country) was further expanding by leaps and bounds. From the overflowing cup, he wrote to Carlton Fuller in Boston, telling of his successes, his satisfaction, and "the sheer joy of life and freedom . . . a freedom that has awakened new perceptions of beauty and allowed me to approach more closely to my potential strength."

The boy in him—the Boy in Golden Shorts—was far from dead as he added: "At the summit of Mont Blanc, after the Frêney, I could sprint as though it were low altitude. Then, after a night at a high hut, we left it 1½ hours later than all other parties and reclimbed Mont Blanc just for the fun of it. We passed the other climbers so early that they were no longer visible below us on the summit ridge."

A few days later, *hubris* flapping in the breeze like a pennant, he was off to the Oberland and "the big project."

Many times before he had camped in the meadows of Alpiglen at the base of the Eiger; but never had it been anything like this. Previously he had been with one or, at most, two companions. Now, in August of 1963, it was with a whole community.

The unifying theme was, of course, his hoped-for *direttissima* ascent. Along as prospective partners (with hostilities at least temporarily shelved) were Gary and Stew Fulton. Tom Frost—though, to John's disappointment, not interested in Eiger-climing—was on hand as a sort of observer-consultant. His law examinations behind him, Konrad Kirch appeared, with the thought of "Maybe, just maybe"; as did the Frenchman, Pierre Mazeaud, with whom John had been long corresponding. These might be called the hard core of the encampment. Around them swirled and eddied an outer ring of other climbers, semi-climbers, non-climbers, old friends, new friends and non-friends, who had been attracted by the lure of the Eiger and John's new full-scale celebrity. Further, it was no all-male assemblage. There were wives, girl friends, and would-be girl friends. There were Marilyn, Johnny, and Andréa. Most improbably of all, there were, for a while, John's father and mother, dropping by for a visit. Though their son had now been climbing for ten years, this was their first sight of him, ever, in a mountaineering milieu; and it is understandable if, when they left, they were more perplexed than before.

John's own eye, however, was less on Harlinville than on other campsites roundabout. As always, a forecast of settled weather was attracting climbing teams to the foot of the Eiger, and on his arrival there were already three of them established there: one Italian, one Spanish, and one Japanese. He was not greatly concerned about the last two. They were planning to climb the north wall by the old zigzag route, which was by now *vieux jeux* to him. But the Italians, he soon learned, were, like himself, *direttissima*-minded, and though only a twosome, were a team of formidable reputation. As a consequence, he was impatient to get going; for he considered the "Eiger Direct" his very own brainchild, and it would be a bitter blow to him to see the prize snatched away.

For a *direttissima*, of course, a whole new route had to be worked out: both by observation from below and then, step by step, on the mountain itself. With the thought of blending the two phases, John approached Fritz von Almen, proprietor of the hotels at Kleine Scheidegg and owner of the best telescope in the area, suggesting that he become in effect a partner in the venture—following the climbers' progress through the lens, and directing them by radio along what seemed the most promising lines of attack. Von Almen, however, declined so great a responsibility. So it was up to John & Company, before starting, to work out as detailed a plan as possible. This, plus the complex sorting of food and gear, took time, and it was no comfort to see the Italians already stringing ropes on the lower part of the face. To add to the tension, a large delegation from the press had established itself at Kleine Scheidegg and was dramatizing an Eiger "race" between Italians and Americans.

Then, inevitably, came the prime enemy. . . . Weather. . . . Forecasts to the contrary notwithstanding, a series of storms moved in; rain fell below and snow above, and the north wall vanished in tiers of windblown cloud. In the tents of Harlinville, guitars strummed, wine corks popped, and the assorted couples, married and otherwise, alternated between lovemaking and fighting. ("That was no climbing camp," said one of its denizens later. "It was a gypsy camp, except with tents instead of wagons.") There were reports of hashish and marijuana on the premises. As always, when there were girls around, there was talk that John was having an affair. Or several. But Marilyn, in retrospect, derides the notion; and with herself and the Eiger both at his elbow, she would seem, this time, to have a point.

What one knows happened is that he watched, he waited. . . . And during the wait his group of potential climbers began to erode. Tom Frost and Pierre Mazeaud took off for other mountains. Konrad Kirch, an Eiger-climber but no Eiger-lover, watched the avalanches roar down the face and changed his "maybe" to a "no." Then Gary, whose relations with John were still touch-and-go, decided, first, to become

192

only a support member of the team, and later to withdraw entirely. ("He felt that he needed psychological adjustment," John wrote cryptically to a friend.) This left only Stew Fulton as a qualified partner; and John, now hard put as his project crumbled around him, decided to suggest to the two Italians that the four of them join forces.

Before he could do so, however, a whole new train of events was set in motion. One early morning, during a break in the weather, all three of the other teams—Italian, Spanish, and Japanese—began the ascent of the north wall. Through the day they moved up in separate parties, bivouacked for the night, and the next morning continued to climb, until yet another storm closed in upon them. Through the telescope at Kleine Scheidegg, John could see, in brief glimpses, that the Italians and Japanese were stopping, then descending, but the two Spaniards, unaccountably, still pushed on. Though they were higher than the others, they were still far short of the great cleft called the Ramp, which on the Eiger was the accepted point of no return. And to John their decision to climb farther seemed reckless and foolhardy.

So it was to prove. The storm continued, grew worse. During the next day, and the next, through rents in the clouds, watchers below could see the climbers still ascending, though very slowly; and on the next, at last, they were past the Ramp and on the Traverse of the Gods. By now, however, they had been five days on the wall, the last four of them in foul weather, and it was certain that they must be near the end of their tether. One hope only remained for them: they were now close to the snowfield of the Spider and high enough so that they could possibly be rescued from above. Down at the Eiger's base, fellow mountaineers girded themselves to see what could be done.

One of them was Toni Hiebeler of Munich, a top-ranking German climber and leader of the team that in 1961 had climbed the north wall in winter. On the afternoon of the rescue decision, in clearing weather, he started up the west ridge of the peak, accompanied by Roberto Sorgato, one of the Italians who had been trying the *direttissima*, and three Spanish friends of the pair on the wall. At two the next morning, John followed with the other Italian, Ignazio Piussi, both heavily laden with food and equipment. The plan was that the first group would climb to the west shoulder of the peak, which overlooks the upper north face, and from there try to determine by search and shouting whether the two Spaniards were still alive. If so, the two

193

groups together would go on to the Eiger's summit, and from there John and Piussi would rope down the face to bring such help as they could to the stranded men. Meanwhile a more general alarm would be sounded. As in 1957, when the Italian Corti was rescued, a platoon of climbers would carry cable and winch to the summit, and if all went well, the Spaniards would be hauled to safety.

Such was the blueprint. But it was not to be. When, toward dawn, John and Piussi reached the bivouac of the advance party, it was to learn that there had been neither sight nor sound of the Spaniards. Nevertheless, the two went on themselves to the west shoulder—only to see and hear nothing. While they were there John's walkie-talkie crackled, and word came up from Scheidegg that, through the telescope, a body and rope had been found on the snow of the Spider. No second body was visible, but the upper section of the rope was hidden, and it was presumed that the other Spaniard lay dead at the end of it. A little later a helicopter search confirmed what had been seen from below. It was obvious that the Eiger's *Mordwand* had claimed its twenty-fourth and twenty-fifth victims.

The would-be rescuers descended. During their brief venture John had been much impressed by the Italians, Sorgato and Piussi—especially Piussi, a giant of a man, who had coursed up and down the west ridge as if it had been a country lane. And back at the base of the peak he made his delayed suggestion that they join forces with himself and Stew Fulton. The Italians agreed. In spite of defection, disappointment and disaster, a strong team seemed at last to have been assembled for the *direttissima*. . . . But again, it was not to be. . . . After a short break, the weather resumed its storming. Already, the four climbers had been Eiger-watching for a full month, with little exercise or conditioning, and at John's suggestion they broke camp and moved to milder altitudes for a bout of practice climbing near Geneva.

Here the campaign reached full anticlimax. During a workout on the well-known cliffs called the Salève, John had one of the few falls of his career, a forty-foot solo drop. Tougher than ever, he was not seriously hurt; but by the time he was through aching and limping his three companions had to take off for home. To seal the doom of further exploits, the summer was drawing to an end. The Eiger, from all reports, was now more impossible than ever. Picking up Tom Frost in Chamonix, John made the classic retreat to the Calanques, on the

Mediterranean, and finished out the season on their sunlit crags and blue waters.

Again the mountain would have to wait for the flea to return.

The town of Leysin is in the heart of the western Alps, near where the upper Rhone River flows into Lake Geneva. It can be reached from Geneva, from the Rhone Valley, or across the mountains from Chamonix and the Oberland, and as you come to the river delta road signs announce that you are approaching the twin towns of Aigle-Leysin. They are, however, far from identical twins. They are not even very close together; for Aigle is on the flatland of the delta, whereas Leysin, reached by corkscrew road or rackrail train, clings to a mountainside high above. In years gone by it was a peasant village. During much of the nineteenth century and the early part of the twentieth, it was one of Switzerland's many health centers. Today it is largely a resort, with its old sanitariums converted into hotels, clubs, and schools.

The Leysin American School, to which John and Marilyn reported in September 1963, is one of two institutions under the same directorship, of which the other is called the American College of Switzerland. The school, covering the four years from ninth through twelfth grades, had at the time an enrollment of about 130; the college, with a two-year course, roughly half that many; and both were co-educational, drawing their students from American families who, for one reason or another, were living abroad. Marilyn's teaching was to be wholly at the school. John was officially in charge of physical education for both school and college. But he soon discovered that the collegians, for whom athletics were not compulsory, were largely not of the type to become involved by choice, and most of his work was on the high school level. Predominantly, though not exclusively, his charges were boys.

In finding a home, the Harlins were lucky. A mere two minutes' walk from the school were small twin chalets called Castor and Pollux, and into Pollux they moved, as the best and last of their many homes. Like the school, and indeed all of Leysin, it was on a steep slope facing southward, and before them, in a vast cyclorama, spread the upper Rhone Valley and beyond it the snow-capped range of the Dents du Midi. These were not, to be sure, always visible. "Here," wrote John, "the elevation is such that often clouds float below the town, their tops gradually rising until you are isolated in mists. At this point the sun is sometimes obscure, sometimes shrinking down on your two or three acres and on the rolling masses of white. Then you are swallowed, and cold mists seem to enter your heart. You want to run uphill into the blinding sun, to the color and warmth you know are waiting above."

One did not have to run up. There was a winding auto road; at their doorstep was a cable lift; and from the high meadows above Leysin one could see in all directions across the domain of the Alps. To the northwest only were comparative lowlands—the green-clad hills and valleys surrounding Lake Geneva. To the southwest, beyond the Dents du Midi, the vast range of Mont Blanc filled the sky. To the southeast rose the Matterhorn, Monte Rosa, and the other giants of the Pennines. To the northeast, in the Oberland, was the trinity of Jungfrau, Mönch, and Eiger. When the confines of town or school or home closed in on him, like the clouds, all John had to do was move a little upward to find himself at the very hub of the world he loved.

In school, Marilyn's work was more demanding than his. Through the Air Force years she had kept up her biology, but she had long since grown rusty at chemistry, which she was now also teaching, and had to struggle to keep ahead of her pupils. John was, on all fronts, doing what came naturally. The school, housed entirely in one converted sanitarium building, had little in the way of an athletic plant, and there were no organized team sports of either the American or European variety. But this was all right with him, for he had left games behind him with his football days. What he was interested in was what he was increasingly to call "character building through adventure," and his prime means to this end were climbing and skiing. In the indoor phase of his program the emphasis was on calisthenics and wrestling, both designed to bring his charges to the highest peak of conditioning.

As always with those exposed to John, some loved his methods— and him. And some hated both. As always with John, he poured himself out for those who were attuned to him and all but ignored those who weren't.

With assistants on hand, he was not tied to workaday routine. In fact, no little of his value to the school lay in his fame as a mountaineer, and he was allowed great leeway in his comings and goings.

In October, for the third time, he attended the mountain film festival at Trento. And even out of season, as far as big game was concerned, there was ample time and chance for lesser climbing. Roundabout Leysin was a fine assortment of rock outcroppings, ranging from an old quarry almost in his back yard to peaks of considerable size and challenge; and on some of these—the Tour d'Ai, the Sphinx, the Grand Mirroir, and others—he was soon doing climbs that, in difficulty if not in scale, compared to ascents in Yosemite or on the Chamonix Needles.

In general, the simpler climbing was done with his students at the school; the more ambitious with old mountain friends, among them Gary and Konrad, who periodically paid visits. Also among the visitors was Lieutenant Sandy Bill, now at last out of hospital after his fall of the previous spring. But Sandy was not yet able to climb again; only to hike up to the base of cliffs, to watch John enviously as he maneuvered above.

Already it was in John's mind—indeed one of his major projects—to make Leysin a mountaineering center of the Alps. Soon after his arrival he was writing top climbers all over Europe and America, inviting them there; and John being the salesman he was (when the product was mountains, not encyclopedias), there was a steadily growing response. Back in Bernkastel, the "mountaineering room" in his home had been the attic. Here in Chalet Pollux it was the hillside semi-basement, and as often as not it was occupied not only by masses of gear but by gear-users as well. Increasingly, mountaineers, if not mountains, were to come to Mohammed.

In the community of Leysin the Harlins were soon well established —John more so than at Bernkastel, for his French, though long unused and still weak on verb endings, was far better than his German. Marilyn's was already more than adequate. And the children, with Johnny in grade school and Andréa in kindergarten, made the new linguistic switch with consummate ease. Most of the native population —shop- and innkeepers, craftmen and farmers—were of course neither mountaineers nor intellectuals, and like small-townsmen anywhere, had their share of provincialism. But John was to find a far closer rapport with them than with their counterparts in the Rhineland, and with not a few he became close and affectionate friends. Bernkastel, for him, had been an incidental way station. Leysin was a self-chosen home.

With the community of the American School, on the other hand, things were much as they had been back in Hahn. To the conventionally minded—who here, as there, were in the majority—he was again the maverick, the queer one, whose "footfall rang in a universe that was not theirs." To a few—the more adventuresome and freewheeling—the sound of that footfall was a call to dream and action, and John's personality the most compelling they had ever known. As in previous venues, there were defectors from the ranks of those who began by admiring him. ("He may have been great," said one, "but you got awfully tired of hearing him tell you so.") But there were also those who at first rejected him, only in the end to become converts. "In the beginning I disliked him," said one of his feminine faculty colleagues, a Russian emigrée married to a Swiss, who was old enough to be his mother. "He seemed nothing but a physical engine, a sort of dictator-athlete. . . . But as I came to know him I found so much beneath that. He had humor, understanding, compassion. His strength of spirit was as great as his strength of body." When people were converted to John, it was rarely a halfway affair of mere "liking." He became a central figure, a major influence in their lives.

En famille, by and large, things were smoother than before. Happy in his work, John was less restless, less demanding, and Johnny and Andréa were reaching ages where he found them interesting. Increasingly now, he would be spending more time with them: on outings and picnics; on hikes and easy climbs and cave explorations; when winter came, in skiing on the surrounding slopes. And this pleased Marilyn no less than the children. Though his eye, and sometimes the rest of him, still tended toward sexual wanderings—with the usual spate of accompanying gossip—there were fewer scenes, no open liaisons, and their marriage seemed to have weathered the worst of its crises.

"Do you know something, Mara?" he said. "We're going to grow old together."

15. Superjohn

One John Harlin wrote to Carlton Fuller toward the end of 1963:

"I have never before had the opportunity of watching a seasonal change in the mountains. Every moment is a treasure of experience. There is a quietness about autumn that is restful. With the lowering snowline there is a floral sleep, and the storms that bring the snow seem out of place in their violence. The greens are replaced by ambers and ochers, while an occasional late flower is a smile on the sober mountainside. Sometimes silence can scream of potential energy, but the quiet of our autumn is the restfulness of peace."

Another wrote:

"I am becoming an animal of strength by climbing and training every day. I have never had an opportunity such as this, and it seems to be turning me into some sort of mountain ape. Oh well, it is better than being in a zoo! Significant climbs have been: first ascent SW face of Tour d'Ai, second ascent of the Grand Mirroir, direct-aid first ascent of the Sphinx *à gauche*. I am keeping up my flying by giving instruction at the Montreux airport. Other projects include . . ."

One project he did not finish was this letter; others had higher priority. Foremost among them was winter climbing, and foremost in this, a return to the Eiger. He had not yet been on the north wall in winter. Few climbers had. But he had reason to believe that a *direttissima* might be more feasible at this season, when, in the grip of frost, there was less stonefall and avalanching. At the end of the past summer he had suggested such a venture to the Italians, Sorgato and Piussi, and they had agreed to try it.

In January, however, the Italians were not yet able to get away from their home bases. And the mountain ape was raring to go. As substitute partner he enlisted a Munich friend of Konrad Kirch's, a young physicist and part-time ski instructor named Hans-Albert Mayer, and soon after the first of the year they checked in at Kleine Scheidegg. They had no dreams of impossible glory. An "Eiger direct," especially in winter, would, they well knew, require more attacking force than a mere twosome could generate, and they therefore contented themselves with seeing how things would go on the old zigzag route.

The answer was not too well. On the first day, following what for John was now the milk run, they climbed up past the First Pillar, the Shattered Pillar, through the Difficult Crack, and bivouacked in a snow hole near the Hinterstoisser Traverse. So far, so good. The weather was clear, the footing firm. But during the night came double trouble, in the form of an upset stomach for Mayer and a realization by both that their clothing, and especially their boots, were not warm enough for winter Eigering. By morning, Mayer was weak from nausea; their feet were going ominously numb; and short of suicide, there was nothing to do but descend the mountain.

Next came what can only be called a one-day wonder. With his first partner *hors de combat*, John found another in the person of Martin Epp, an accomplished and ambitious Oberland guide, and shifting sights from the Eiger, set out for the north face of the neighboring Mönch. This battlement of rock and ice, almost a mile high, had been scaled just once before in winter, in a siege that took four days. But it was no *Eigerwand*, and Epp believed that, in the perfect weather now existing, two strong climbers could do it in one. John was ready to try. After a preliminary night in a hut at the foot of the face, they made their start at four in the morning, and "moving with well-machined teamwork," made fantastic progress. At noon, unslinging his walkie-talkie, John called Marilyn, who was with a school skiing party near Kleine Scheidegg, and reported that they were already more than two-thirds of the way up. But other than this, there was little talk on the ascent. As on the Frêney Pillar with Tom Frost, he and Epp "climbed encountering this or that adventure without communicating by words, but by a silent communion of experienced mountaineers." And as on the Frêney, too, the end was total success. By midafternoon, after less than twelve hours' climbing, they were atop the Mönch—with an easy descent route—in another notable victory of John's climbing career.

Sorgato and Piussi had not yet come up from Italy, but he was still in no mood to bide his time. With Rick Horn, a climber-skier from Colorado who was one of his assistants at Leysin, he took off for the Mont Blanc range and the Aiguille de Blaitière. On this rock spire he had long had his eye on two climbs: a new *direttissima* up its sheer west face, and a first winter ascent of the face by a route known as the Brown Crack. This being winter, the Brown was the choice; and he and Horn did a noble job on it, surmounting all its worst difficulties before turning back, short of the summit, in the face of an oncoming snowstorm. More impressed than if they had gone to the top, the French and Swiss press hailed the climb both as a triumph of skill (for what they had done) and of judgment (for what they had not).

Then Leysin again. . . . The Eiger again. . . . And this time the Italians were there. Indeed, instead of two, there were four of them, for Sorgato and Piussi had brought along two companions, thus bringing the team to what they felt was the ideal size. Throughout the autumn there had been much correspondence about ways and means, routes and equipment. And now, at the base of the peak, there was time for more preparation, as the Eiger, with its usual perversity, went into a phase of storm. This being a *direttissima* assault, the path of ascent would be a new one virtually all the way up the north wall— starting with the takeoff place, a few hundred yards east of the old one. And here, in late February, with the return of fair weather, the climb at last began.

In effect, they were not merely on a new route but a new mountain. There was no First or Shattered Pillar, no Difficult Crack or Hinterstoisser Traverse. After the preliminary snow slopes and broken cliffs, the wall soared up to the First Icefield in a bulging precipice that was later to be called the First Band. On this, through the first day, the five battled their way upward, contending with great steepness, great cold, and endless ice-clogged crevices which had to be laboriously cleared before pitons could be hammered into the rock. Still—as always in hard climbing—John rejoiced. He was on his Eiger again. He felt strength welling within him. Looking up, he thrilled to "the harmless powder snow avalanches, starting thousands of feet above and coming down like great veils, occasionally pluming out from the face in the wind." . . . Then, moments later, peering down into a nearby couloir, it was to see the mountain in its other guise: "—a blackened arm, with the hand in a position of supplication, sticking out from the snow." . . . It was obviously that of a climber long since fallen. And there was nothing to do. Toward dusk they found a snow cave dug by a German party who had made an unsuccessful *direttissima* attempt a few weeks earlier; and here they dug in for the night.

Theirs was a strangely assorted team—with four Italians plus one American from Kansas City, by way of California and way stations. And even the Italians were strangely matched: especially the two close partners, Roberto Sorgato and Ignazio Piussi. Sorgato, slight and lithe, was a member of a prosperous Milanese family and a university student of business administration. Piussi, a bear of a man of peasant stock, came from a mountain village near the Yugoslavian border, where the chief occupation was in theory dairying but in practice smuggling. And it was he, particularly, by whom John was impressed. For one thing, by his power. (He was one of only two men he had ever known— Paul Revak being the other—who he felt might be his match in physical combat.) For another, by his daring. (On their descent of the Eiger's west ridge the previous summer, he had launched into a wild glissade down its snow slopes, which even John, for all his derring-do, had been hard put to follow.) He was all man, this giant from Venezia Giulia, and almost literally, a yard wide.

Like most peasants, however, he had his set ways of doing things, and they differed vastly from John's. The ex-Air Force pilot, with his walkie-talkie, paid close attention to radioed weather reports. The bear from the hill country favored his nose and a wet finger. In eating, John relied on prepared and concentrated foods that would give him a maximum of nourishment from a minimum of bulk. Piussi's pack bulged with sausages, cheeses, and fat loaves of bread. A particular irritation to him was John's practice of often climbing without gloves, so as, by controlled exposure, to inure his hands against frostbite. (Anyone but a crazy American would stay comfortable while he could.) And John in turn was annoyed by Piussi's ironclad rejection of anything new. On the "Eiger direct," to be sure, there was no gladiatorial confrontation. Ignorant of each other's languages, they could not even argue, except through the multilingual Sorgato. But storm clouds often hovered as the two proud and powerful men matched tradition against tradition and will against will.

As for nature's storm clouds, they were, for the time, permissive. During its second day on the face, in continuing fair weather, the team worked its way up the steepness of the First Band. They had not gone far when they encountered a second gruesome reminder of the Eiger's history: this time a dismembered leg that, from boot and trouser, they identified as belonging to one of the two Spaniards who had been lost on the wall the previous summer. Again, there was nothing to do. They climbed on. In the early afternoon they reached a point, about 2500 feet up, where the wall began to thrust outward in a huge overhang; and here they established their second bivouac. With several hours of daylight remaining, however, John and Sorgato reconnoitered another few hundred feet up the precipice, while Piussi and the two other Italians brought up supplies and made a habitable camp.

That evening came the first bad portent—at least for John—when Radio Geneva reported approaching foul weather. And the next morning the report was repeated. With conditions still satisfactory on the mountain itself, it was decided to go on with the climb, but as a precaution, to return that night to the already established bivouac. Reversing the roles of the previous day, John and Sorgato now worked at hauling loads, while Piussi and the other two went up in the lead; and on their return in the evening they announced that they had strung fixed ropes all the way to the First Icefield. With this, the First Band, the initial obstacle on the *direttissima*, had been mastered. That night, the spirits of the climbers were high and hopeful.

The weather, however, put an end to that. On the morning of their fourth day on the wall, not only the radio but the sky announced the coming storm, in terms unmistakable even to the skeptical Piussi. With a few hours of grace left to them, they all ascended the fixed ropes to the First Icefield, and even probed for a way on the wall above it.

But then the wind rose. Snow-laden clouds moved in. Roping down to their bivouac, they traversed to the nearby tunnel windows of the Jungfraujoch Railway, which provided a welcome, if undramatic, escape hatch.

Their effort was at an end. They did not have the resources to wait out the storm and then renew the attack. But before their tunnel descent to the valley, one final touch was to be added to their defeat. During one of his radio talks with Kleine Scheidegg, John had reported their discovery of an arm and a leg; and now, when he called from the tunnel windows to announce their abandonment of the climb, word came up that the Grindelwald police urgently required one or both to establish legal proof of the climber's death. The arm was too far below to retrieve. But the leg was fairly close by. Roping down, John found it, put it in his pack, and prusiked back up to the windows through the wind and snow of the rising storm. There were times when mountaineering was less fun than at others.

Up the Leysin hillside from the American School and Chalet Pollux stood another erstwhile sanitarium that was now the Club Vagabond. Half hotel, half youth hostel, it had become a year-round center for wandering, non-studying students—largely American, Canadian, and British—who for one reason or another loved the mountain world. On winter nights the skis were ranged in long rows against the outer walls; inside flowed beer and *Glühwein* and the sound of voices singing. Sometimes it was Joan Baez or Bob Dylan on the hi-fi. Sometimes it was the denizens themselves, joined in chorus, and one of their favorites, locally composed and improvised, was known as *Big John Harlin:*

> . . . *alone on the Eiger*
> *with his ice ax in his hand,*
> *hell bent for death and glory*
> *to climb the Murderwand. . . .*

How far the tongue was in the cheek depended on the singer. Some knew John only by name and fame, or as an on-and-off visitor to the Vagabond: a powerful figure of a man in a red jacket or sweater, shoving his long blond hair back from his eyes as he talked earnestly, spellbindingly, to fellow mountaineers. Others knew him well—the mountaineers, old friends, new friends (and enemies) at the school and college—and for some he was a hero, for some an anti-hero, but for all he was squarely at stage center. . . . "He was like a king with his court," said one. . . . "Like a film star with his fans," said another. . . . "Like something out of Wagner or *Ein Heldenleben.*" . . . "He was full of charisma." . . . "What John was full of," said still another, "was bullshit. But he was a bullshitter who *did* things, and we all knew it."

More than ever, the myths multiplied around him. As a boy (or a man, or a child), he had killed a man (or several men) in Rome (or elsewhere). As a boy (or child), he had climbed the north face of the Matterhorn (or was it the Eiger?). He had been a brilliant dress designer with Balmain and Dior. He was a graduate of Annapolis. He had been an All-American in football and a medal winner in the 1960 Olympics. Even Marilyn reaped her kudos, for she was both a Doctor of Philosophy (or possibly Science) and one of the world's top women mountaineers. Presumably she had been so busy climbing and writing dissertations that she had failed to notice that John had had more mistresses than Don Juan and Casanova combined.

Beth Little of Sequoia High School had noted it years before: John had an aura. The golden shorts were gone, but the blond god remained. At the Club Vagabond they chanted, *"It's a bird—it's a plane —it's Superjohn!"* . . . "And do you know," said one of the chanters, "sometimes after a few beers I wasn't sure if we were kidding or not."

If there was one thing that outnumbered myths, it was projects. He would return to the Eiger, of course. He had plans for bigger climbs than ever on the *aiguilles* of Mont Blanc. But also, as in the days of HASL, his thoughts were moving out past the Alps to farther horizons. With Konrad Kirch, Pierre Mazeaud, and others, he was envisioning a joint German-French-American attack on K2 in the Karakorams. Beyond that, and on a still larger scale, was what he called his "Great Walls of the Earth" venture: an expedition, or series of expeditions, to various huge unclimbed mountain faces in several continents, from Yosemite to the Andes and Norway to Nepal. About this latter he wrote enthusiastically to Carlton Fuller, in the hope that the American Alpine Club might help in its financing. The first reply was not encouraging, but he kept on planning and corresponding.

He did not limit himself to the realm of mountains. With Marilyn he revived their much-discussed idea of going to back-country South America—or now, perhaps, British Columbia—for a two- or three-year experiment in subsistence wilderness living. To old friend Arne Arneson, still at Hahn, he was writing about a possible scuba diving trip to Tahiti or East Africa. And also Africa-oriented, though very differently, was a correspondence with Roy Brown, now doing public health work in Uganda, in which he explored the possibilities of federation for the new nations of that continent. Just what he expected to *do* about African politics is unclear. But the irrelevance or "far-outness" of a scheme never fazed John in the slightest; nor did the fact that most of his projects, in terms of time and place, were mutually exclusive. In their proliferation, however, he was perhaps being more realistic than fanciful. Even to him it must have been apparent that the odds were high against such Grand Designs, and in sheer number there was at least added hope that *something* would materialize.

Closer to home, he was still nurturing his dream of starting his own school. From the beginning, he had thought of his job at Leysin as a short-term stint, designed to give him a working acquaintance with academic affairs; and more than ever before he was casting about for the many components that would make the plan work. Further, he had now set himself a simpler and more immediate goal: the establishment at Leysin of a mountaineering school that would operate during the summers. Unlike the "big" school, this would require no property and little money. The key ingredients would be his own talents and reputation, plus an able corps of assistants, and both were readily available.

Finally, and underlying all else, there was his desire to write. Since coming to Leysin he had revised the two short stories he had written at Bernkastel and sent them off (so far unsuccessfully) to American magazines. In his account of the Fou climb, prepared for the *American Alpine Journal*, he had consciously striven to get away from the usual technical dry-as-dust style of journal prose and enliven the story with color and comment. For the last Eiger climb with the Italians, he had reached an agreement with *Life* that, if the venture was successful, he would write the story—for a handsome fee. And though the *if* had not been realized, he was hopeful that a similar deal could be made for future enterprises. Most keenly and ambitiously of all, he wanted to write a book: a book based on his experience both as mountaineer and flier: not merely an account of events and accomplishments, but a penetration in depth into the twin "dimensions" of his life. In his desk at Chalet Pollux he already had a drawer full of notes for it. And he had a title: *Introspection Through Adventure*.

He had not yet, however, forged chains strong enough to hold him to that desk. He was up and off to the school gymnasium, and from there to his ski classes on the winter heights. Indoors and outdoors, he was a hard taskmaster. "Boy, how he used to torture us with chinning and pushups!" one of his students recalled. "But there was always a grin somewhere underneath, and when you'd done what he wanted you to, you felt like a champion." Up on the white slopes, too, it was *la vie dur* that he offered: no up-in-a-lift and a downhill breeze, but rugged cross-country going "that would leave tongues hanging right down to the snow." The softies became experts in excuses for non-attendance. The tough ones sucked in their tongues and earned the nod of the master.

As he had hoped, he was attracting many topflight climber-skiers to Leysin, and several became his full- or part-time assistants at the school. Among them were Stewart Fulton, along with his brother Alec, and in their wake a squad of other Scots and Englishmen. They were a colorful lot, this new breed of British mountaineer: a by-product of their country's "mod" revolution and a far cry from the traditional Oxbridge gentleman-sportsman. Stew Fulton was by trade an electrician. Another, Don Whillans, was a plumber. Most had come to the mountains from the working class districts of Britain's big industrial cities, and they were a rough-and-ready, brawling, hard-nosed crew. Along with their toughness, characteristically, went a barbed, often bitter wit, and at Leysin not a little of it was directed at John. His Grand Designs, his talk of mountaineering esthetics and introspection, were to them, in a word, bullshit; and it was they who composed the mock-heroics of the *Big John Harlin* song. But they were the first to admit that he was a bullshitter who could perform.

Among Americans who became part of the scene were Ted Wilson, from Utah, and Tom Walsh, late of Stanford, who in the days to come were to be among John's closest friends. Konrad came and went. As did Gary. Like John, Gary was feeling the urge to write—in his case a novel—and in the off seasons for mountaineering was wandering and odd-jobbing around Europe. More often at Chalet Pollux was his now long-time girl friend, Claude Guerre-Gentons, who had become very close to the Harlins, and particularly Marilyn. "Girl friend" seems scarcely the *mot juste* for her, nor does "mistress"; for she was a remarkable young woman—a university graduate, a *lycée* teacher of classics in Grenoble, and on the side no mean mountaineer. From the beginning, Gary the Footloose had made it clear to her that he was not the marrying sort, and this she had wholly accepted. Indeed, she had decided that, whatever her status, she wanted a child by Gary, and early in 1964 she gave birth to a son. Though he was now rarely around and contributed nothing to their support, French law permitted Gary—as he wished—to acknowledge legal paternity. And from now on, while his father roamed, there was often chez Harlin, along with Johnny and Andréa, a third and youngest child named Laurent Hemming.

In the spring came a visitor of a different sort. Jerry Robertson, now a helicopter pilot in the Air Force, reappeared—this time not from the States but on leave from Vietnam, where he was instructing Viet airmen in the ways of the chopper. And the reunion left John with ambivalent feelings. On the one hand, he was still no Hawk; his abhorrence of war's insensate destruction remained as strong as when, at Hahn, he had requested transfer from fighter-bombing. On the other, he had been trained for years in the skills of combat flying, with never the chance to put those skills to the test. He would have loved, just once, to gun up into that wild blue yonder and show a North Viet Red Baron how a plane should be flown.

It was never to happen. Jerry left. John remained. And on balance, one feels, he was not too regretful. He was a fighter, yes; but a warrior, no. When he did battle, it was with a will, a drive, a power that few men ever, anywhere, have been able to match. But as an antagonist he preferred a mountain to his fellow men.

As at Bernkastel, his parents made frequent appearances. In another two years, his father, at sixty, would reach the mandatory retirement age for a TWA pilot, and there was much talk of a partnership in John's school project, with John I in the role of business manager. There was even a venture with his mother in prospect (to be added to the list, perhaps, as Project 99B): the establishment in Leysin of an art and gift shop. One prospective item for sale about which he was enthusiastic were twisted cypress snags from the cliffs of the Calanques, on the Riviera, and he went so far as to place a "feeler" ad in the

European edition of the *New York Times.* In the end, nothing came of the scheme, but it at least indicated further progress in John's relationship with his mother. He was on far easier ground with her as a man than as a boy.

He himself went again to the Calanques that spring, along with Sandy Bill, now wholly recovered from his accident. And Marilyn, too, got down to the Riviera, taking a group of her biology students to the Oceanographic Institute in Monaco. Then, with summer, there came for her a long-planned and far bigger trip: a two-month visit, with Johnny and Andréa, to home country in Washington. It was the first time in four and a half years that either she or John had set foot in America.

Summer. . . .

The sun shone (sometimes).

And John returned to the heights.

Item One in his program, however, was not *what* but *with whom.* Without its having been put into so many words, he and Gary had reached a realization that they could no longer climb together amicably. Konrad Kirch was off on a German expedition to the Hindu Kush in Afghanistan. Other old companions also proved unavailable for one reason or another, and for his first effort he teamed up with a young American named Lee Herral, one of the many peripatetic climbers who had been drawn into his orbit at Leysin. His objective was unfinished business on the Blaitière—this time not the Brown Crack, which he had all but climbed during the winter, but the other route on his mind, the west face direct. Their attempt ended when John, leading high on the peak, took a jarring, though not crippling, sixty-foot fall. But a week later he was back—now with Frenchman Pierre Mazeaud as partner—and together they accomplished a first ascent in two days of rugged going.

Next: the Eiger. Again, always, the Eiger. Having had a winter *direttissima* try with the Italians, he now wanted to see how it would go in summer, and with two other Frenchmen, the guides René Desmaison and André Bertrand, launched an attack in early July. As he had feared, the stonefall on the direct route was tremendous. On the sheer walls they were repeatedly hit by plunging debris. But they escaped serious injury, and after thirty-six hours had climbed well past his previous high point to the upper margin of the Second Icefield. As usual, temporarily clear skies had brought out rival teams: one of them none other than old confreres Sorgato and Piussi. If the weather had held, there might have been an interesting and productive joining of forces. But—the usual but—the weather didn't. On the third morning, clouds moved in, the wind rose, snow lashed the mountainside, and all hands had to beat a retreat.

The storm continued. French and Italians went their separate ways. After a quick look-in at Leysin, where school was recessed for the summer, John returned to Chamonix—and yet another campaign. For years now he had had his eye on the west face of the great spire called the Aiguille du Dru. Back in 1960, with Jerry Robertson, he had made an abortive attempt on it; in 1961 he and Gary had eyed it speculatively; and in 1963, with Konrad Kirch and Tom Frost, he had made a second unproductive stab. Like virtually all the great Alpine walls, it had been scaled by several routes, including one forged by Gary and Royal Robbins in 1962. But it had not yet been done *direttissima*—in the clean straight-upward line that was now John's climbing passion—and he was resolved that he, of all men, was the one to do it. During the rest of this summer and into the next, it became for him a project almost as compelling as the Eiger.

His first choice as partner would have been Robbins, who not only knew the peak but was perhaps the finest rock climber in the world (and the Dru was all rock); but the Californian was back home and unavailable. By correspondence, however, he had recommended a young mountaineer named Rafael Tejada-Flores, Bolivian by birth, American by adoption, who was currently in the Alps. And by mid-July John and Lito, as he was known, were together at the base of the Dru. . . . More technically, one must add, the Petit Dru. The famous west face of the *aiguille* is not part of its main mass but of a slightly smaller sub-peak. . . . Still, there was nothing *petit* about it except its name. As they began their climb, the sheer, diamond-shaped wall rose above them in 3500 feet of soaring granite.

On the first day, the attack went well. With another climber, an Englishman from the Cambridge Mountaineering Club, in support, they negotiated the lower reaches of the face, known as the Gray Ledges, and when night came, bivouacked at the top of the ledges, already at an airy height. Above them, however, was still the monolithic part of the precipice, speaking loudly, said John, of "small man, damn big mountain." And the next day they were inching on through a world of verticality and bristling overhangs. "At the top of one of these," John recorded, "I bade Lito take the lead to give me a rest. I was anchored just on top of the lip of the overhang on a small ledge to the side of my anchor pins. A little above me, Lito and a flake disagreed as to relative security, the pin popped out, and down came Lito. I was pulled from my stance. The anchor held, while I in turn held Lito from falling an additional 150 feet by the rope around my back." Lito was caught all right. But not his pack. Down it went, first falling free, then bumping and bouncing 1500 feet to the foot of the mountain. And with it, and the food and gear it contained, went any hope of continuing. Through the rest of the day, disgusted, they rappeled down the precipice—to be greeted en route by the added indignity of a crashing storm.

In quest of sun and solace, they went off to the Dolomites. Then Lito had to move on, while John returned for a second go at the Dru with Pierre Mazeaud and Roberto Sorgato. On this one there was no fall, but the storm came earlier: almost at the same spot where Lito had tumbled. And again there was retreat and evacuation—this time, for John, until the following year.

With Sandy Bill, he went off once more to the Calanques. Then, returning to the Mont Blanc area, he joined up with still another new partner, a twenty-two-year-old Scotsman named Dougal Haston. In spite of his youth, Haston was already known as a top climber, and the previous year had been one of the second British team to climb the Eiger's north wall. In appearance, and largely in manner, he was very different from most of his hard-bitten compatriots: tall, slim, and fine-boned, with the face of an actor or a romantic poet. But on a mountain he was a tiger, and John was happy to have him as a ropemate. The goal they set themselves was the Shroud, a huge icy gully, never climbed, that furrows the wall of the Grandes Jorasses close by the Walker Spur.

One menace of the route was falling rock. Another was its extreme steepness: from 75 to 85 degrees, almost all of it on ice. At such an angle the use of an ax was impossible. They climbed on the front points of their crampons, stabbing the wall with ice daggers and inserting protective screws at intervals of ten feet or less. "All movement," said John, "was delicate and took intense concentration. The ice ascended and ascended for two thousand feet, with no ledge nor opportunity to place a rock piton for a comparatively secure rest. I had to fill my mind with images of security to continue to pressure myself up that great gray sheet." After a full day of this, plus a long search, they found a ledge of loose boulders on which they huddled for the night. But the next dawn brought storm warnings and rocks roaring down the gully. After a further advance of a few rope lengths they faced up to the fact that they were courting disaster, and called a halt. As it was, their descent, in rappel after rappel, proved almost as difficult as the climb upward, and toward its end they were enveloped in one of the worst storms of the year.

That was the end of the 1964 summer campaign. Marilyn and the children would soon be returning, the school at Leysin reopening. In terms of certified successes it had not been up to previous seasons; out of many attempts, the Blaitière had been the only peak climbed to the top. Yet John was far from dissatisfied. His goals had been immensely ambitious. He had enjoyed the struggles, learning much in the process, and had got on well with most of his partners. In particular, he had got on well with Dougal Haston—indeed, considered him an almost ideal teammate—and no sooner was the Shroud venture over than he was talking to him earnestly about the Eiger Direct.

Another by-product of the summer—and an important one—was its effect on his marriage. Not since his early days in the Air Force had he and Marilyn been separated for so long a period, and in spite of his activity he found he missed her vastly. As always, he was an erratic correspondent. It was from Washington that she wrote, during a long silence, "Still no word. Are you alive? For God's sake *LET ME KNOW.*" Yet, when he did write, it was as he had written years before when they were a boy and girl in love. . . . "Mara, I don't think I can describe the loneliness, the complete desolation. . . . I miss you so. I love you ad infinitum. . . . Oh Mara, Mara. . . ."

They were human—and almost nine years married. The second honeymoon would not continue quite as rapturously as all that, but after the

212

summer's separation their relationship was unquestionably better than before. He knew now, very clearly, that he needed her; that, much as he prized freedom, he was no Gary Hemming, built to roam untrammeled. Proof positive, at least for Marilyn, came on the late August day when she and the children arrived back in Europe, landing in Luxembourg, and found him waiting at the airport. "Down in the Oberland it was perfect Eiger weather," she said wonderingly, gratefully. "And yet there he was, meeting *me*."

Administratively, the Leysin American School was not a Gibraltar among institutions. When it began its 1964 fall term, it was with a new headmaster—the sixth in its three years of existence—and the usual large turnover in faculty, putting the second-year Harlins among the comparative veterans. Back home, during the summer, Marilyn had attended courses at the Friday Harbor Marine Laboratory of the University of Washington, and now felt herself on sounder footing in her teaching. John's staff of athletic assistants was able and dedicated. Whatever the problems of the school, they were happy there, and with each other.

. . . Or at least as happy as John knew how to be, in his restlessness, his ambition, his eternal drive to the elsewhere. As always, he was enormously active. Scarcely a day passed on which he was not up on the peaks around Leysin, either as instructor with his students or, with fellow experts, performing ever more difficult feats on their walls and buttresses. For Marilyn, hope sprang eternal that he would ease off on his more ambitious and dangerous ventures. As after his 1962 Eiger climb (and perhaps overweighting his appearance at the Luxembourg airport), she again wrote to her parents: "John is losing his enthusiasm for high-powered climbing." But again, this was strictly wishful thinking. Through the fall, like a Chief of Staff in the Pentagon War Room, he was meticulously plotting the next year's campaigns on Eiger and Dru.

By mail came an actual communiqué from the military. He had at last been promoted to the rank of captain—in the Air Force Reserve. But it was a voice from the past, without meaning or relevance. He was far more interested in his fourth annual trip to the Trento Festival, at which he was now an accredited star of the first magnitude.

213

And in an invitation from London to address the Alpine Club, oldest and loftiest of mountaineering organizations. Up the hill, in the lounge of Club Vagabond, the voices sang louder than ever of

> . . . *direttissima, glory on the wall*
> *for Big John Harlin, greatest of them all.* . . .

Then came another invitation, from farther afield than either Trento or London; and in December, a few months after Marilyn's return, he was off on his own first trip to the United States in almost five years. It was as guest of the American Alpine Club, with expenses paid, and in Boston he was the principal speaker at the club's annual dinner. Introduced by President Carlton Fuller as "a mountaineer extraordinary," he told of his climbs on the Eiger and elsewhere and interjected a strong plea for more internationalism in mountaineering. American climbers thronged to hear and meet the Man of Mystery who, in absentia, had become the best known of them all. And he, for his part, met many potential partners for future ventures. Most exciting to him was an invitation to join an expedition, already organized and financed, to Kangchenjunga, third highest mountain in the world. With it, his long-held hope of climbing in the Himalayas seemed at last about to be realized. But in the end there was again disappointment, when political permission from India failed to materialize.

Other activities and projects multiplied. In Boston, he spoke also before a large turnout of the Appalachian Mountain Club. In New York, he submitted some of his writings to a literary agent and was much heartened when the agent showed a lively interest. In Washington, he presented several plans for both mountaineering and writing to the National Geographic Society, which was also receptive. And everywhere he promoted interest in his projected school of mountaineering, which he now hoped to launch during the following summer. When he returned to Europe, it was with no contracts or advances in his pocket. But he had built some sound bridges toward the future, and was never again to feel as isolated as in the past from his own country and countrymen.

Not the least of his experiences on the trip was his flight back across the Atlantic. The plane was a TWA jet; its captain was John E. Harlin I; and this was the first time since childhood that John had flown with his father as pilot. Later, he wrote to his mother from Leysin:

"My admiration for Dad was heightened, if that's possible, by the great opportunity of watching him at the controls of the 707. It's not that he just flew it, but flew it with that rare ability of being so ahead of it. There existed a tremendous margin of safety that most pilots don't approach. It was a thrill I'll never forget."

It was not often that Superjohn was a passive spectator. But he knew a good job when he saw one.

16. Perspectives

". . . on the uppermost european up, the upperest up of mont blanc, in winter too and three were we and strong but mindwisely tormented by the alternative downs from the uppermost up . . . Of we three was john harlin and a plan of boldness and burningly down the hidden frêncy and bivouac and up and bivouac until it was done and down for the glory of winter firsts. We three wax winter strong at 14,000 feet and are reflectingly proud for no other reason than that it is difficult. . . . Nothing idealistic here. Brutal harsh physical and mental strain tempered by the magnificent feeling of overcoming and watching others overcoming. Incredible impressions of scenery and performance stored for retrospective enjoyment. Downward, fantastic stormcloud-filtered sun hazily touching alpine strugglefields. . . ."

James Joyce had not come to the mountains. It was Dougal Haston writing in the *Scottish Mountaineering Club Journal* of a ski trip in the winter of 1965. With Bob Boucher of Colorado, a new mountaineer in winter too and three were we and strong but mindwisely tormented on the Leysin roster, he and John made a three-day tour of the highest peaks in the Alps: carrying seventy pounds each; fighting wind and snowstorm; now racing, themselves at wind-speed, down miles of whiteness; now with skis on their shoulders, hip deep in whiteness, struggling to gain a yard of steep uphill. With markings hidden by blown snow, they took turns falling into crevasses. But they were either caught by their skis or held by their rope, and were pulled out uninjured. When they came down to Chamonix, it was from a high-level trek that had been accomplished in winter only once before.

It had been John's original hope to make a first winter ascent of one of the Frêney Pillars, but old debbil weather had precluded even a serious attempt. And such, too, proved the case with the Eiger. He and Dougal Haston had now definitively become partners for the north wall *direttissima*. Throughout the winter, by observation and report, they kept their eye on the mountain. Once, during a fair spell, they actually set foot on it, emerging from the railway windows and reconnoitering up to the First Icefield. But conditions were bad. Soon new storms came. The climb of climbs had to be deferred, at least until summer.

In Leysin, John continued his skiing. Increasingly, in his non-teaching hours, he went out with his family; for Marilyn had developed a love of the sport, in its less rugged aspects, and the children were already well past the novice class. Johnny, in particular, was something of a nine-year-old wonder: a slight, almost fragile-looking boy, as his father had been at his age, but quick, graceful, and controlled on even the steepest of runs. Big John, on the other hand, was still primarily a "muscle skier," possessed of fantastic strength and endurance, but no virtuoso in technique; and in sheer style of performance Johnny often outshone him. Half of John glowed with paternal pride. The other half, the half that was still small boy himself, was rather less than delighted that a peanut—even his own peanut—could excel him.

With his teenage students he had no such problem; none was yet up to Johnny's standard. And once this led, literally, to the brink of disaster. During a skiing session on the heights above Leysin, two of the boys lost control while schussing and, veering off course, went tumbling down a steep ice slope. Even for John, the slope was unskiable. Removing his boards, he started down on foot, taking with him one of his abler charges, a boy called Dal Cottrell. But after a few steps Dal slipped and also tumbled. Lunging to catch him, John was

218

knocked from his footholds. Presently, instead of two, there were four figures sprawled at all angles at the bottom of the ice slope. But again the Harlin luck held good, with no more than bumps and bruises for either himself or his flock.

Soon after came the most ambitious of his school skiing projects. This was a traverse of the famous *Haute Route* of the Alps, a high and formidable trail leading across miles of wild mountain country between Zermatt and Chamonix. And he and the best of his students made about half the distance, up and down over glaciers and passes, before bad weather drove them off and down by way of a transverse valley. It is interesting, perhaps significant, to note that the start of the trip marked John's first return to the Zermatt area since the long-gone summer of 1955. In his past five years of intensive activity all over the Alps, he had not once climbed in the surrounding range of the Pennines, with its Matterhorn, Weisshorn, Monte Rosa, and host of other great peaks. Now, setting off on the *Haute Route*, he was at the very foot of the Matterhorn's north face, where he and Rip Collins had once groped through baffling darkness. But what thoughts went through his mind, as to what he had once done—and not done—there, must be left to our imaginations.

Winter withdrew. The snows receded upward, and skis were relegated to sheds and basements. In their place were rope and ax, piton and carabiner, as John and companions headed toward the wall of the Grand Mirroir in the nearby Argentine Valley.

"... A day in spring," he wrote joyfully; "a scented day, cool air, warm sun, and life bubbling from every seam. . . . We crossed the stream high, where two forks cut the volume of water. Leaving the valley behind, we gained altitude through meadows and gullies, gradually passing from one zone of spring to another—from a land ecstatically awake to one still a little drowsy from the long winter's sleep. . . . While the valley of the Argentine slowly miniaturized, the great tilted mirror of rock rose more and more proud. One always becomes aware of a certain personal insignificance and pretentiousness under these walls, just as they in turn seem small when flying above them, and *ad infinitum* from perspective over perspective. . . ."

His own perspectives were, as always, multiple. And some were far, and some were near. One of the nearest was what he had decided to call the International School of Modern Mountaineering (ISMM—director: John Harlin), which would begin operations during the coming summer. What small financing was needed would come from Bev Clark, the wealthy young Englishman he had met in Wales in 1960, who, like so many others, had been drawn by John to Leysin and now made it his part-time home. Allan Rankin, the Canadian co-owner of Club Vagabond, would provide board and lodging for clients, and American Ted Wilson would serve as business manager. Back in the States, brochures, prepared by John, were being distributed by Tom Frost, Royal Robbins, Jim McCarthy, and other well-known mountaineers. And as fellow instructors, along with his already existing staff at the Leysin School, John was confident he could enlist top climbers from many countries.

It was his hope, of course, that the venture would be profitable. But money *per se* never ranked high in his priorities, as against the propagation of the Harlin creed. Among ISMM purposes, as stated in its brochure, were: *To enable the individual to introspect into his character and then build upon it through analysis and adventure. . . . To strive, through the study of perfection in the sport of mountaineering, to understand and express our lives in the environment of our choice.* Here as ever, behind more mundane matters, loomed the image of the Grand Design.

Also tailored to large ideals was his still simmering project of an academic school. It would, he had now determined, be called the Summit School. It would be located in, or close to, Leysin. It would be international and multilingual. For it, too, he had prepared a brochure, listing as its objectives:

1. *Thorough academic preparation for discerning universities*
2. *Understanding of the world community*
3. *National and international leadership*
4. *Character building through adventure*

But this had not, like the ISMM prospectus, been printed and distributed. For the Summit, the perspective from dream to reality was still a long one.

Meanwhile, of course, there were the summits of another sort. He was corresponding with Haston and others about the Eiger. And knowing by now that *direttissimas* were complex, and therefore expensive, ventures, he was in quest of backing from a magazine or newspaper.

For the second objective, the Dru, he already had what he considered the ideal partner: Royal Robbins, the great Yosemite cragsman, whom he had first met in the Calanques in 1962. He had again seen Robbins during his American visit, with the upshot that he was coming to Leysin for the summer as a staff member of John's mountaineering school. And with the Dru a mere few miles distant beyond the Dents du Midi, it would be easy for them to get there during breaks in the schedule.

As throughout his mountain career, he not only planned his ascents; he trained for them. Indeed—now that the Air Force no longer competed for his time—his training was probably as complete and rigorous as an athlete has ever undertaken for any sport. Workouts in calisthenics, climbing, skiing were merely a part of it. He not only often climbed without gloves. He skied without them: holding snowballs in his hands, when they were free, to toughen and inure them. He took meticulous care not only of the more obvious components of his physical engine, such as muscle and wind, but of all of it—skin and bone, eyes and ears, teeth and toes. Directly before and during a major climb, he paid great attention to diet. And in this, biologist Marilyn, who had strong opinions on the subject, aided and abetted: plying him with liver for breakfast, blackstrap molasses, yogurt and wheat germ, carrot and dandelion juice. Others joined the Italian Piussi in making fun of his menus. "Let them," said John. His goal was a perfect engine, perfectly fueled.

—Not only that, but more. He went beyond the engine to the engineer, beyond the body to the mind and nervous system. They too should be exercised, he believed. And he wrote: "In a life-threatening situation most people's minds and consequently their bodies are overloaded. So they give up, through fear and lack of self-control. It is possible to make an accurate analysis of physical reserves, and to make an unemotional coordinated application of these reserves. The result is perfect physical and mental control of mind and body in this particular experience."

Control, self-control, are the key words here. And the key to John's credo of all-out effort. He was convinced that mind and will "can make the body do things it doesn't want to." And not only can but must. One of his skiing pupils had not forgotten the day when, up on the slopes, he told John he was feeling cold, and John replied, not jokingly,

"It's good for you to be cold." He was a man of many mystiques, and not the least of them was the mystique of the Ordeal; of overcoming the ordeal and, through it, weakness and fear. If he demanded much of others, he demanded still more of himself. If he found joy on the heights, he endured much to win it. Another of America's best mountaineers, Yvon Chouinard, has written of climbs such as John's that they can be made only by those "who have the desire and perseverance needed to withstand the intense suffering which is a prerequisite for the creation of any great work of art." And that is precisely what mountaineering was to John Harlin—a work of art. And of love.

Now summer came, his eighth summer in the Alps, and sixth in succession. . . .

But it was far from up and off to high conquest. For one thing, holding him down, there was the opening of the climbing school, and for another there was the weather. By now, the reader is probably sick and tired of Alpine weather; and so too are the alpinists, who will assure you that each succeeding summer is the worst in man's memory. The summer of 1965, however, *was* the worst. So badly did it start, even at the relatively low level of Leysin, that John took his first school group down to the Calanques for their indoctrination.

Back on home grounds, between storms, the classes continued: on the Sphinx, Tour d'Ai, Grand Mirroir, and other rock peaks roundabout. Royal Robbins had appeared and served as second-in-command. Stew Fulton and Don Whillans were on hand, together with another front-rank British climber, Mick Burke; and on a lower level of expertise, Bev Clark, Allan Rankin, and Ted Wilson helped out. Intermittently, old partners of John's appeared, among them Gary Hemming and Konrad Kirch. But notably absent, at least to the students, were several impressive names that had been announced in the brochure. In another of his "instant fusions" John had listed therein virtually the whole aristocracy of Alpine climbing; and as had happened before, hope and fact did not totally jibe.

In this, its first year, ISMM was scarcely besieged by clients. And this was just as well, for it was not running like clockwork. Staff members, with climbing projects of their own, had a way of vanishing without warning. As in other ventures, John was strong on the "big picture," weak in what Bev Clark called "squalid details," and there was a spate of strayed equipment, forgotten lunches, and scrambled bookkeeping. Most serious, perhaps, was a weakness in adapting instruction to the capabilities of individual students. John liked to think he was interested in beginners. But he wasn't. The teaching he enjoyed was at the Ph.D. level. What he wanted of the novices was for them to stop being novices as quickly as possible; and some, finding the climbs on which they were taken too rich for their blood, dropped out in short order.

These are the minuses. But there were also plusses. And they too were largely centered on John. Elsewhere in the Alps there were a few schools and hundreds of individual guides who taught climbing; but one is safe in doubting if any even approached him in breadth and depth of purpose, or in missionary zeal. In certain items, his brochure promised more than he could deliver. But his Grand Design, as expressed there, was no hogwash, and all who came to him found it out. In John's company, or under his tutelage, you did not merely climb a mountain; you lived a mountain. It was an adventure not only of the body but of the mind and spirit. Many things in ISMM still needed straightening out, but even in its first year it was something new and exciting under the Alpine sun.

—If there had been a sun.

Day after day, the Leysin peaklets were draped in mist, and from the observation points above the town there was little to see but miles of storm. The Eiger, always slow to return to good condition, appeared definitely out for the summer; but John and Robbins clung to hope for the Dru, whose vertical granite would shed snow more quickly. Twice during July they drove to Chamonix and climbed hopefully up to its base. Each time, however, they barely made a start before fresh storms repulsed them.

Finally, toward mid-August, they made a third try—the fifth for John in two years. And this time (by now, almost to their astonishment) they were able to keep going. As ever, the break in the weather had brought out "armies" of other climbers, and beneath the west face of the Petit Dru they found themselves in an international camp of French, Germans, Austrians, Britons, Czechs, Poles and Japanese. On the morning of takeoff, however, the crowd dispersed onto various routes. John and Royal were alone as they moved up toward the start of the unclimbed *direttissima*.

They were a formidable pair: probably the two outstanding American mountaineers of their day: the one a long-proved master of mixed Alpine climbing, the other an unsurpassed cragsman. And they were also a strongly contrasting pair in almost every way. John was the "blond god," big and powerful. Royal was slight and wiry, with dark hair and a close-trimmed beard. John was the "grand designer," the dreamer, the mover and shaker, often careless of detail. Royal, by profession a teacher of skiing and climbing, was precise, methodical, meticulous, both in plan and action. So different were they in personality and outlook that—as developed later—they could not, in the long run, get along. But as of here and now on the Dru, their differences spelled strength, not weakness, and they made a magnificent team.

Their initial route followed that pioneered the previous year by John and Lito Tejada-Flores: up the broken rock of the so-called Gray Ledges, then onto the sheer monolith of the west face proper. Royal, too, had been on the wall before—on his successful climb with Gary Hemming in 1962. But that had been on a non-direct route, off to the left of their present one, so that, step by step, this was new terrain to him. Nevertheless—or more likely, therefore—he asked to take the lead as far as John's earlier high point, and in several hours of strong going they reached and passed it. "This seemed like a gateway to success," said John, "as the Hinterstoisser had seemed on the Eiger."

They had luck with their first bivouac, for they found a roomy ledge. And luck with the night, which was cold but clear. Starting off in the morning, John assumed the lead, and again the hours went by as they nailed their way up the granite precipice. Royal, technician *par excellence*, had, in Yosemite, devised a complex but effective new way of hauling up the heavy packs required for a multi-day climb; and this helped their progress. As did their wide, well-engineered assortment of chrome-molybdenum pitons. There were places, however, where even the most ingenious molly was not usable: pitches with no cracks whatever, or cracks so situated that hammer blows might dislodge huge blocks of rock. And here "skyhooks" were used. These were bits of metal, like small pitons in hook shape, that were not driven into the wall but merely hung from flakes or tiny ledges to support rope and climber. And the sense of security they provided was strictly minimal. Said John of trusting his weight to one: "It cannot possibly hold. But it does." And added, "Happiness is a belay ledge after a pitch like that."

There was almost endless verticality. When it stopped it was to become overhangs, and the overhangs in turn became "roofs." But it was not the technical climbing that was to be the worst of it. That came, ironically, when they were out from under roofs, on straightaway going.

It began with a sinister whine high above. Royal, now again in the lead, shouted down a warning—but too late. Invisible in its speed, but with the force of a cannonball, a rock hit John on the thigh. There was "a sound, an impact, and white-hot pain. Incredible pain that overwhelms, that seems to go to the core of one's being." In the first moments of agony he was sure that his leg was broken; and so it would have been with almost anyone else. But John's thighs, like the rest of him, were heavily muscled, hard as oak. Though the pain continued, he was at least still able to move his leg, and realized that there was no break, only serious contusion. Still, in the position they were in, that was bad enough.

Calling to Royal, he told him to go on up to the next belaying stance. Then he himself followed. His method of ascent was by prusik—hoisting himself by movable clamps up the rope that Royal had secured above—and he tried to favor the injured leg as much as possible. By the nature of what he was doing, however, he had to bend and straighten it, over and over, and in the course of the 135 feet he had to climb the agony was almost unendurable. Several times he broke down. He had cried once as a boy when he shot the dik-dik in Ethiopia. He had cried once as a man when he thought he was losing Marilyn to Jerry Robertson. Now for the third time in all those years, he cried again—partly with pain, and partly with the misery of seeing a fine adventure turn, in a senseless instant, to apparent disaster.

When at last he reached Royal, they discussed what should and could be done. There was no way off the face to either side. Even for two sound men, descent would be questionable, for, on the overhanging wall, many rappels would leave them hanging in space. That left one way—up—and John said he would try it. On their radio they called Royal's wife, Elizabeth, who had accompanied them to camp at the base of the Dru, telling her of their predicament, and asking that a party come up another easier side of the peak to help them down from the top.

225

For a cripple, even an easy down can be harder than a difficult up; and they did not want to fight the mountain to the bitter end, only to find themselves marooned and helpless on its summit.

At last they moved on again: slowly, grimly: Royal leading, John prusiking after. And even apart from his injury, the going was harder now because of increasingly loose and rotten rock. "I could scarcely place two pitons in a row," said Royal later, "without the second loosening the first. The entire route we were on is being steadily pried from the mountain by water freezing in cracks. It will one day all come down together in one enormous rockfall. It was an awful, eerie place. . . ."

And as for John:

"When one has deliberately to torture oneself by continuous movement of an injury," he said, "there develops a curious sensuousness to the pain. One tends to analyze its dimension in different terms, from color to form. So up I move trying different ways of contracting and extending the torn muscle. About the only relief is the quality change of the pain varying from sharp spikes of accent to round deep rendering. White to red—Bach to Wagner—cry to groan."

If his was the mystique of the Ordeal, he was now experiencing it to its fullest. And now too, more than ever in his life, he had to call on his powers of control. If in the fullness of life there were many Johns, here on the mountain there were at least two: the one struggling and suffering, the other watching, directing, controlling him. It was not mind over matter. It was mind over pain, over weakness. Here on the wall of the Dru, he put his credo to the sternest test it had ever met. . . . And it served him well.

He ground on. The hours ground on. Through the afternoon—toward dusk—and then they made their second bivouac. Beneath them was a narrow shelf; above, the largest overhang on the wall "spread its wings of shelter." The pain in his leg, though still bad, was no longer excruciating. The demands he had made on it had helped rather than hurt, but he had no way of knowing how much it would stiffen during the coming hours of inaction. "The night," he recorded, "brings apprehension, while those ballerinas, hope and confidence, dance in the shadow of a stone roof."

The ballerinas prevailed. In the morning, though bruised and battered, he was still mobile, able to follow, if not to lead on the rope.

It was again the Dru, not he, that posed the major problem; for the roof above, that for the night had been a shelter, now loomed as the major obstacle on the climb. It proved, however, to have a weakness—a deep crack splitting it vertically through its center—and dangling from skyhooks, Royal reached it and wormed his way up and through. John followed by prusik. Again Royal led, John followed. And so it went through their third day on the wall. During the afternoon came proof that word of their project and problems had circulated in the world below: for a helicopter appeared, rising out of the valley mists, its occupants craning with binoculars and cameras. Then it veered away and vanished, leaving them again to the solitude of rock and air.

On that third day they gained less height than on the previous two. But by its end they had put all the wall's worst difficulties beneath them and knew that, barring fresh catastrophe, they had the game in their hand. No catastrophe struck. Miraculously, the weather, which had smiled on them from the start, still held through the night, into the next morning. And in the morning, too, John's leg was so much better that he was able not only to follow Royal on the rope but to share the lead. After the adventures and trials below, the last hours of the ascent were almost anticlimactic. Toward midday, they moved up off the last pitch of the wall onto the steep but not vertical ridge known as the Bonatti Pillar. And from here, after a few more rope lengths, they traversed to the *voie normale* (the conventional route) on the far side of the peak. The actual oft-reached summit, a few feet above, did not interest them. They had made their climb. First of all men, they had achieved a direct ascent of the west face of the Petit Dru.

The mountain did not let them off without a farewell salute. Three and a half days of almost perfect weather was as much as the Alpine gods could tolerate, and thunderheads were darkening the horizon as they roped their way downward. With the bad, however, there also came good; for presently there were shouts from below, and they were intercepted by their "rescue team," dispatched by Liz Robbins, in the persons of Bev Clark and Lito Tejada-Flores. With John's remarkable recovery, no rescuers were needed, and he was somewhat embarrassed at having rung a false alarm. But it was nevertheless good to have company for the rest of the descent—particularly when the clouds moved in and enveloped them in full storm.

First it rained. Then it snowed. And through them both, lightning flashed down on the mountainside, shocking all of them except Royal. With the resultant slowing of progress, yet another bivouac was necessary, and they spent a night on a precarious ledge with the tempest roaring around them. In the morning, things were no better. Snow continued to fall heavily, and the peak had "a white, sliding, cold skin." But still they moved on down—"and though the descent is slow and treacherous," said John, "I feel exhilaration. Finally, on the glacier, I feel like a dog tugging at a leash. I think to myself that it is wrong to feel so energetic."

Wrong, no, one would say. . . . Astonishing, yes.

At glacier's end, "with shouts, laughter and seat-glissades," they reached a high mountain hut. Liz Robbins was there. And so was Marilyn, who had hurried over from Leysin when she got word of John's injury. Other climbers were there, full of admiration and congratulation. Reporters were there, and photographers, and a television crew brought up by helicopter. Down in Chamonix came an orgy of baths, food, and glory.

They returned to Leysin. And the weather to normal. At lower levels, it was still possible for the mountaineering school to function, but with the summer slipping away, all thoughts of the Eiger had to be dismissed. In this, for once, John was not too disappointed. His many confrontations with its north wall had by now convinced him that winter was the best time for a *direttissima* assault.

Before summer ended, however, he squeezed in one more major climb. This was a successful first ascent, in evil weather, of the easternmost of the two Brouillard Pillars, on the south flank of Mont Blanc near the Pillars of Frêney. His companions were three first-rate British climbers whom he had met in the course of his mountain travels; and with one of them, Christian Bonington, he formed the same close friendship as with Dougal Haston. Indeed, they were scarcely off the Brouillard before he invited Bonington to join Haston and himself in their next-winter go at the Eiger.

In early September the climbing school ended its first season. And soon thereafter the Leysin American School began its fall term. The institution was still having its troubles—now more spectacularly, with its former director in jail charged with embezzlement of its funds. And for different reasons, another member of the past year's staff was also missing: to wit, John Harlin. Marilyn returned to her teaching. But he, after much thought, had decided to resign, so as to devote his full non-mountain time to writing.

As usual, he had projects going on many fronts. With his two old short stories revised and more in the planning stage, he was in correspondence with *Playboy, True,* and *The Saturday Evening Post.* For the *American Alpine Journal* he had prepared a detailed and colorful account of the Dru adventure; and he was launching on what he hoped would be a series of mountain articles for an English-language newspaper in Geneva. Closest to his heart, however, was his flying-mountaineering book, *Introspection Through Adventure.* About it, he was corresponding both with his New York agent and a London publisher, and he had high hopes of finishing it by winter's end.

At his recommendation, Royal Robbins had supplanted him as athletic director at the school. But in spite of this, and with increasing evidence, the two recent partners were finding that they could not get on. Some of the trouble, one surmises, stemmed from their post-Dru reception by the press. John, already an Alpine celebrity, had been further lionized, whereas Royal, less known in Europe, had been largely ignored; and the latter, though no publicity-chaser, would have had to be more than human not to be annoyed. But beyond this, it would seem, it was simply a matter of incompatible personalities: of the "blond god" romantic and the no-nonsense professional. From Royal's point of view, John was disorganized, careless of the truth, bemused by his image of himself as a grand-design hero. In his own word, he became "disenchanted." For John's part, Royal struck him as plodding, unimaginative, and a bit of a cold fish. Of the two, John was the temper loser, and when annoyed he would flash out angrily. But he was also a quick forgiver of others' transgressions and a forgetter of his own. Royal was not. Whereas for John, to the end, their trouble was "some sort of misunderstanding," he, on the contrary, took the fixed, uncompromising position that here was a man he did not like.

As indicated, he was not alone in this. Whether in politics or business, aviation or mountaineering, a man as strong as John Harlin makes enemies. And even among his friends there were those who found him sometimes hard going. One of them recalls a time in a mountain hut when John, "like a general to a private, told me to go outside and check the snow. He played the part so naturally I damn near did; then catching myself said 'Check it yourself'—and John apologized." Another, taking an easier line, said, "He becomes so dominant that when you disagree with him you just don't bother talking back." And for still another, on a middle course: "John seemed to me to be possessive with people. He always had his own little entourage. And I had the feeling that if you got sucked into this you could lose or subvert your own personality and goals to his."

Seldom part of the entourage, as compared to earlier days, was Gary Hemming. The old friends were still old friends—by no means enemies—but increasingly their points of view differed on matters of importance to them both. Specifically, they held widely variant opinions on the subjects of promotion and publicity. Gary considered himself a "purist" in mountaineering. For him it was strictly a communion between himself and mountain, and he wanted no part of the commercialism with which the more spectacular aspects of the sport had become invested. John's "purity," in contrast, was well diluted. No less than Gary, he abhorred the cheap sensationalism of a certain part of the press. But he had no objection whatever to his feats being recorded and applauded, and believed that a valid way of raising the money needed for a big climb was through contacts with newspapers or magazines. To Gary this was not only distasteful; it was close to sacrilege. In John's dealings with the press—after Fou and Dru, and now working again toward the Eiger—he saw the machinations of a corporation or film star burnishing an image for public exhibit.[1]

John begged to differ. But he was well aware of his image. It looked up at him from hundreds of press clippings. It emanated from him as he sat of an evening in Chalet Pollux or Club Vagabond—the last of the Cherokee Hapsburgs in the midst of his court. From the background, perhaps, he could hear courtiers singing *Big John Harlin,*

> *. . . alone on the Eiger*
> *with his ice ax in his hand,*
> *hell bent for death and glory*
> *to climb the Murderwand. . . .*

[1] Ironically, in the summer of 1966, Gary was to receive as much publicity for a mountain exploit as ever John had on any venture. This was the leading of a spectacular rescue of two German climbers from high on the Dru, as a result of which he was hailed throughout western Europe as "the American beatnik of the peaks."

and he knew that a certain amount of *lèse majesté* was being committed. But he knew, too, that the song would not be sung at all if there had not been something in it to sing *about*.

Superjohn waxed bigger, brighter—and vanished.

In his place was Otherjohn.

He was the quiet one, the loner. He walked the trails above Leysin, as he had walked the hills above Bernkastel and Redwood City. Returning to Chalet Pollux, he closed the door and for a long time did not come out. Marilyn was at school, Johnny and Andréa at their other schools. His companions were Kuzma the cat (Maus had died) and Rongo, a young Belgian shepherd dog, and they knew how to be quiet when a writer was writing.

He wrote:

Do you feel the sun?
Do you feel the rain?
Do you love these things,
These inputs of sensation?
Then you are alive, and
This is your reality.

And:

The sounds
The colors
The motion
The warmth
The cold
The touch
The smell
With patterns and intricate forms penetrating above and below the
  limit of our perceptions,
While always this kaleidoscope turns to another moment in time.

And:

A man strains for a handhold and drives a piton that secures
him to the mountain that is godlike in its permanence. But he
clings between permanence and a space without limits. It is then
that the profession of mountaineering becomes an illusion, a falsity

231

eroded by the acid of man's own transience and the brevity of his instant of time. As the warmth of life rushes out, his body reacts in a spasm of the animal's desperation to live. When the web hangs on the rock and we have survived, an awe emerges for the simplicity required to endure.

"He could be a brute," said his friend Ted Wilson. "But he could also make you tingle with perception." . . . And now, alone at a desk, he strove for ever more perception, as he had so often on the mountain heights. . . . He knew that there were diverse roads to it. During the past months he had read and reread Aldous Huxley's *The Doors of Perception* and was aware of the role that drugs were playing in the thinking and experience of a new generation. There had been marijuana and mescalin at hand in the 1963 "gypsy camp" at the foot of the Eiger; pot and hashish at Garmisch during the skiing season; and now LSD, in small quantities, was finding its way to Leysin. He was interested—fascinated. The expansion of experience, and resultantly of consciousness, was precisely what he considered the living of life to be all about. But except for one mild bout with pot, and another with morning glory seeds, he himself had not experimented with drugs. Nor did he now. One reason was his concern for their possible aftereffects while he was climbing. Another was that, as with liquor, he felt no need for what they could give him. He could take his psychedelic "trip" on his own—as he had one day, memorably, in Garmisch, when he had emerged from a sauna bath into the winter landscape and *heard* the snowflakes falling around him.

He believed in his hearing, his seeing, his whole arsenal of perceptions. He believed, as he put it, in what he saw behind his eyelids. But there was no faintest trace in him of hippie cool or quiescence, as he strove with each dimension of experience to project it from private inwardness to outward expression.

He wrote:

You are brought up to believe that a flower is beautiful and a spider is ugly. Yet the same criteria you have used to consider the flower beautiful are often present with the spider. Even more, for the spider, like a mobile, has movement and is more delicate in form. What if a species of spider turned out to be far more intelligent and advanced than you? Could you accept these individuals? Or would you be revolted?

He wrote:

> *You are my light, my love, my life,*
> *Oh little bug.*

He was now thirty years old, and in the autumn of 1965 he and Marilyn reached their tenth anniversary.

They had lived through a lot. John and his life being what they were, they would unquestionably live through a lot more, as long as they remained together. But on the record, they seemed prepared and able to do it. A few years back, as their affair was breaking up, Mary X had written John: "Your love of your wife is paper thin, but tied with steel bonds, unbreakable." And if she had perhaps been wrong about the paper, she had been right about the steel. John wandered. He had to wander—to women, as to mountains. But he had also to come back to his Mara, whom he needed and loved.

As for Marilyn's part of it, there were those who thought she lived in bondage to his willfulness and dominance. But she herself did not see it that way. And in her children and her teaching she had non-John outlets that occupied and fulfilled her. "I had other things to live for," she has said, "and did not love John any the less for them. So I could give him the freedom I could not have given if I had been wholly consumed by him."

Here, perhaps, the "scientist" speaks. But she was also a woman who, after ten years of marriage, still thought of her husband as a man above and apart. "John offered me a world of feeling, observation and participation," she said, "that I could never have experienced on my own." And as for his demands and transgressions: "One cannot measure him by the yardstick used for ordinary men. It would be like measuring an elephant in microns."

Of the Mary X affair, she had expressed the opinion that "most of all, she was good for his ego." And that ego needed tender care and feeding, there is no question. The narcissist in him was far from dead. As was the recurrent old-Adam need to prove his virility. In this, as in other aspects of his life, he was not far from the traditional mold of the Ernest Hemingway hero, and indeed of Hemingway himself—

233

forever needful, in Morley Callaghan's words, of "romantic enlargement of himself." At Leysin, as elsewhere, he found women anxious to be helpful, and his flights from their attentions were not always precipitate.

And where, in all this, was his precious concept of *control?*

The answer would seem to be that he was far more successful exercising it in a plane or on a mountain than in the complex give-and-take of human relationships. Here he continued to be volatile, passionate, stormy—with Marilyn, other women, friends; in fact with everyone with whom he was emotionally involved. And his old drive toward violence still lay close beneath the surface. In his thoughtful self (and here he was non-Hemingway) he hated violence, witness his rejection of hunting as a sport and bombing as a profession. But in personal confrontations he was quick to anger, and more than once in Leysin reached the verge of serious trouble.

Beyond this, and in different context, there lurked the question of when and if he might do violence to himself. No man, however much in "control," could year after year take such risks in the mountains without the percentages stacking against him; and there were not a few fellow climbers who felt he was "pushing his luck," "asking for it," and—as the British put it—"someday going to be chopped." Dal Cottrell, his prize pupil in school athletics, had a less defined, more mystical feeling about it. With all his other teachers, he said, he could easily visualize what they would be like ten or twenty years later. "But with Mr. Harlin, no. There was, somehow, just no way of seeing him as an older man."

John himself was of course not unaware of the hazards of all-out mountaineering—or of the fact that experts could be "chopped" as well as novices. One of his close friends, a young Swiss named Erich Friedli, had been killed in a fall the previous winter; and now, in the autumn of 1965, all Europe had been shocked by the deaths of Marc Martinetti and Lionel Terray—the latter the pride of France and, along with Walter Bonatti, the best-known climber on the Continent. Of Eiger climbing John had said, "The odds are about one in three that you get it." But neither the toll of his colleagues' lives nor the threat to his own held him back from his ventures. In his book of values—unchanged since he had commented on the death of Ann Pottenger back at Stanford—that was "part of it all."

Of a man who lived as he did it is bound to be asked: To what degree was he himself motivated by a death wish? . . . That he was more conscious than most men of death and its imminence is unquestionable. As is the fact that he consciously and willfully courted it. Time and again when he set out for the mountains, Marilyn had cause to remember his words to her when their marriage was young: "One day, perhaps, we'll have the *great adventure* and never come back." On his climbs, of course, it was *I*, not *we*, who did the adventuring. But there came a day in Leysin when she was briefly a part of it, in an experience she could never forget. The two of them were skiing alone together, high above the town, and at last, with dusk approaching, it was time to go down. They did not, however, descend by the normal route. Elsewhere on the mountainside was another route, a steep and wild one called the Black Trail, which was posted as closed because of avalanche danger; and almost before she knew what was happening, she and John were skiing down it. Though she tried not to show it, she was greatly frightened. The very name of the trail was eerily menacing, and in the fading light she could see snow masses above them breaking away and sliding downward. In the past, John had spoken to her of the experience of "absolute terror." And now she herself lived through it—not only in the apprehension of physical danger but in her knowledge that he was courting it for them both. But what for her was terror was, for him, exhilaration. As they moved down the mountain in the shadow of death, his response was a mighty "Y-A-A-A-A-R-V-O!" and a grin.

Not always, though. He knew the shadow when he saw it, and there were times when he examined it and looked inward at himself. One night in the Calanques he had wandered alone in moonlight—now climbing, now musing—and of that night he wrote: ". . . I knew that if I climbed on it would be to prove something. It would be a performance, and I would not be satisfied until I killed myself." He had stopped climbing, at least with his body; but his thoughts moved on. ". . . The cliffs and pinnacles guarded the finger inlet. I was again spectator. Yes, if I were killing myself I must not push that far yet. I must be careful. Later maybe, later. Then I knew how much I yearned for that ultimate experience—and how fear had masked it. By piercing that mask, that shell of a body, I wanted to physically transcend the personal with a perspective reality—to find a vivid moment of truth. But not quite yet. . . ."

The ultimate experience—the ultimate adventure—was never far from John's thoughts. Again like Hemingway and his heroes, he awaited and did not fear "the gift of death." . . . But note well that the last words of his thanatopsis are *not quite yet.* Before the gift of death there came the gift of life; and if a death wish seemed sometimes manifest in him, it was because his life wish was so strong that it probed the bounds of the possible. What he demanded most of all was intensity of experience—whatever it led to—and to gain it he would undergo any risk or ordeal. With the great lone sailor of the seas, Sir Francis Chichester, he believed that "the difference between man and the lower animals is that the human being has the ability to draw on reserves he never knew he had. . . . You have to push yourself to the limit, or otherwise you don't know what you can do."

Aged thirty, he had done a fantastic lot. Now, beyond thirty, he proposed to do more. First on the Eiger Direct. Then on other mountains—the world's mountains—straight up to Everest: specifically the unscaled south wall of Everest, a climb as hard as the Eiger at twice the altitude. Always, in the future as in the past, his must be the line not of least but of most resistance; what most men would call the hardest way, but what to him was the esthetic way, the way that in itself was a work of art. . . . *In itself* bears repeating. The thing attempted *for its own sake.* . . . From his perspective, it was less the accomplishment that mattered than the challenge, less the result than the potential that could achieve the result. It was in the struggle to bring potential to reality that he found the meaning of life.

Said his friend, Flight Surgeon Leon Canapary, who has since become a psychiatrist: "Above all else, John wanted to be a champion. I think he believed that if he worked at it hard enough, he could make himself, literally, invincible."

Said Sandy Bill: "His life cup was filled above the brim."

But it was Ted Wilson who, gropingly, almost by accident, but perhaps more accurately than anyone, put his finger on the Harlin pulse-beat. "John was always trying to be something he wasn't," he began—then stopped, corrected himself. "No, that's not it," he said. He thought a moment. "What he was trying to be, always, was something he *was*."

17. The Flame

Still another friend once said of John that "he flamed up a mountain."
He was not speaking of speed or spectacular performance, but of motivation and desire; of his conviction that, however great John's strength
and endurance, he climbed a mountain less by physical means than by
an act of will. The will, the flame, did not wait to manifest itself until
there was rock and ice beneath his feet. Stoked and banked, nourished
and kindled, it was what got him onto a mountain in the first place.

And the second. . . . And the tenth. . . .

By the beginning of 1966, even he would have had a hard time saying
how often he had been on the Eiger. There had been his successful
ascent. There had been several sustained and several abortive attempts,
in summer and winter, *direttissima* and otherwise. There had been
super-reconnaissances and sub-reconnaissances, plus days, weeks and
months of stormbound Eiger-watching. At an estimate, John had by
now been actually on the wall some dozen times and roundabout it
between twenty and thirty.

Some of his bouts with it had been quickly mounted, almost spontaneous. Others had been long and carefully planned. For this 1966 campaign, however, preparations were far more thorough than ever before; and it was to be the nearest John—or anyone else in the Alps—ever came to a full-scale, Himalayan-type expedition.

The most important of items, the composition of the team, had been long since determined. Scotsman Dougal Haston, John's companion on the Shroud and the Mont Blanc ski traverse, had now in effect been signed on for a year and a half. And as third man in the task force—and a new associate for John—there was a young American named Layton Kor. A Coloradan by residence and bricklayer by trade, Kor had in the past few years soared into the top rank of U.S. rock climbers. John had met him at the Boston meeting of the American Alpine Club in December of 1964; the two had of course talked mountains, and specifically Eiger; and during the fall of 1965 he had come to Europe—and Leysin—with the Eiger very much on his mind. He had never before climbed in the Alps, and was only moderately experienced in snow and ice work. But his record on American rock (with such as Royal Robbins and Tom Frost) was vastly formidable, and John was pleased to have him as a partner.

These three—Kor, Haston, John—would be the nucleus of the team. But there would also be an additional semi-member in the person of Chris Bonington, with whom John had scaled the Brouillard Pillar the previous summer. A man of about John's age, a few years older than Haston and Kor, he was in the forefront of English mountaineers, with a record that spanned Himalayas, Andes, and Alps, including the first British ascent of the Eigerwand; and John had originally hoped he would be a full-fledged team member. Bonington, however, was a married man, plus a father; and he wrote to John: "I shall be coming out for the Eiger do and wish you the best of luck. One part of me—no, most part of me—longs to be with you on the barstard, yet I think I owe it to Wendy to be cautious this once." Then he added, in a thought rich in reverberations for lives such as his and John's: ". . . though the more I think of it, the real danger to a climber isn't on things like the Eiger in winter, but just in doing a lot of climbing over a long period."

Though thus limiting his scope, he would nevertheless have two important functions in the venture: one as support man, the other as photographer. And in the second role he would be performing professionally. After much negotiation, John had secured a backer for the project, the *Weekend Telegraph*, of London, which was to pay for newspaper rights on a sliding scale based on degree of success. Chris, an expert with a camera, had worked for the *Telegraph* before, and now would do so again: making him a triple asset to the team—physically, artistically, financially.

After manpower (plus money), the essential items to be assembled were food, clothing and gear, and on these all hands labored through the fall and early winter. Dougal was in charge of snow and ice equipment, Layton of rock "hardware," Chris of matters photographic. But for most of the rest John was quartermaster as well as commanding officer, and presently the basement at Chalet Pollux resembled a regimental supply dump. There was the best cold-weather clothing available, including custom-made boots that he had designed himself. There were ropes, axes, pitons, carabiners, daggers, ice screws, hammers, crampons. There was bivouac gear for both shelter and eating. And there was food, in its most nourishing and concentrated forms. On the mountain, it was planned, each man would carry fifty pounds in his pack and another twenty in climbing gear hung around his body: enough in John's estimate for a ten-day campaign.

Over the Christmas holidays, with preparations well along, he went with Marilyn and the children to London, staying at the home of Bev Clark and his wife. Here he gave lectures, met with Dougal and Chris, and firmed up arrangements with the *Telegraph*. Then early in the year it was back to Leysin for final readying—plus Eiger-watching and Eiger-waiting. Layton was already there. Through most of January the Alps were racked by storms; but toward month's end there came a general clearing, and John sent word to Dougal, in Scotland, to come at once. He reached Leysin on February 1. The following day, in a chartered helicopter, the three teammates flew over to the Eiger and made several runs at different levels along the north wall, finding it in the best of winter condition.[1] And on the third, after much rushing about, they drove from Leysin to the Oberland and caught the last

[1] Owner and pilot of the helicopter was Hermann Geiger, known as "the Glacier Pilot" and long famed in the Alps for his rescues in the wildest terrain. Ironically, he was killed, later in 1966, when his plane collided with another during a routine takeoff from his home airport in Sion, Switzerland.

train up from Lauterbrunnen to Kleine Scheidegg. Fritz von Almen, the proprietor of the hotels there, put them up at a bargain rate at one of several annexes, the Villa Maria; and there they were at the foot of their mountain.

Much had happened on its north wall since John's 1962 climb, interspersed among his own recurrent tries at a *direttissima*. In 1963 had come its first solo ascent; in 1964 its first ascent by a woman, as well as its first *descent*, by a party who had reached its top by an easier route. And in 1965 it may or may not have had its first suicide. This involved a Japanese climber, who had been injured high on the peak, and whose companion had gone on to the summit and then descended for help. While rescue operations were being mounted, he plunged to his death, in circumstances that made it appear a deliberate act; and whatever the case, he brought the sum-total of Eiger fatalities to twenty-six. As for *direttissima* attempts, other than those in which John had participated, there had been some half-dozen to date. On these, no lives had been lost. But all had been defeated by weather, and none had pushed farther than John's own high at the top of the Second Icefield.

Over and over, he and his partners studied the photographs of the face that they had taken from the helicopter. And to this were added long sessions at von Almen's telescope, plotting their prospective route, upward—upward. For the lower part of the climb, John proposed to follow, approximately but not exactly, the line he had previously taken, first with Sorgato and Piussi, then with Desmaison and Bertrand: up the broken cliffs of the base to the railway windows; up the precipice called the First Band, to the First Icefield, the Second Band, the Second Icefield. Beyond this, at the bulge of the Flatiron and the niche of Death Bivouac, their path would, for the first and only time, meet the old zigzag route up the wall. Then, while the old route veered off toward the Ramp and the Traverse of the Gods, their new one would follow a direct line past a huge vertical pillar toward the lower web of the Spider. In the Spider they would again be near, but not actually on, the old course. For this time they would climb on its right side instead of the left, and at its top emerge through new Exit Cracks to a still higher icefield called the Fly. Finally there would again be the Summit Icefield: now, however, not at an angle toward the

242

Mittellegi Ridge, but straight up toward the Eiger's summit.[2] . . .
Indeed the whole ascent, from start to finish, would be as *straight up*
as human skill and ingenuity could make it. This was the whole purpose and meaning of their venture.

Two days after the others, Chris Bonington arrived from England,
and what might be called the three-and-a-half-man team was now complete. Their first project was a day of workout climbing on the peak's
west ridge, which they hoped to follow quickly with the real thing. But
the Eiger, in good Eiger fashion, promptly entered a full week of in-
termittent storm and snowfall. There were individual days when a
start, or even a full climb, could have been made on lesser mountains.
But John was waiting for a forecast of a long stretch of fair weather—
and this did not come. While it waited, the team skied daily (minus
gloves), rehashed plans, rechecked equipment, and grew steadily better
acquainted *as* a team.

That it was a strong one was self-evident. Three of the four of them—
John, Dougal, and Chris—had already scaled the north wall by its
"regular" route; and Layton, though new to the peak, had a reputation
as a cragsman that was almost legendary. In the plan of battle it was
he who would lead on the worst of the verticalities and overhangs.
Dougal would be the specialist in snow and ice. John would, as always,
be over-all leader and coordinator. And Chris, as good an all-round
climber as any of them, would (in addition to his photography) be a
certain pillar of strength in his role of support.

Further—and this was far from always the case in multi-member
parties—it quickly became clear that theirs would be also a congenial
team. John, Dougal, and Chris had already climbed, well and happily,
together, and were enough of a piece, in outlook if not in personality,
to avoid serious friction. It was with the professional toughs of British
mountaineering that John had his troubles: the hard-nosed, no-nonsense breed who thought him a "bullshitter," and who he in turn found
unimaginative and dull. Chris and Dougal, however, were of another
breed—the former a Sandhurst graduate, the latter a one-time philosophy student at the University of Edinburgh—and if, in the realm of
ideas, they did not always agree with John, they at least knew what he
was talking about.

[2] For a pictorial depiction of both routes, see photograph following page 144.

As for Layton Kor—in a way the outsider on the team—he was a horse of a different color. Tall, rangy, and relaxed, he was far from a tough; but with a background of high school plus bricklaying, he was also far from the intellectual-introspective type so common in American mountaineering. One of his favorite stories was of an earlier climbing partner who had said of a mountain sunrise that it was "better than Mozart." To which Layton added, grinning: "Afterward, I kept thinking it was even better than Fats Domino." He was not, in short, a man who could be expected to share deeply in John's philosophy of mountaineering; to think of routes as "esthetic" or "orchestrated," or of an ascent as "a work of art." Nevertheless, he took to John—liking and admiring, if not wholly understanding him. And John returned the sentiments in full measure. Though men of differing viewpoints and values, and even of vocabularies, they were soon closely knit in the bonds of friendship. . . . As indeed were all four of the team now poised for the Eiger Direct.

In mid-February they at last made their first physical move toward their objective. For some time they had been discussing the ethics of taking a large part of their loads up by train to the railway windows in the north wall, thereby saving themselves much drudgery on the first two thousand feet of the climb. And in the upshot it was decided to do so. With three heavy packs, Dougal and Chris rode up from Kleine Scheidegg to the Eigerwand Station, clambered out through its opening, and established a cache in a nearby snow-hole. Then they returned to base, to await the day when they would climb up and retrieve it.

They were to wait longer than they expected. . . .

For the next day there was a calamity. Skiing on the slopes near Scheidegg, John, presumably bored with conventional locomotion, tried a one-legged *wedel*—fell—and dislocated his shoulder. Even when eased back into place, it was stiff and sore; and when, that same afternoon, he went down to Grindelwald to see a doctor, he was told the obvious fact that he could do no climbing for a while to come. He was dejected and disgusted. All the more so because it had been a typically Johnian sequence: weeks of rigorous, dedicated training followed by a careless, totally avoidable accident. But at least he was convinced that, now as always, he would make a quick recovery; and

244

as added quasi-comfort, the weather was still no good for Eigering. Accompanied by Layton and Dougal, he took off for a visit to Leysin.

(On the same day, by a not-too-neat happenstance, there arrived in Kleine Scheidegg a young journalist named Peter Gillman, assigned to write the story of the climb for the *Weekend Telegraph*. When he discovered that his protagonists were simultaneously disappearing, he phoned his London office for instructions and the next day doubled back homeward. Except for John's shoulder, things were not exactly popping around the Eiger.)

Marilyn had not gone to the Oberland. She had her teaching to do, the children to take care of, and besides, she hated sitting around at the foot of a mountain waiting to see what would happen to John. This year she was happier than ever in her school work: free of chemistry and teaching only biology, now both at the American School and the College. And son Johnny, for his part, was preparing for his examinations (in French) for entry into secondary school. Also—and far from incidentally—he had qualified for the Topolino (Mickey Mouse) international junior ski championships, to be held in March in Trento, Italy, and was counting the days in a delirium of anticipation. Proud and delighted, his father went out schussing with him on the practice slopes, but presumably did his *wedeling* on two legs, not one.

Also on hand, on one of his out-of-the-blue appearances, was Gary Hemming; and it must have been a strangely poignant experience for the two Rover Boys to be together, with the one launched on his greatest mountain venture and the other having no part in it at all. There was not, however—nor had there been—any talk of Gary's participating in the current campaign. It was understood between them that, though they remained friends, they were no longer climbing partners; and it was almost as an outsider that Gary sat by, as John, with Layton and Dougal, went on Eiger-waiting and Eiger-planning.

In such time as was left over, John struggled to keep up with his other projects: some old, some new. One involved his own skiing—an invitation having come to him to compete, this time as a reserve officer, in another series of military meets. He was the prime mover and implementer of a recent decision by the American Alpine Club to join a European-based federation of such clubs, the *Union Internationale des Associations d'Alpinisme*. On the school front, his "Summit" project was for the moment dormant, but for his climbing school, ISMM, he was full of plans. One was to develop a group clientele, drawn from such organizations as the Sierra Club, in California, and the Appalachian Mountain Club, in New England. A second was the creation of a magazine, to be edited by Marilyn and called the *Alpine Mirror*. A third was to expand activity to include winter and spring skiing; and he was discussing with Hermann Geiger an operation called "Wings and Skis," whereby clients would be flown to high and hitherto inaccessible ski runs throughout the Alps.

Writing, other than note-jotting, would have to wait until he was down from the Eiger. But through the past fall he had made good progress, and he still hoped to have *Introspection Through Adventure* in finished form before the new year was far along. . . . As for climbing: even the Eiger towering in the foreground could not shut out the shapes of other, greater peaks beyond. Increasingly, his dream of dreams was the Himalayas—and particularly the south wall of Everest, whose base was 9000 feet above the Eiger's summit. But with Asia in ferment, political permissions were hard to come by, and he therefore also had in mind some ambitious alternatives. Foremost among them, now, was a variant of his long-cherished Great Walls plan: a sequence of hardest routes on the greatest peaks of the Americas, from Alaska to Patagonia. And about this, as well as Everest, he was corresponding far and wide.

For a long while Marilyn had been hoping that each of his seasons of "extreme" Alpine climbing—and especially Eiger climbing—would be his last. And now, finally, there seemed to be hope ahead. There was not much left to top such feats as he had performed on Dru and Fou, Frêney and Mönch; once he had climbed the Eiger Direct, there would be nothing. And John was no hand for repeat performances or diminuendo achievement. He believed that he was a part, a leader, of a "climbing revolution," a forward surge in ambition and acomplishment that in the past few years had brought mountaineering into a new stage of development. Of its stages he had written: "First, there is the climbing of the summit by the easiest possible route. . . . Second, there are the different ridges and faces to be tasted, still by the easiest route possible. . . . Third, there is the *direttissima*, the esthetic line of attack." He and his generation had brought this third stage to fruition in the Alps. With the Eiger Direct accomplished, it would reach its ultimate point. But on greater mountains elsewhere, notably in the Himalayas and Andes, climbers were just completing the first stage. Most of the second and the whole of the third still remained to be achieved. And here, he believed, lay mountaineering's future—and his own.

That he would give up climbing, or reduce the scope of his climbing, was unthinkable. Mountaineering was no mere sport to him. It was his profession. It was his life. And he proposed to keep it just that, as long as life itself lasted. The scene of activity might change. Indeed, more than might; it was sure to. There would be new ventures, new horizons, a broader canvas for his "works of art." But the essence of things would remain as always. The man and the mountain. The challenge and the response. The struggle. And the risk.

These would go on. And in her heart Marilyn must have known it. At age thirty, John's perspectives had lengthened, deepened; but they had not changed. He would continue as he had started, on the high road, the hard road, and she, like all women of men of adventure, would have to pay a price. By now, she was used to paying it. She would be able, one thinks, to go on paying it. At the very start of their marriage she had said that she would not try to stop him from doing what he wanted, for then she "would lose what he *was*, the man I loved and married." She had lived by that. She would continue living by it. And whatever else lay ahead, there would at least be the comfort of knowing that the shadow of the Eiger had lifted at last.

Soon now. . . .

But not yet. It was she herself who took the phone call from Kleine Scheidegg and ran down to the basement of Chalet Pollux to tell John and the others: "A German team has started on the wall. There are eight of them!"

It was a bombshell. They had known that a German attempt at a *direttissima* was in prospect, for John had been asked, several months before, if he would be interested in joining forces. But that the climbers should show up at this moment was wholly unexpected. . . . And in a team of eight: an army! . . . In short order, John, Layton and Dougal were in their car racing back to the Oberland.

That same day, they learned on arrival at Scheidegg, the Germans had made an initial probe of 1500 feet up the easier first quarter of the face, fixing ropes and carrying loads before descending for the night.

247

And the next morning, February 20, they themselves launched their first move onto the mountain. John's shoulder was not yet strong enough for this sort of climbing. He stayed below, working on logistics with Chris Bonington, while Dougal and Layton formed the vanguard. For two pitches above the base they used the ropes left in place by the Germans. Then branching off on their own, they moved up through the morning, past the German high point, to the cache that had been left six days earlier near the railway windows. Here, about 2000 feet up, they dug a bivouac platform out of the snow. Then, with the weather clear and several hours of daylight remaining, they moved on farther up the wall.

To the bivouac, the going had been largely on ice and snow, and Dougal had led. Now came the rock of the First Band, and it was Layton's turn. Soaring sheer, smooth and almost holdless, the precipice was a stern challenge to his skills, as slowly he maneuvered higher, hammering the slimmest pitons, threading the rope that would become the lifeline of their advance. It took four hours to gain ninety feet. Then with dusk approaching, they roped back down to the bivouac site.

When they had started in the morning it was an open question as to whether theirs was a reconnaissance or the actual start of the big push. If the weather held, they would spend the night at the bivouac and push on higher the next day, with John and Chris following as soon as John's shoulder permitted. If the weather broke, they would descend to base for another session of watching and waiting. . . . The Eiger being the Eiger, the weather broke. . . . By the time they reached the bivouac, the wind had risen and black clouds were moving in with the oncoming night. They would have liked to keep on downward. But as they weighed the issue snow began to drive in, and they decided that, with darkness plus storm, a further descent was too risky. They managed something to eat and drink and dug into their bivouac sack. During the night the storm rose to full pitch, and by the next morning it was so bad, even down at Kleine Scheidegg, that Chris Bonington came up by train to the railway windows to see if he could be of any help to them. By the time he arrived, however, they had taken the bit in their teeth and begun the descent on their own, thumping into the shelter of the Villa Maria while the storm still raged at noontime.

248

Indeed, it raged for three more days, in what proved the worst storm of the winter. The team was immobilized. So were the Germans. And as they waited in the close confines of Scheidegg the rival climbers became acquainted. Most of the Germans were from Stuttgart or nearby, and though all were new to the Eiger's north wall, they were among their country's best climbers, with wide experience elsewhere. They had two co-leaders, Peter Haag, aged twenty-eight and an engineering student, and Jörg Lehne, thirty, who worked for a Stuttgart publishing and printing house. And it was this firm, the Belser Company, that was the financial backer of their venture.

That the venture was a big one—and not only in manpower—was instantly apparent. And further, by Alpine standards, it was a highly unusual one. John, along with other top mountaineers, envisioned a future in which Alpine techniques would be brought to the Himalayas. But the Germans, reversing the process, were now bringing Himalayan procedures to the Alps. Specifically, they did not plan to climb onto the Eiger and keep climbing, in a steady upward advance. Instead, as on an Everest or K2, they would move up a distance, carry supplies, establish a camp; then repeat the process, higher and higher, again and again; maintaining a continuous shuttle up and down the mountainside until the whole of it was coordinated in a chain of camps and routes. The camps would not be dismantled as height was gained, but maintained throughout the siege. Ropes, once affixed, would be left in place, to insure easy descent and reascent. And the team of eight would be split into two groups: one up ahead forging a way, with the other, below, involved in porterage and maintenance. As for time involved, they had plenty. John's estimate for his own party was ten days on the wall, itself an almost unprecedentedly long period for an Alpine climb. But the Germans were planning no less than an eighteen-day campaign, and had food and gear for an even longer one if it proved necessary.

The talks at Kleine Scheidegg were friendly. Both teams respected each other; and besides, by the nature of the climb ahead, they would be in such close daily contact that hostility would be both ludicrous and dangerous. Nevertheless, there was no delight on either side at the turn of events. Virtually all climbers agree that competition—and particularly of the face-to-face variety—is the bane of mountaineering; yet here was a situation in which it was automatically produced. Also, no climber likes a "crowded" mountain, and here was a guaranteed built-in crowd. John's thoughts went back to 1962 on the Eiger, when he and Konrad Kirch stared down in dismay at the "army" behind them. But then, at least, it had been in small units, like their own twosome. Now, as companion-rivals, they would have a veritable *panzer* force grinding up the peak.

All this. And more too. . . .

For if there is one word worse than *competition* in the mountaineer's lexicon, that word is *publicity*; and now it was certain that there would be plenty of this as well. To begin with, the Eiger Direct is the most spectacular climb that can be performed in the Alps. And the most public as well; for whereas most mountain routes are hidden away among other mountains, this one is wide out in the open, as if on a great vertical stage. Further, if competition is anathema to climbers, it is sheer joy to the press, and already a horde of reporters and cameramen were zeroing in on front-row seats at Kleine Scheidegg. The Germans—or at least their sponsor, the Belser Company—were realists in such matters. Far from hiding their light under a bushel, they had with them a Swiss named Harri Frey, hired by Belser as ground manager and public relations man. If there was—and there obviously was—going to be a flood of publicity emanating from the foot of the Eiger, they wanted to retain as much control over it as was possible.

As for John: he was, as noted, no shrinking violet, no "private purist" like Gary Hemming. He too had found a publisher as backer. He accepted, indeed welcomed, the fact that the *Telegraph* would spread the story of the climb not only in Britain but through the English-speaking world. Like the Germans, however, he wanted a degree of control—his own sort of control, geared to his own standards. To the editor of the *Telegraph* he had written, as a condition of accepting its sponsorship: "All material emanating from your writers must be edited before publishing by Chris Bonington or myself. . . . Good old English conservative diplomacy must be used in all relations with the Swiss at Scheidegg; and the reporting must be accurate and without contrived sensationalism."

With the *Telegraph*, as it developed, things were to go well. But with other elements of the press, where no control was possible, it would be a different story. Largely, it was a compounding of those two "bad words" of mountaineering. The fact that competition, active or potential, existed on the climb generated publicity. Publicity, in turn, generated more competition, real or contrived. Soon the climbers of both teams would be caught in a web, not of their own making, in which they were performing puppets for the delectation of millions.

Soon too, however, they would at least be physically out of it: high in the world they all craved and loved. The storm at last subsided, and again there was readying. On February 25 the Germans returned to the mountain, reached the foot of the First Band, and bivouacked, all eight of them, on the face below. The next morning, John, Layton, and Dougal set off for the Eiger's base, only to find that the recent snowfalls were now thundering down the wall in huge avalanches, and to beat still another retreat to Kleine Scheidegg. On the same day the Germans stayed holed up in their bivouac, also unable to climb. But on the twenty-seventh two of them forged a route partway up the First Band, close to the line taken by Layton and Dougal a week before. The rest worked at carrying up supplies and excavating a large camping cave which they called the *Eispalast* (Ice Palace) near the foot of the Band.

Meanwhile, below, the British-American team was acquiring reinforcements. One was the returning *Telegraph* reporter, Peter Gillman, now back for the duration; and John was delighted to find him a sensitive, strictly non ballyhoo-type of young man with a sound knowledge of what mountaineering was all about.[3] The other, also an Englishman, was Don Whillans, now an athletic instructor under Royal Robbins at the Leysin American School, who had been given two weeks leave from his job at John's request. A topflight mountaineer who had often climbed with Chris Bonington, his function on the Eiger would be to help out with transportation problems at the lower levels; and no team could have hoped for a stronger man in support.

There was still, however, the little matter of getting the show on the road, the team on the mountain. And on the morning of February

[3] In addition to his *Telegraph* dispatches, Gillman, in collaboration with Dougal Haston, later wrote the story of the climb in book form. It was published in England under the title *Eiger Direct*, in the United States as *Direttissima*, and is the source, the present author is happy to acknowledge, of much of the material in this and the following chapters.

28, what they hoped would be the big push began. The advance guard, after some reshuffling of assignments, consisted of Layton, Dougal, and Chris (with John and Don Whillans scheduled to follow the next day), and in short order they had reached the foot of the First Band and were visiting with some of the Germans in the *Eispalast*. Then, while Chris remained there to take pictures and start a snow-hole of their own, Layton and Dougal prusiked up the Band on fixed ropes to their earlier high point and set to work on the virgin rock beyond. Some of the Germans were working on a parallel line only a few yards to their right, but the teams climbed independently of each other. For a while, Layton, in the lead, made tremendous progress. Six-foot-four in height, and with a corresponding reach, he was able to find cracks and hammer pitons far beyond the range of most climbers; and presently a good part of the First Band was beneath them. Then, as usual, the Eiger turned mean. Snow started to fall. Fresh avalanches began, and they had to turn back. On the descent, Dougal's rappel rope jammed and flipped him backward, leaving him upside-down for a few bad moments on the side of the precipice. But he managed to extricate himself, and they continued down to the bivouac site, where Chris awaited them. Here, in worsening weather, Layton decided that he wanted to keep on going all the way to Kleine Scheidegg, and proceeded to do so, while Dougal and Chris settled in for a blowy night on the wall.

In the morning, things were no better. They waited until after noon to see if wind and snow would ease off—but they didn't. So they followed Layton down. Meanwhile, John and Don Whillans, according to schedule, had started from Scheidegg toward the base of the wall, but also finding conditions impossible, had beaten a retreat. By evening, the whole team was back in the Villa Maria, none the worse for wear, but much the worse for frustration.

Most frustrated of all was John. Almost a month had now passed since he had brought his team to Kleine Scheidegg—and there they still were. The weather, which in winter was supposed to be reasonably stable, had been atrocious. Thanks to his shoulder, he himself had not yet so much as set foot on the Eiger. The Germans had not only appeared from nowhere, but were now perched 2000 feet up in their camp on the north wall. Rubbing salt in the wounds was the now ubiquitous press, some of which, in the absence of real news, had taken to manufacturing it. AGAINST THE GERMANS, read one caption above a picture of John, Dougal, and Layton, while the accompanying article went on to beat the drums of nationalist rivalry. SPRINT UP THE EIGER, shouted a front-page headline, which John had the pleasure of reading in a hotel *Bierstube*.

For a day and a night there was a diversion. Marilyn drove over from Leysin, and for one dine-and-dance evening the Eiger was remote in darkness beyond the hotel's picture windows. In the course of it, too, one of the "other Johns," an old, almost forgotten John, emerged, and the mountaineer again became a couturier—of sorts. As she dressed for dinner, it developed that Marilyn had forgotten to bring a garter belt. Her stockings sagged. And John would have none of it. In an improvisation that would have won a nod from Balmain, he taped the tops of her nylons securely to her thighs, and for the evening had a wife whose legs he approved of. Then the next day, with Marilyn gone, he returned his attention from hosiery to mountain.

He paced the wide terraces of Kleine Scheidegg; then the narrow confines of his room. He fiddled with gear. With a restless hand he pushed back the long yellow hair that fell over his eyes. A dozen times and more on the night of March first he looked from his window at the winter sky, and as the night advanced it grew clearer; the stars emerged and gleamed. He swung and kneaded his shoulder, and now at last it was all right. If it remained clear into the morning there would be still another setting out, and this time it would be himself and Layton in the lead.

If—if—if—

He slept.

And the morning *was* clear. The dawn was luminous. After an early breakfast he and Layton rode up in a ski lift to the foot of the Eiger's west ridge; then skied across the snow slopes to the point where their fixed ropes hung down from the north wall. Here they removed their skis and turned upward. His feet trod Eiger ice, and his hands touched Eiger rock. To a casual observer, that morning, he would scarcely have seemed a man who "flamed up a mountain." He moved slowly, deliberately, at first a little stiffly. . . .

But the flame, though hidden, was there. Never in his life had it burned more brightly.

18. The Rope

The rope is the symbol of mountaineering. And its *sine qua non*. Other paraphernalia, from the familiar ice ax to the most exotic chromolly or skyhook, are used in special situations and conditions; but the rope is uncoiled whenever terrain becomes difficult or dangerous—which means when mountaineering begins. In its origins, and still largely in practice, it is a protective device. Two knowledgeable climbers roped together are not twice, but a hundred times as safe as if they were climbing alone. But in the course of mountaineering's development it has also been put to other, more sophisticated uses and become an implement of offense as well as defense. The maneuver of the rappel, or roping down, enables a climber to make swift descents of sheer or overhanging pitches that, by conventional methods, would take hours or be wholly impossible. And on the ascent—at least on peaks big and hard enough to require back-and-forth progress—the fixed rope, attached to the mountain by piton and carabiner, is a means of locomotion as well as a lifeline.

Going up, to be sure, someone has to fix the rope in the first place. The bare mountain has to be climbed before a rope can be climbed. But once the first man is up and has lowered one, there is no need for his struggle to be repeated. On a steep incline, the rope is continuously there as a handhold. On verticality or overhang, where it falls free, it can be ascended directly, by prusik; and for a long *direttissima*, such as on Fou, Dru, or Eiger, prusiking becomes the normal method of progress. To the uninitiated it may appear dangerous in the extreme, with the climber suspended in space and often revolving as the rope turns with his shifting weight. But actually it is not—unless he panics—and *direttissima* climbers are not the sort who are apt to do that. Indeed, prusiking is one of the few maneuvers they will normally do wholly on their own, without the protection of belay from another.

Not only rope techniques have changed over the years, but ropes themselves. Once made of hemp, they are now fabricated from nylon or similar synthetics: stronger, lighter, more resilient, and far less subject to stiffening or kinking when either frozen or wet. For long in advance, John and Dougal had been searching for what they considered the ideal line for the Eiger Direct, and in the end had chosen one made of a fiber called perlon. Some was of 50-meter length and 11-millimeter thickness, to serve as belaying rope in normal climbing; other of 100 meters and 7 millimeters, for use as fixed rope and in hauling packs. Unlike old-style hemp, it was not "rope-colored," but woven of strands of varying hues. And on the morning of March 2, when John and Layton began their ascent, it was a bright thread of color that led them upward toward the grayness of the heights.

There were few overhangs, hence few prusiks, on the first 2000 feet. These would begin in earnest on the First Band. They did not, however, go on to the Band this first day, but stayed at its foot, enlarging the bivouac snow-hole that Chris Bonington had started a few days before. Far from a decision of the moment, this signaled a change in strategy which John and his team had been weighing for several days: a switch, at least in part, from their original "Alpine" concept of the climb to the Germans' "Himalayan" pattern. There now seemed little chance of the ten successive days of good weather which were essential to making the climb in one sustained push. And a retreat to Kleine Scheidegg for every storm would impose an impossible drain on both time and energy.

The alternative was to fashion a refuge similar to the Germans' *Eispalast*, big enough to hold all of them; then, farther on, a second such shelter, probably at the site of the old Death Bivouac; and with two such secure and well-stocked depots, they would be at least reasonably self-sufficient on the mountain. Further, with a smaller team than the Germans, they would then be able to move faster. But even so, their original ten-day timetable could obviously not be met. This in turn meant that more food and gear would be needed; so while John and Layton worked on the snow-hole, Dougal and Chris were involved in quartermastering in the valley below.

There followed a spate of what Layton called "yo-yo climbing." The next day, after a night in bivouac, he and John, first prusiking, then climbing on their own, got all the way to the top of the First Band, while those below brought fresh supplies to the foot of the wall. In the evening—with many loads still to be brought up—John and Layton descended to base to help. The following morning, with the others doing the porterage, Dougal and Chris (who by now seems to have forgotten his self-imposed limitations and was functioning as a full-time climber) took the lead and, beyond the First Band, worked their way up a steep gully system toward the First Icefield. During the up-and-down sequences there were problems and minor crises. One of the fixed ropes on the First Band was found to be wearing in places, and a new one was strung alongside it. In a mishap in the course of a prusik, Dougal lost two climbing clamps plus a camera. But there were no serious setbacks, and over-all progress continued. On the night of March 4, for the first time, all four team members camped in the enlarged snow-cave at the foot of the First Band.

A few yards away, most of the Germans were still in residence in their *Eispalast*. They too had been moving upward, with two of them now in a small bivouac near the top of the Band. But their line of advance, to the right of the British-Americans, had been proving a hard one, and two jarring, though not serious, falls had slowed them up a bit. By now, for John & Company, they were no longer mere bundled, helmeted figures but recognizable individuals, with back-home occupations of engineer, mechanic, carpenter, toolmaker. Their names—in addition to co-leaders Jörg Lehne and Peter Haag—were Karl

Golikow, Siegfried Hupfauer, Rolf Rosenzopf, Günter Schnait, Günther Strobel, and Roland Votteler. Linguistically, there were of course communications problems, varying from man to man; but it was nevertheless friendliness rather than rivalry that increased as the two groups followed their almost elbow-nudging courses. Cheeriest of the Germans was mechanic Golikow, whose invariable greeting, delivered with a grin, was his one phrase of English, "It's a hard life!" . . . And so it was. But for the moment, also a good one: the life all of them, from whatever country, would have chosen over any other on earth.

There had now been three consecutive days of fair weather. If it held for another, John's team was prepared, for the first time, to move higher en masse. . . . But it didn't. . . . Cloud and hissing spindrift greeted them on the morning of March 5, and it was decided that Layton and Chris would go down for further load-hauling, while John and Dougal stayed at the snow-hole. They spent the rest of the day housekeeping—as did the Germans next door. But when the following morning dawned in splendor they were again on their way. Topping the First Band and the gullies above, Dougal led for several precarious hours up a succession of crackless, ice-coated slabs. Then John, taking over, moved on up the Second Icefield toward the base of the Second Band. This time there was no turning back at the high point. A bit of poking with axes uncovered a natural snow-cave, and in this they holed up for the evening and night.

Meanwhile, at the other end of the yo-yo, things were so fantastically different as to strain the imagination. On other mountains one came down from a camp to a camp; at most, to a primitive hut. But on the Eiger it was to a luxury hotel. To steak, wine, table linen, dance music, hot baths, clean sheets. To headwaiters in striped trousers and women in evening gowns. For all the climbers, moving up and down, it was a heady, even dizzying experience. But of the lot, it was Layton who most enjoyed it (as he least enjoyed cramming his 6-feet-4 into the dimensions of a bivouac), and he indulged in yo-yoing whenever possible. To him, the rigors of frequent descent and reascent were amply repaid by the creature comforts he found below. And in the end he set what is probably a unique mountaineering record by gaining weight during the course of the climb.

However, it wasn't all cakes and ale at Kleine Scheidegg. Don

Whillans was still working on loads and logistics—a job on which Layton and Chris now briefly joined him. Peter Gillman, who had quickly become a devoted member of the team, was not only writing his dispatches for the *Telegraph*, but also talking with John several times daily by radio, supplying him with detailed weather forecasts, and acting as general coordinator of affairs below. Wendy Bonington, Chris's wife, arrived from England and settled in for the duration as all-around Girl Friday. Marilyn, this time with Johnny and Andréa, came over again for a weekend, and the three of them spoke with John, very publicly, on the radio: for her, an experience no less frustrating than exciting, but for the children a thrill from beginning to end. John's old friend, Air Force dentist Cleve McCarty, came and went several times, as did assorted other friends and acquaintances (though not Gary), until the scene resembled a reprise, with more affluent overtones, of the Eiger gypsy encampment of 1963. There was even—as then—a bevy of female camp followers on hand, devoted to the T.L.C. of whichever heroes happened to be at the lower end of the yo-yo.

The Germans, too, had their entourage at Scheidegg, centered on publicist Harri Frey. And around him and Gillman and descending climbers, reporters and photographers swarmed in ever-increasing numbers. From both Germany and England came television crews, and the English one, besides filming scenes of climbing at the Eiger's base, staged an interview with Layton, Chris, and Don Whillans. First Layton described the progress and problems of the climb. Then it was Whillans' turn, and he was asked if, as a climber of his stature, he was unhappy at being a mere porter.

"No, it suits me fine," said the sardonic Don. "This way, I don't have to go high."

"How many times had you been up to the bivouac cave?"

"I made it halfway, once."

"Would you say there's a race on between the two teams?"

"If it's a race," said Don, "it's the slowest in the world."

Chris was then asked about criticisms that both teams, with their backers and retinues, were commercializing, and therefore cheapening mountaineering. He replied that "no one does a climb like this just for money"; then went on to point out that for so big an enterprise the money had to come from somewhere, and that the press was the most logical, often the only, source.

However, the criticism increased—along with the publicity. The more sensational press kept drumming on nationalistic competition. In soberer newspapers and journals, conservative mountaineers declared that this was not true Alpinism, and that the standards of the sport were being degraded by the application of Himalayan siege tactics to a smaller peak.

The public-at-large could not have cared less about such esoterica— including the section thereof that, as skiers, tourists and pro-tem Eiger-watchers, now thronged the terraces and public rooms of Kleine Scheidegg. By the dozen, score and hundred, they swept the north wall with binoculars, or jockeyed for a place at Fritz von Almen's telescope on the rare occasions when it was relinquished by the journalists. A few among them, of course, were knowledgable about mountaineering and understood what was happening on the wall, both physically and spiritually. But for most it was merely a puppet show, a circus, on the great vertical stage, and what they craved was melodrama and sensation. "The ghouls," the climbers called them in their more bitter moments "—waiting for their corpse." And though this was pushing it far, it is true that it was not mountaineering that interested them, but the national "rivalry," the "race."

"British-American team takes 15-foot lead in Eiger climb," wrote a sarcastic Peter Gillman in one of his daily reports.

Intimations of all this came to John during his radio talks with Peter. But for the time at least, it was remote, almost meaningless, in the high and austere world above. On the morning of March 7, with the skies still clear, he and Dougal emerged from their snow-hole, pushed up the remaining stretch of the First Icefield, and set to work on the cliffs of the Second Band. Off to the right, as usual, the lead German pair of the moment, Karl Golikow and Jörg Lehne, were paralleling their course, and Golikow shouted over his copyright greeting, "It's a hard life!" This time it was truer than he knew; for only moments later he came off his holds and fell thirty feet.

Luckily, it was into a drift of snow at the top of the icefield, and he was unhurt. But the mishap led him and Lehne to reconsider their route, and they asked John and Dougal if they could join them on theirs. The answer was affirmative. The Germans edged over. And for the rest of the day the two teams advanced literally shoulder to shoulder.

260

The line John and Dougal had selected, while far from easy, was better than they had dared hope from below: leading largely up a cleft in the precipice that, though choked with snow, offered ample cracks for pitons and even occasional hand- and footholds. The twosomes still climbed on separate ropes, with the Germans keeping to the right of the cleft, the American and Scotsman to the left. But for much of the time John and Lehne, leading, were on almost exactly the same level, moving like Siamese twins joined hip to hip. As they advanced, John and Dougal strung fixed ropes for the benefit of Layton and Chris, who, they knew, had left Scheidegg that morning and would presently be following, hauling loads.

In the late afternoon, the Germans broke off their ascent and rappeled down toward the higher of their two already established bivouacs. With the top of the Second Band very close, however, John and Dougal decided to push on, and in a wild sunset, cold but flaming, emerged at last onto the top of the band. It was a fine and magical moment. But it did not last long, for soon the sun was gone. The flame was gone, leaving only the cold; and around them there was only rock and glare ice, with no prospect of another snow-hole. For four hours, first in dusk, then in blackness, they searched and scrabbled for a spot where they could at least dig out a platform. And at last they found the one, constructed the other, and crawled into their bivouac sack. By now they had no solid food left, only the makings of hot drinks; and with these they kept themselves at least tolerably warm until they fell asleep.

Though the next dawn was another fine one, they did not move on. Not only were they out of food, but low on rope and hardware for a new day's climbing; so they decided to wait until Layton and Chris caught up with them. Toward midmorning they did so, carrying the needed supplies. Then, after a rest, they descended for more loads, while John and Dougal struggled to enlarge the tiny bivouac site. By late afternoon, when the others returned, it was big enough to hold the four of them. But even with all their packs on hand it was discovered that certain important items—among them chocolate, candles, carabiners, and radio batteries—were in short supply; and Layton, the tireless yo-yoer, volunteered to descend all the way to Kleine Scheidegg to get them. He made the trip down in an incredible hour and three-quarters. And by two the next morning (with small chance for creature comforts or weight-gaining) he was on the way up again, reaching the others while they were preparing breakfast.

Again, John and Dougal went out in the lead. And the goal for the day was Death Bivouac. While they had spent the previous day consolidating, the Germans had gone on climbing, and their advance guard was now well out ahead. Further, the weather forecasts, relayed by Peter Gillman, indicated that the current fair spell would soon end; and a storm-lashed night in such a bivouac as they were now leaving could well be disastrous. In contrast, Death Bivouac, despite its name, would offer protection. Almost two-thirds of the way up the Eiger, it was also the natural advance base for a summit assault. Both tactically and for safety, it was essential to reach it this day.

It took some doing. Carrying heavy packs, John and Dougal began by prusiking up a rope left by the Germans; then emerged through a network of gullies at a point near the base of the projection called the Flatiron. Next came a traverse beneath the Flatiron to the foot of the Second Icefield, followed by a long grind up the icefield. At a distance, Layton and Chris followed with more packs, and behind them came two rear-guard Germans, also heavily laden.

By the time John and Dougal reached the top of the icefield, daylight was fading, and ahead lay yet another traverse—this one all on ice and extremely formidable. They were still determined, however, to reach Death Bivouac; so Dougal, removing his pack for better balance, worked his way out onto it, above a sea of gray space. It was hairy going. The ice was so hard that it would take few pitons or screws, and he had largely to hack his way, with ax in one hand and dagger in the other. To make things worse, the weather chose this moment to fulfill the radio forecast, and in the cold dusk a heavy snowfall began. But Dougal still kept going, trailing a rope behind him, and as twilight thickened into night, came off the traverse into the niche of Death Bivouac. By this time, Layton and Chris had joined John at the far end. One by one, using the ill-secured rope, the three followed after. Close by Death Bivouac there was a bulge of snow, which they attacked with hands and axes, and presently they had dug in it a cave large enough to hold them all.

Their day, however, was not yet done. To effect the ice traverse, they had left two of their packs, containing food and cooking gear, at its other end; and now, in night and storm, first Dougal and then

John made the precarious roundtrip to retrieve them. As a final touch, while they were preparing a much-needed hot drink, a gas cylinder burst into flame, causing great scrambling and confusion before it was hurled out into the void. In this, they were at least lucky in their domicile; for, unlike tents and bivouac sacks, snow-holes don't burn up.

It was long past midnight when they finally settled down, pretzeled tightly together in their tiny refuge. And they slept late in the morning. When they peered out, however, it had stopped snowing; according to Peter Gillman, on the radio, the *real* bad weather was not due until the following day; and they decided to make use of the grace that was granted. Having made a photographic record of cave and surroundings, Chris descended to Kleine Scheidegg. John spent the day housekeeping and sorting gear. Dougal and Layton, reconnoitering above Death Bivouac, hacked their way up the Third Icefield, climbed some steep rock beyond, and came to the base of a huge vertical column that had been given the name of the Central Pillar. Here they met the lead pair of the German team, which had established itself in two snow-holes near their own. Holding to the established pattern, the Germans had ascended by a route to the right of theirs, and were now studying its continuation on the right flank of the Central Pillar. For their part, Dougal and Layton worked out a prospective line to the left of the pillar, and returned to Death Bivouac with high hopes that it would "go."

By the next morning, however, the predicted storm was obviously close at hand. Layton, still the master of yo-yo, effected another of his double-quick descents to Scheidegg; but John and Dougal, with ample food on hand, decided to weather it out in bivouac. Ambitiously, but ill-advisedly, the Germans tried another upward sortie, only to be driven down by an onslaught of blizzard. And from then on there was nothing for anyone to do but hole up and endure.

John and Dougal's snow-cave was scarcely a fortress. Excavated from a cornice projecting from the rock face, it had an outer wall of precarious thinness, and the cracks that now and then appeared in it offered disquietingly spectacular views straight down toward Scheidegg and Grindelwald. With the spring thaws, cornice, cave and all would obviously peel off the mountainside. But though close on the calendar, spring was scarcely a current worry, and the heavy snowfall at least had the welcome effect of thickening their protective shell. Further, it formed an effective blockade at the cave entrance, which earlier had been a funnel for wind and spindrift; so that, as the storm continued, they were progressively more secure. They had foam rubber mattresses, besides their rugged clothing, for insulation, and with the wind shut out, the cold was tolerable. There was enough food, enough fuel for cooking, and assorted tablets to stimulate metabolism and circulation.

Still, it was to be a long pull, and a rough one. . . . A day and a night passed. Then another of each. Though neither wind nor snow-fall was continuous, there were no signs of general clearing, and by now the north wall was so draped in unstable whiteness that any major move was unthinkable. Occasionally there were back-and-forth visits with the nearby Germans, five of whom had also remained in bivouac. But communication was limited. Their meaningful conversations were not with their neighbors, but over the radio with Kleine Scheidegg, 4000 feet below.

"What are the survival problems up there?" asked Peter Gillman during one of their scheduled sessions.

"Staying alive," said John succinctly. But being John, he was of course more than half enjoying it, for here again he was engaged in testing himself through the mystique of the Ordeal.

He talked weather with Peter, tactics and logistics with Chris and Layton. Down at the Scheidegg end, a tape recording was being made of their conversations, for use in the sound track of a planned film of the climb (with John himself doing most of the camera work above); and at intervals, interspersed with the regulars, assorted camp followers came on the air with information, questions and greetings. Notable among them, one day, was Marilyn, over again from Leysin for a brief visit. But this time the children were not with her. John's peripatetic parents had again appeared, this time to take grandson Johnny to the Topolino ski meet at Trento, in Italy. And Andréa, too, had gone with them—though not so much for the skiing, Marilyn added, as to gorge on spaghetti and macaroni.

Then it was "Scheidegg out"—"Eiger out"—and the voices were gone. The whole world beyond and below was gone again, and there were only John and Dougal in their cave of snow. Sometimes the two would talk through the hours: of mountains, women, philosophy, food (not food for sustenance, food for enjoyment); and then back through intermediate subjects to mountains. Combining several of them, John found himself speaking of Tahiti, "where there's a pinnacle rising sheer up in the middle of the island like a great phallic symbol." And from there, through some devious route (perhaps Bligh and the *Bounty*), Dougal got off on a recitation of the history of Britain.

Then for hours they would be silent: listening to the storm, trying to sleep. Or John, rummaging in a pack, would bring out and re-read the letters he had received down in Scheidegg. From Johnny: "Try to make it to the top." From Andréa: "Come home soon." From Mara: "Much much much love." Finding another scrap of paper, a blank one, he in turn wrote a note to them: ". . . we are being very safe so don't worry. . . ." *March* ?? he dated it, for the days in the snow-hole were sliding together. But he knew where he was all right, and he wrote it down: *Death Bivouac*.

The next day, when he awoke, he was coughing and feverish. In his first radio talk with Scheidegg he asked if there were a doctor he could speak to, and in short order there were no less than five at the other end of the circuit—four of them women and all French, on an Alpine holiday from Paris. After hearing his symptoms, they agreed that he was obviously ill, but not so seriously as to warrant a descent of the mountain in bad weather. And it was arranged that there would be a second conference the following day.

Meanwhile, between coughing spells, John discussed with Layton and Chris the still baffling problem of how the Eiger was finally, if ever, to be climbed. There were good reasons for John, and Dougal too, to come down for a breather. But also strong reasons for staying up, so as not to give another headstart to the Germans. Like it or not—"slowest in the world" or not—there was, in fact, a race on, and the only way it could be ended was for the two teams to join up. There was much in favor of this, John conceded. But on the other hand, he said, "we don't have this conception of a great group going to the summit. And we don't want to come up on the third or fourth rope as though we were pulled up by the Germans." He was still convinced that, given a break in the weather and a route ahead that was not clogged with rival climbers, he and his smaller, more mobile team could be the first to the goal. It was decided to have a conference with the Germans. Then it was decided not to, lest the approach be construed as weakness. And the matter was tabled.

The following day, he was feeling better, and the conclave of doctors again decided there was no urgent medical need for him to come down. But by now another problem had arisen: the supply of food in the bivouac was running low. And it was one thing to descend the mountain, unladen, by rappel; quite another to ascend it, with heavy loads, through the treacherous drifts of still unconsolidated snow. "Do you think you can make it?" John asked Chris and Layton. "We'll try tomorrow," they told him. For the rest of that day, with Don Whillans, they worked on the preparations, while, above, John and Dougal tried to clean up what was now the shambles of their cave. "Among other things," Dougal announced blithely over the radio, "we are covered with a mixture of Scots-American excrement."

During the past several days the Eiger, from below, had been largely hidden by storm clouds. Peter Gillman and his opposite number, Harri Frey, had kept the press briefed on what little was going on in the bivouacs. But journalists no less than climbers were growing restless, and in the absence of news again began to contrive it. It Started as a Race. . . . Now It's a Rescue blazoned the London *Daily Sketch* the next day, over a story by its Scheidegg reporter that Layton and Chris were setting out for the mountain. As it developed, however, even the "rescue" fizzled; for the avalanches on the wall were so great that it would have been irrational to attempt it.

On the morning of March 16, with cloud still covering the peak and snow falling at Scheidegg, Chris regretfully announced the situation on the radio, and John and Dougal decided to come down. Not only was their food all but gone, John's ailment—now diagnosed as bronchitis—had again become bothersome, and to spend much longer in the cold, cramped snow-hole would mean sure and serious deterioration for both him and Dougal. Toward noon they began roping down the north wall, to be met by their companions at the base. And that evening—after five days at Death Bivouac and thirteen consecutive days on the Eiger—they were back in the incredible world of steaks, wine, women, baths and beds.

There were gaping tourists. There were camp followers full of intrigue and misinformation. There was the press closing in with unanswerable questions.

But there were also those steaks, baths and beds. (Wine and

women could wait.) There was a long phone talk with Marilyn in Leysin. There was a wire from John I in Trento that Johnny had done the Harlins proud in the Topolino ski meet.

On the morning after his Scheidegg arrival, John continued his descent, now by train, to Lauterbrunnen. This was for the funeral of a good friend, Hilti von Allmen, a young and accomplished Swiss guide who, a few days before, had been killed by an avalanche while skiing. Over barely more than a year, the toll of friends, old and new, had been heavy. Recently word had come that Paul Revak, back in Naval flying, had been lost on a flight out of Guantanamo Bay in Cuba. There had been Erich Friedli; then Terray and Martinetti. Now Hilti von Allmen. And all but Paul had died in the mountains.

From Lauterbrunnen he continued on down to Interlaken, where a hospital examination confirmed that he had bronchitis, but was now virtually over it. The next morning, on the train taking him back to Kleine Scheidegg, he read in a newspaper that he was in the hospital with pneumonia, obviously through with climbing the Eiger.

That same morning, in bright but unsettled weather, Layton and Chris had returned to the wall and this time kept going. By the time John was on the air with them, they had climbed all the way to the foot of the Central Pillar, on reconnaissance, and were now back in Death Bivouac, which had been untenanted for just two nights. The forecasts, as relayed by John and Peter Gillman, were still uncertain. But when the next morning dawned clear, Layton and Chris again went up to the Pillar; and before it ended, this day, March 19, became the key one of the climb to date.

The Germans were still working on a route to the right of the Pillar. But Layton and Chris agreed with John and Dougal, who had first studied it, that the true and better line lay to its left. The big problem was to reach the left-hand base of the Pillar in the first place, for it was separated from their point of observation by a smooth, almost vertical wall. The leading of a traverse across it was obviously a job for Layton, the Yosemite cragsman; and off he went on it—climbing bare-handed, using his great reach, hammering pitons, hanging stirrups, stepping into them—then repeating the process, again and again. There was no hold anywhere, except what he made for himself. Behind and beneath him was a gulf of space. But he kept going, and he made it, in a masterful three-hour performance. Even with the rope there, Chris was at first leery of following him. But he did. And at the far end they found, as they had hoped, that the climbing to the left of the Pillar would be steep but feasible.

The Germans on its right side, however, were on that same day reaching an impasse: an overhang of snow blocking their route, that appeared sure to collapse under pressure of hand or ax. That evening at Death Bivouac, their co-leader, Jörg Lehne, asked Layton and Chris if, when they reached the top of the Central Pillar, they would lower a rope to help them; and the two agreed. Then, the next morning, Lehne suggested that, instead, the teams join ropes on the left of the Pillar. And again Layton and Chris agreed. In the upshot, Layton and Karl Golikow, leading, with Chris and Lehne following, crossed the airy traverse, reached the top of the Pillar, and from there climbed on almost to the lower web of the Spider. The true heights of the Eiger were being reached at last.

Down below, when he got the radioed reports, John was delighted with the progress but of two minds about the joining of forces. On the one hand, he was a sincere internationalist, with a thorough distaste for the "race" that had willy-nilly developed. Yet he was also sick and tired of having his Eiger ventures embrangled with others. In a combined force with the Germans, his own smaller team would inevitably become, or at least seem, the junior partner. On its own, he was convinced it could reach the top before them.

It was, however, impossible to play Napoleon, or even an effective platoon leader, from Kleine Scheidegg. Decisions had to be made almost from moment to moment, as situations changed; above all, as the crazy weather pattern changed. Over the radio, on the evening of March 20, he told Layton and Chris that "the forecast is a go, is a go." Then he and Dougal prepared to climb on up and join them. Don Whillans, the day before, had had to return to his work at the Leysin School. But his place had been taken by fellow Englishman Mick Burke, whom John had also brought onto the school athletic staff; and now Burke helped with the packing of loads for the final push.

Final?

After so long, so many ups and downs, it was hard to believe. Yet John was convinced that, at last, it was so. The advance guard had almost reached the Spider, three-fourths of the way up the wall. Soon he and Dougal would be up there too. They would make their last bivouac in the Spider, or perhaps even higher, in the small icefield called the Fly. From this height there would be no retreat, even in storm. They would hold their gains, push on still farther. Beyond Spider and Fly . . . to the Summit Icefield. . . .

Yes, this was final.

In his room at Villa Maria, John readied his gear. He peered from the window, paced restlessly, pushed his long hair back from his eyes. Then, quiet for a few moments, he reread the letter that had come earlier that day from Marilyn, in Leysin.

It ended:

Don't play with the gods up there. It appears they are jealous of you and thus manifest their wrath in peculiar ways. To convince you, mortal man, that you ought not to defy them, they have inflicted the worst winter, journalists, competitors (for security I am happy they are there) . . . your shoulder, your lung problems, and then Hilti! Now the "blond god" returns. Perhaps by now the others submit, and when they do, you will finish in fine spirits, fine weather, and rapidly return to the hearth of Pollux. Yet the battle may not be over. We all give our support through this last stretch.

At 1 A.M. he and Dougal ate a steak breakfast that Mario, the maitre d' at Kleine Scheidegg, had arranged for them in a small room off the main restaurant. Then, in their full winter climbing gear, they clumped down a hall past the open door of the hotel bar. From inside came the hum of voices, the clink of glasses, and a few curious glances from late drinkers for whom it was still yesterday.

There was the frozen night. White slopes.

Then the mountain.

". . . the web hangs on the rock . . ." John had written. And now here was the web. The ropes. The fixed ropes, the prusik ropes, the controversial ropes that had changed Eiger climbing from an "Alpine" to a "Himalayan" venture, and that alone would enable John and Dougal to catch up with the others high above. As a companion had said, John could flame up a mountain. As Marilyn had said, he was the blond but mortal god, filled with hubris, challenging the true gods, dark and eternal. But now, again, flame and hubris were well hidden, as yet again he began the milk run on the lower walls of the mountain. Outwardly he seemed rather his own "flea returning," climbing routinely, mechanically on his web of rope.

First they moved in darkness. Then in dawn. Then in sunrise. At the campsite below the First Band they picked up a few items of food. Then they went on higher, prusiking the bands, hand-roping up the icefields, and toward noon reached their old domicile at Death Bivouac. For the next few hours they were alone there. Chris, after his high exploits with Layton and the Germans, had descended to Scheidegg; and from there, when the time came, he would set out with Mick Burke, following the west ridge to the Eiger's summit, to serve as combined support and photographic team at the hoped-for climax of the climb. As for Layton, he was still above them, with the Germans. From the entrance of the snow-hole they could see his tiny figure, roped to Lehne and Golikow, leading the way into the main icefield of the Spider.

On the way up, John's bronchitis had again become bothersome and he had had some bad fits of coughing. But now at the bivouac he felt better. Perhaps the sight of Layton so high had something to do with it. By the next day he and Dougal, too, would be that high, and higher. The weather, since they had begun climbing, had been perfect. And the latest forecast received had indicated that it would remain so for three more days.

Then latest became next-to-latest, as on the following radio rendezvous, at 4 P.M., Peter Gillman glumly announced that the madhouse pattern had changed again. Zürich and Geneva were now both announcing the approach of a cold front—meaning a storm—that would strike the Eiger region in about twenty-four hours.

"Christ!" they said. "Aren't we ever going to get a break?"

When, later, Layton came down to join them, he was pleased with the day's progress, but he too turned gloomy when he heard of the new turn of the screw. To heighten the irony, the night was fine; the next morning was fine. But the forecasts, as received then, were still for a storm that evening, and as John said, "You can't stake your life on their being wrong." It was decided that Layton, who had had several consecutive days of all-out climbing (and was still as pro-

Scheidegg, anti-bivouac as ever), would go down for brief R & R; and he forthwith took off. Meanwhile, John and Dougal would ascend to the Spider by the now-existing fixed ropes, establish a supply dump there, and return to Death Bivouac for the night.

Such, at least, was the revised plan. But at about noon, before leaving, they had still another radio talk with Scheidegg that turned everything upside-down again. Item One: A figure, obviously one of the Germans, had been seen through the telescope on the ice of the Fly—meaning that, in terms of time, the ascent from Spider to Fly was much easier than had been anticipated. Item Two: Zürich and Geneva had now amended their forecasts to the effect that the approaching cold front had slowed. Its attendant storm would now not reach the Eiger until the following night.

Decision, redecision, was instant. With fixed ropes now in place, John and Dougal could still reach the Fly by dark and bivouac there. The next morning, within good striking distance, they would go for the top; and even if storm caught them there it would not greatly matter; for by then they would have both the escape route of the west ridge and the help of the Bonington-Burke support team. . . . As for Layton, his descent had been a bad break for him. But not an irreparable one, for he could start back up, at his own incomparable speed, and climb with the second German echelon, which had not yet left Death Bivouac. In fact, he had said before leaving that he would do exactly that if circumstances warranted.

Thus it was set.

"Scheidegg out," said Peter. . . . "Eiger out," said John.

And again he and Dougal were climbing.

—Or rather, this time, Dougal and he, for Dougal was ready before him and moved up first on the fixed ropes. Ahead of him was one of the Germans, Sigi Hupfauer, carrying supplies, and the three men worked in cooperation. When Hupfauer, out of sight above, was off a prusik line, he would shout down for Dougal to start; and then Dougal in turn, when he was up and off, would shout down to John. They moved strongly and steadily, with the ropes both leading and supporting them: up to the base of the Central Pillar—across to its left-hand side—up a chimney to the top of the Pillar—then up still farther toward the lower web of the Spider.

"The sky," said Dougal later, "was deep blue, and the line of the fixed rope glittered brightly. . . . It was a day for appreciation. I felt I was on the way to completion of my greatest dream. The many years of hard-won experience were at last going to be put to as searching a test as one could find in the climbing world." . . . Then he added: "John and I had become very close friends on the previous trials. There was no other person with whom I wanted to share this unique experience."

Just what John felt, or how he would have put it, we do not know. But his emotions could scarcely have been less strong and deep than Dougal's. Even more than his companion—more than any man, of any nation—he had dreamed the Eiger dream and waged the Eiger struggle: over many years, in many seasons: on the old route, on the new. On the new, in particular, he had been the planner and challenger, the mover and shaker, the man of all men who craved the *direttissima,* the Eiger Direct. And now at last it was in his grasp. One more fair day and he had it. On this penultimate day, March 22, he was moving strongly, surely, toward that one supreme goal he had sought in his life.

By three o'clock they were approaching the Spider. Hupfauer, indeed, was already at its lower margins; Dougal was prusiking up the last fixed rope beneath it; and John was at the foot of the next-to-last, ready to climb. It spanned a pitch of some 150 feet, largely vertical, but overhanging toward the top, so that for most of its length it fell free, well away from the wall. This meant that a man ascending it, particularly with a heavy pack, would swing and revolve in the air above 4000 feet of nothing. But John had performed the maneuver hundreds of times on dozens of mountains. He had been performing it all the way up from the bivouac, and the prusik he was now beginning was just another link in a chain. He tied into the line with a carabiner, adjusted his stirrups and sliding clamp. Then he heaved himself upward. Above, the bright thread of the rope hung taut with his weight against the gray of rock, the blue of sky.

At 3:15, on the terrace of Kleine Scheidegg, Peter Gillman, as he had done so often in recent days, was peering up at the Eiger through Fritz von Almen's telescope. Searching for John and Dougal, he swung the lens slowly upward along the route to the Spider; then suddenly stopped, as what might have been a tiny flame fell through his circle of vision against the rock of the mountainside. But it was not a flame. It was a figure dressed in red. "It was stretched out," said Peter, "and was turning over slowly, gently, and with awful finality."

19. "Goodbye John"

"It was a happy scene," Dougal Haston wrote later, "sitting on the tiny ice step at the foot of the Spider."

With him were Sigi Hupfauer and another of the Germans, Roland Votteler, and above Jörg Lehne was prusiking up a fixed rope that had already been installed between Spider and Fly. Soon John should be joining them; a half hour was the usual interval between climbers on a prusik ascent. But when it had passed, he had not appeared. After an hour, he had still not appeared.

The three men on the ice step tried to talk of other things. Then it came time for Hupfauer to go up to the Fly, and he started off. Votteler was scheduled to descend to Death Bivouac for more supplies, and as he began rappeling told Dougal that he would keep his eye open and give John a hand if he were in any difficulty. After several long minutes alone Dougal could stand the waiting no longer. With Hupfauer now off the fixed rope above, he himself began prusiking up toward the Fly. But at the end of the first rope's length he stopped, when he saw a figure ascending below him. "Sudden terrific elation swept through me," he said. "Then shattering depression." For it was not John. It was Votteler. Reversing directions, Dougal quickly rappeled back down to him and was told that the second fixed rope down from the Spider had broken near its upper end. There had been no sign of John, said Votteler. But it was possible that the rope had parted just as he was beginning the prusik, and that he had fallen only a short way or not at all.

John had been carrying his team's only walkie-talkie. Dougal had no way of reaching Kleine Scheidegg, to learn if anything had been seen from below. But the faint hope held out by Votteler was short-lived. For the other Germans, up in the Fly, had their own radio, and now, presently, as Dougal stood wretched and helpless, Hupfauer appeared above and called down:

"John's dead."

Through the Scheidegg telescope, the red shape that Peter Gillman had seen falling had been located on a snow-slope at the foot of the north wall. But several climbers on both teams wore red clothing, and for a while it was not known who had fallen. Then, at 3:50, Layton Kor and Chris Bonington set off on skis, and guided on radio by Peter Gillman, who remained at the telescope, they reached the body in forty-five minutes. It was John. Together his two friends sat down in the snow and cried.

On word from Scheidegg, a party of guides came up from Grindelwald and took the body down by train to the town mortuary. There an autopsy was performed, and the list of lethal injuries filled almost a page in the subsequent report. Interestingly—in death, as so often in life—the description of John had his brown eyes as blue.

Meanwhile, Wendy Bonington had been dispatched to Leysin to bring Marilyn the tragic news. But while she was still on the way, Don Whillans phoned from there by chance and was told by Peter Gillman what had happened. With his wife, he arrived at Chalet Pollux a few minutes before the story was broadcast on Swiss radio. The next morning, Marilyn gave instructions that the body be brought from Grindelwald to Leysin.

Up on the Eiger and down beneath it, both teams were immobilized in shocked disbelief. John had been one of them. Now he was gone.

A flame had burned. Now it was out. The first impulse of everyone was that the whole venture be abandoned. . . . But as the night of March 22 wore on, second thoughts took over; values were weighed and examined. Germans above spoke to Germans below. They made their radio available to Dougal, so that he could talk with Chris and Layton. And in the end the two teams reached a joint decision. . . . They would go on. They would go on, because if there was one thing in the world they knew, it was that John would want them to. Further, they would continue not as separate parties but as a single united team. And if it was granted them to reach the top, they would give a new name to their line of ascent. The Eiger Direct would become the John Harlin Route.

No less than Dougal Haston, Layton Kor had become greatly attached to John. His grief was deep and wrenching. But on the morning of March 23 he again started up the north wall from Kleine Scheidegg, in the hope of finishing the climb they had begun together. At Death Bivouac—now a more macabre name than ever—he would join up with the Germans who were still based there and go on with them in a second echelon. Dougal, who had spent a miserable night bivouacked in the Spider, would join with the Germans who were also camped there and climb on in the vanguard. The ever-changing weather forecast now had storm due for late the next day, the twenty-fourth, but by that time, it was hoped, all hands would be on the summit or close to it. . . . In any case, they were going to make the try.

While Layton prusiked up alone, however, and Dougal moved with the high German group from Spider to Fly, another climber was on an enterprise of his own. This was Karl Golikow—he of the "hard life" with a grin—and his mission was to inspect the series of fixed ropes between Death Bivouac and the Spider. The upshot was that he found several, besides the one that had broken, that were frayed in one or more places; and the Germans, when this became known, made a major change in their plans. All those above the ropes would go on toward the summit, but those below would turn back. When Layton arrived at Death Bivouac he learned of this decision, and after much deliberation and soul-searching he came to his own conclusion that the only sane course was for him, too, to descend.

With him, from his investigation, Golikow brought down key bits of "evidence" relating to John's fall. He had in his pack both the upper end of the broken rope and a section of a slab of rock over which it had hung, and in the grain of the rock there could still be seen threads and fibers that had been rubbed off by friction. The rope, like all those used by John's team, had been a new one, made of perlon, and like all the ropes used for prusiking, was of 7-millimeter thickness. It had been put in just two days before the accident by Layton and Chris, as they climbed with the lead Germans between the Central Pillar and the Spider. At the top, above the slab that had caused the friction, it was still, when Golikow reached it, firmly tied to two heavy pitons. And the pitons were still firmly embedded in the mountain wall.

There was, however, another piton in the wall that had more of a story to tell: one of the pitons supporting the next rope below the one that had broken. When he came to it, Golikow saw that it was bent and askew, and clinging to it were a few bits of red-colored fabric. This could mean only that John had hit here. And this in turn meant, almost certainly—for the piton was some hundred feet below his falling point—that the impact, if it had not killed him, had at least knocked him out. For what it was worth, it could now be assumed that he had been conscious for only a brief part of his 4000-foot fall.

From the outset, controversy had bubbled and boiled around the Eiger Direct. Now in the wake of a sensational death, it was more intense than ever: in the cockpit of Kleine Scheidegg—among mountaineers everywhere—throughout the European press. There had been the "Alpine-Himalayan" issue. There had been the nationalistic "race." Now compounded with these were charges that the climbers were being callous and inhuman in continuing the climb after John's death. Three decades after it had begun, the debate raged again as to the moral justification for an activity which, in the name of sport and adventure, took such a toll of life. The Ogre of the Alps was back again on center stage: the Eiger's *Mordwand*—its Murder Wall—which had now claimed its twenty-seventh victim.

More specifically, discussion centered on how John had been killed. And beyond the *how*, on *why*. In the official report of the Rescue Service of the Swiss Alpine Club (which submits such statements—plus bills for services rendered—on all mountain fatalities in the country) it was noted that the rope that broke had a thickness "of 7 mm!" And without further comment, underlining and exclamation point showed clearly enough its opinion of so thin a line. To this, partisans of the climbers replied that 7-millimeter rope was standard and universally approved for prusiking; and that to carry up heavier fixed lines, on an ascent where as many had to be used as on the Eiger *direttissima*, would impose an impossible weight burden on the climbers. As for other second guessing: Yes, it was true that there would have been no fall if everyone, while prusiking, had been belayed by a teammate; or if all fixed ropes had been constantly inspected as by Golikow at the end. But here, too, the demands on the climbers—in this case on their time—would be impossible. As it was, the climb was taking weeks. With such precautions, it could go on forever.

So the arguments went, back and forth, pro and con, with no agreement—just as they had through all the years since the Eiger's wall was first challenged. . . . No, longer than that: far longer. Through all the years of man's adventuring, which means through all the years he has existed. . . . For it was the age-old, ageless argument—the same on mountain or sea, in air or space, anywhere on earth or beyond where man seeks to extend his domain—of what risk is justifiable in the pursuit of his ends.

This was the *why* of death on the Eiger: the general, the public question. But for some there was also a personal, private question: not *why was someone killed*—but *why John?*

Including Chris Bonington as a full-time climber, there were twelve men on the mountain, so that the basic mathematical odds on anyone were eleven-to-one. Even allowing for the fact that John was a few pounds heavier than Sigi Hupfauer and Dougal Haston, who immediately preceded him up the fatal rope, the odds do not swing far off from that figure. He was second to none as an all-round climber, was the most experienced of all on the Eiger, and while prusiking, one can presume, performed no error of commission or omission. In terms of the event, the ultimate happening, he was simply a man in the wrong place at the wrong time.

Still, he was not a statistic in an actuarial table. He was himself, John Harlin, who had returned to the Eiger again and again, and had got himself into such a place—or places like it—time after time. When word of his death spread, many things were felt by those who had known him, but the rarest of them was surprise. In the Club Vagabond, at Leysin, there had long been those who thought that Superjohn was "asking for it," and that the day would come when he would "get chopped." His one-time student, Dal Cottrell, was soon to say, "There was no way of seeing him as an older man." Chris Bonington had written: "The real danger isn't the Eiger in winter, but just in doing a lot of climbing over a long period." . . . And John had done a vast lot, of the most extreme sort, for many years.

For all her grief and desolation, even Marilyn was not surprised. During all those years she had lived with this possibility; and though she knew better than anyone that John's craving was not for death but for life, she knew too that death, when it came, was in the dimension in which he had lived. It was the size, the strength, the blazing intensity of that dimension that left her and all who knew him—if not surprised—then stunned and incredulous that what had been so alive, so vital, was now, in an instant, nothing.

Said Konrad Kirch: "It is not a symbol we have lost, but an incarnate force."

And Bev Clark: "I'd have thought the Eiger would break before John did."

In death, now, he made the journey he had made so often in life— from the Oberland to Leysin. And behind him, on the Eiger, the long drama he had set in motion entered its last act. Layton and the four Germans who had been below the broken rope, at Death Bivouac, descended to Kleine Scheidegg. Dougal, with the four lead Germans— who were now Lehne, Hupfauer, Strobel and Votteler—set off on what he called "the loathsome prusik" from the Spider to the Fly. From there, on March 23, Lehne and Strobel went on to forge a way toward the Summit Icefield, while the others scraped and hacked to fashion yet another bivouac platform out of rock and ice.

Even after all they had been through, it was not in the nature of the Eiger to smile on them at the end. That afternoon, ahead of schedule, the storm came—first in heavy snowfall, then in battering winds—and for the next two days it was again a duel to see which would break first: Eiger or man. In their blanket of cloud, they were totally hidden from below. Radio communication all but broke down. As planned, Chris Bonington and Mick Burke beat their way up the west ridge, to be on hand in support when *the moment* came. But the moment was delayed and delayed, and they themselves, in the howling storm, had to dig into a snow-hole close beneath the summit. Up after them came three of the four Germans who had descended (the fourth had been taken ill), plus Toni Hiebeler, the Munich Eiger-climber, who had been standing by at Scheidegg—making a total of six men in a wild and frozen vigil on the heights.

On the north wall itself, the battle was unremitting. From the Fly, on the twenty-fourth, Dougal led for much of the way up through the network of cracks that veined the precipice above. Then, on fixed ropes, he descended with two of the Germans for another night in the Fly, while the two others improvised an even higher bivouac near the top point that had been reached. All that night it stormed. The next day it stormed. And all five were now close to the end of their strength. In spite of gloves, their fingers had become stiff as sticks; frostbite was gnawing at their feet; and between the driving snow and the rime frozen on their faces, they could barely see where they were heading. John Harlin was gone. But much that had been part of him was still there in that white cauldron through which they struggled. The Harlin Ordeal. The Harlin Control. . . .

They kept on.

And on March 25 came climax. In the morning, Jörg Lehne and Günther Strobel set off from their high bivouac; Dougal, with Sigi Hupfauer and Roland Votteler, from the Fly. Hour after hour they crept upward, emerging in turn from the cracks in the precipice; reaching the Summit Icefield; hacking and cramponing their way up the icefield, through midday, into afternoon . . . until at last, incredibly, they heard voices *above* them; they saw figures above them on a level ramp of snow, dimly visible through the scud against a storming sky. At four o'clock, Lehne and Strobel were on top of the mountain. An hour later, Dougal, Hupfauer and Votteler were there. Their companions in the two support teams welcomed them, embraced them, and led them down to the huge snow-hole they had dug in the west ridge a short distance below the summit.

As usual, there would be a price to be paid to the Ogre. All were suffering, in varying degrees, from frozen feet, and three of the Germans subsequently lost some or all of their toes. But their job was done, the goal achieved. Beneath them, no longer a dream but a reality, lay the prize they had striven for so hard and so long: the fabled *direttissima*—the Eiger Direct—now and forever the John Harlin Route, straight up from base to top.

If this, their victory, was not enough reward, something more was awaiting them when, the next day, they came back down to Kleine Scheidegg; something that in itself was enough to compensate not only for their effort and hardships, but for the criticism and controversy that had clouded the venture from the outset, and especially in the days since John's death. It was a telegram addressed to the *Anglo-American-German United Team*, and it read:

WE EXTEND TO EACH OF YOU OUR HEARTFELT GRATITUDE FOR YOUR CONTINUING THE CLIMB IN JOHN'S SPIRIT. WE REALIZE YOU CONTINUED UNDER THE MOST DIFFICULT AND HAZARDOUS CONDITIONS. WE CONGRATULATE YOU UPON YOUR SUCCESS AND PRAY FOR YOUR SPEEDY RECOVERY.

It was signed by Marilyn Harlin and John's parents.

The same storm that racked the heights of the Eiger blew, on March 25, through the town of Leysin. At this lower altitude, its winds were less ferocious, but the snow fell heavily, clothing town and mountainside in gleaming white.

Marilyn had decided that John should be buried there. More than anywhere he had lived, Leysin had become his home. The surrounding Alps were his home. Off to the southwest, beyond the Dents du Midi, was the range of Mont Blanc. To the northeast, beyond Leysin's own mountain mass, was the Eiger.

John's father and mother were there for the funeral. After returning with the children from the ski meet in Trento, they had, in their usual globe-girdling fashion, taken off again: John I for the Congo and Sue for the States. But Marilyn had managed to reach them, and now they were both back, numbed with shock and grief.

Konrad Kirch was there; he had come from Munich. And Layton Kor was there, wearing a too-small white shirt he had borrowed from Chris Bonington and a black tie that Peter Gillman had borrowed from John to wear at Hilti von Allmen's funeral.

Chris and Peter were not there. Peter was still inextricably involved in events at Kleine Scheidegg, and on this same day, Chris, with Mick

Burke, was at the very climax of the climb on the summit of the Eiger. So too, of course, was Dougal Haston. And the Germans. Both teams had sent Marilyn wires of regret and condolence.

Gary Hemming was not there; he had gone to Paris. Besides, he did not approve of anything as formally establishmentarian as a funeral. But later he returned to Leysin to visit with Marilyn.

The service was held in Leysin's Protestant church, conducted jointly by the local Anglican and Swiss ministers; and a Catholic priest said a prayer. But as John would have wanted, there was little formal ritual. Konrad Kirch spoke in both English and French, and a representative of the Swiss Alpine Club saluted John as a "brother." In attendance, besides family and close climbing companions, were others who had known him in the many aspects of his life. Through the storm, they had come from Chamonix, from many parts of Switzerland, from Germany and beyond. And finally, of course, there were those whose home was also Leysin: the staff and students of the American School, other resident outlanders, local officials and townspeople, in a social, national, and linguistic mixture such as had never before joined for an occasion in the small mountain community.

From the church, the mourners followed the hearse to the cemetery, on a hillside near town. They walked up on snowy paths to where a grave had been prepared near the top of the slope. And here, as the coffin was being lowered, an incident occurred to contribute a final apropos touch of Harlin controversy and Harlin myth. The story varying with the teller, a girl, either French, British, or American, who either had or had not been one of the camp followers at Kleine Scheidegg during the climb, either did or did not faint, cry out hysterically, or attempt to throw herself into the open grave.

Marilyn herself has said she noticed no such incident. And in any case, the mourners soon moved down the hillside through the snow, leaving only the gravediggers by the flower-strewn grave. One of the floral pieces was from Dougal, Chris and Peter. Another was from the German Eiger climbers, and on its ribbon, in English, were the words *Goodbye John.*

As these lines are written, John's death is more than a year in the past. Marilyn is now back in her home country, working toward her doctorate in botany at the University of Washington, while the two children go to school—their first English-language school—near her parents' home in Olympia. Andréa is taking ballet lessons and asking how many years she has to wait before she can have a baby. Johnny has decided that, when he is grown, he wants to be a naturalist and forest ranger, with plenty of skiing on the side, and some mountaineering as well.

Not on the Eiger, though; the Eiger is his father's. His own eye is on the Matterhorn.

Glossary of Mountaineering Terms

Abseil—(see *rappel*).

aiguille—a rock spire or needle.

artificial climbing—ascent by means of direct aid (q.v.); usually consists of hammering pitons or bolts into the mountain, hanging stirrups from these, and then standing in the stirrups.

belay—the securing of a rope to hold the fall of another climber. The rope may be passed around the body, hitched over a natural projection, or threaded through a carabiner, which is in turn attached to a piton affixed to rock or ice.

bivouac—a temporary or impromptu camp.

bolt—used for the same purpose as a piton, where no cracks exist in the mountain rock. Pitons are hammered into cracks; for a bolt, a hole must be drilled.

carabiner (in German, *Karabiner*)—a metal snap-ring, used in conjunction with a piton, through which a rope is passed to hold it in to the mountainside.

chimney—a steep, narrow cleft in a wall of rock or ice.

col—a pass, or the low point of a ridge.

cornice—a projecting mass of snow or ice.

couloir—a gully.

crampons—metal frames, with projecting spikes, that are attached to the soles of boots for use on steep ice or snow.

crevasse—a deep crevice or fissure in a glacier, caused by its downward movement.

direct aid—the ingredients of artificial climbing. Pitons, bolts and stirrups used not merely for protection but to make a climb possible.

étrier—French for stirrup.

fixed rope—a rope attached to the mountain by pitons and left hanging, so that following climbers in a party can use it for ascending, and all members, in case of need, can use it for descent.

free climbing—ascent by normal means, using only natural hand- and footholds.

friction climbing—adherence to the mountain by friction of some part of the body, rather than by a hold or stance.

glissade—sliding down a snow-slope.

ice dagger—a steel blade about six inches long, used in climbing steep ice.

ice screw—similar to an ice piton, but screwed instead of hammered into place.

jamcrack (or *jam crack*)—a crack or crevice in rock which can be climbed by jamming in part of the body, usually elbow or knee. Sometimes used as a verb, meaning the process of doing this.

jumar—a type of clamp used in prusiking (q.v.).

peg—piton.

pitch—a section of a climb, usually defined by belaying points or the length of rope being used.

286

piton—a metal spike of varying shapes and sizes, to be hammered into ice or cracks in rock. In free climbing it is used, in conjunction with the rope, for protection; in artificial climbing, for actual assistance in the ascent.

prusik—a method of ascending a fixed rope with the help of either knotted slings or clamps. The slings or clamps slide up the rope, but not down, thus helping the climber hold the gains in height achieved by the use of arms and legs. The word is used as a verb as well as a noun.

rappel (in German, *Abseil*)—roping down. The maneuver of making a steep or free-hanging descent by means of a rope attached to the mountain and either passed around the body or through a friction device.

sling—loop of rope or tape.

stirrup—a sling hung from a piton or bolt, in which a climber stands when there is no natural hold or stance.

tape—nylon webbing, used to make slings.

tension traverse—a traverse on which the climber keeps in position by using the pull of the rope against him.

traverse—the horizontal or diagonal crossing of a mountainside. Also the crossing of a peak from one side to another.

A Note About This Book

The text of this book is set in linotype Electra, designed by the American artist W. A. Dwiggins in 1935. Electra is a typeface noted for its elegance and clarity. The layout, typography, line drawings, and binding were designed by Earl Tidwell.